RESOURCE MANAGEMENT FOR ELDERLY WELL-BEING

A Holistic Approach to Financial Planning and Security in Retirement Years

By: Dr Lisa L. Cole Martin

innovativeink
PUBLISHING
A Division of Kendall Hunt

innovativeink PUBLISHING
A Division of Kendall Hunt

www.innovativeinkpublishing.com
Send all inquiries to:
4050 Westmark Drive
Dubuque, IA 52004-1840

Print ISBN: 979-8-3851-4298-9
Ebook ISBN: 979-8-3851-4299-6

Published in the United States of America

Contents

About the Author v
Preface vii

CHAPTER 1: INTRODUCTION TO RESOURCE MANAGEMENT FOR THE ELDERLY 1

What Is Resource Management? 2
Interdisciplinary Influences on Resource Management for the Elderly 3
The Aging Population and the Need for Resource Management 4
Challenges and Issues in Resource Management for the Elderly 5
Ethical Considerations in Resource Allocation 7
Overview of the Certified Financial Planner Financial Planning Process 8
Discussion Questions 10

CHAPTER 2: ESTABLISHING CLIENT-PLANNER RELATIONSHIPS 11

Building Trust With Elderly Clients 11
Understanding Unique Needs and Goals 12
Communication Strategies for Effective Planning 13
Discussion Questions 15

CHAPTER 3: GATHERING AND ANALYZING DATA 17

Collecting Financial Information **17**
Assessing Current Financial Status **18**
Importance of a Net Worth Statement and Personal Cash Flow Statement **19**
Net Worth Statement 20
Personal Cash Flow Statement 21
Identifying Key Financial Documents **22**
Discussion Questions **24**
Continuing Case Study: Darren and Lisa Harmon **25**
Introduction to the Continuing Case 25
Objectives 25
Client Information 25
Personal and Financial Background 26
Financial Assets and Liabilities 26
Estate Planning Information 34
Continuing Case Study—The Harmons—Cash Management **34**
Chapter 3 Case Assignment 3.1 34

CHAPTER 4: IDENTIFYING GOALS AND OBJECTIVES 37

Setting Short-Term, Mid-Term, and Long-Term Goals **37**
Prioritizing Financial Needs **40**
Aligning Goals With Retirement Plans **41**
Discussion Questions **43**
Continuing Case Study—The Harmons—Smart Goals and Objectives **44**
Chapter 4 Case Assignment 4.1 44

CHAPTER 5: DEVELOPING A FINANCIAL PLAN 47

Creating a Budget for Seniors 47
Budget Categories Percentages Recommendations 50
Financial Progress Ratios 51
Allocating Resources for Healthcare and Living Expenses 52
Planning for Unexpected Costs 54
Discussion Questions 56
Continuing Case Study—reating and Evaluating a Budget 57
Chapter 5 Case Assignment 5.1 57

CHAPTER 6: RETIREMENT PLANNING 59

Understanding Retirement Accounts and Benefits 59
Maximizing Social Security Benefits 60
Pension Plans and Annuities 61
Discussion Questions 63
Continuing Case Study—Allocating Resources for Healthcare and Living Expenses 64
Chapter 6 Case Assignment 6.1 64
Continuing Case Study—Planning for Unexpected Costs—Large Future Irregular Expenses 66
Chapter 6 Case Assignment 6.2 66

CHAPTER 7: INVESTMENT MANAGEMENT 69

Risk Assessment and Tolerance 69
Diversification Strategies 70
Investment Vehicles for Seniors 71
Continuing Case—The Harmons—Investment Planning—Addressing Financial Goals 73

Chapter 7 Case Assignment 7.1 73

Continuing Case—The Harmons—Retirement Planning and Retirement Income Forecasting 76

Chapter 7 Case Assignment 7.2 76

CHAPTER 8: ESTATE PLANNING 79

Wills and Trusts 79

Powers of Attorney and Healthcare Directives 83

Minimizing Estate Taxes 85

Minimizing Estate Taxes and Maximizing Wealth Transfer 87

Types of Advanced Estate Planning Techniques 87

Discussion Questions 89

Continuing Case—The Harmons Evaluating and Updating the Estate Plan 90

Chapter 8 Case Assignment 8.1 90

CHAPTER 9: TAX PLANNING 93

Understanding Tax Implications for Seniors 93

Tax-Efficient Withdrawal Strategies 94

Utilizing Tax Credits and Deductions 95

Discussion Questions 97

Continuing Case—The Harmons—Elderly Related Tax Planning 98

Chapter 9 Case Assignment 9.1 98

CHAPTER 10: GOVERNMENT BENEFITS AND ENTITLEMENT PROGRAMS 101

Social Security, Medicare, and Medicaid 103

Veterans' Benefits and Other Government Programs **104**
Eligibility Criteria and Application Processes **106**
Interaction Between Government Benefits and Financial Resources **107**
Discussion Questions **108**
Continuing Case—The Harmons—Government Benefits and Entitlement Programs Analysis **109**
Chapter 10 Case Assignment 10.1 109

CHAPTER 11: HEALTHCARE AND LONG-TERM CARE PLANNING 111

Medicare and Medicaid Overview **111**
Long-Term Care Insurance **112**
Types of Long-Term Care 113
Long-Term Care Insurance and Other Financing Options **114**
Managing Out-of-Pocket Healthcare Costs **116**
Discussion Questions **118**
Continuing Case—The Harmons—Analyzing the Interaction Between Government Benefits and Financial Resources for Retirement **119**
Chapter 11 Case Assignment 11.1 119

CHAPTER 12: INSURANCE PLANNING 123

Types of Insurance for Seniors **123**
Evaluating Existing Insurance Policies **126**
Making Informed Insurance Decisions **127**
Discussion Questions **128**
Continuing Case—The Harmons—Healthcare and Comparing Long-Term Care Policies Options **129**
Chapter 12 Case Assignment 12.1 129

Continuing Case—the Harmons—Insurance Planning for Retirement.................... 131
Chapter 12 Case Assignment 12.2 131

CHAPTER 13: SOCIAL SECURITY AND PENSION ANALYSIS 135

Social Security Benefits Overview 135
Strategies for Maximizing Benefits 137
Pension Options and Decisions 139
Discussion Questions 141
Continuing Case—The Harmons—Evaluating Social Security and Pension Planning 142
Chapter 13 Case Assignment 13.1 142

CHAPTER 14: HOUSING AND LIVING ARRANGEMENTS......................147

Assessing Housing Needs 148
Financial Considerations for Downsizing 148
Exploring Senior Living Communities 149
Discussion Questions 152
Continuing Case—The Harmons—Evaluating Housing and Living Arrangements in Retirement 153
Chapter 14 Case Assignment 14.1 153

CHAPTER 15: INCOME AND CASH FLOW MANAGEMENT....................157

Managing Monthly Income 157
Cash Flow Strategies for Stability 158
Planning for Variable Income 159
Discussion Questions 161

Continuing Case—The Harmons—Housing Mortgage Affordability/Analysis 162

Chapter 15 Case Assignment 15.1 162

CHAPTER 16: SPECIAL CONSIDERATIONS FOR BLENDED FAMILIES AND MULTIPLE GENERATIONS 165

Financial Challenges and Dynamics of Blended Families 165

Strategies for Managing Financial Resources Across Generations 166

Inheritance Planning and Asset Distribution in Blended Family Situations 167

Communication and Addressing Financial Concerns 168

Discussion Questions 169

Continuing Case—The Harmons—Planning for Blended Families and Multiple Generations 170

Chapter 16 Case Assignment 16.1 170

CHAPTER 17: PLANNING FOR DISABILITY AND INCAPACITY 173

Planning for Disability and Incapacity in Financial Planning 174

Durable Powers of Attorney, Healthcare Proxies, and Living Wills 174

Guardianship and Conservatorship Considerations 175

Discussion Questions 177

Continuing Case—The Harmons—Evaluating Planning for Disability and Incapacity 178

Chapter 17 Case Assignment 17.1 178

CHAPTER 18: PHILANTHROPIC GIVING AND CHARITABLE PLANNING 181

Role of Philanthropic Giving in Financial Planning 182

Charitable Planning Strategies and Tax Implications **182**
Family Philanthropy and the Impact of Charitable Giving **183**
Discussion Questions **185**
Continuing Case—The Harmons—Philanthropic Giving and Charitable Planning for the Harmons in Financial Planning Analysis **186**
Chapter 18 Case Assignment 18.1 186

CHAPTER 19: MONITORING AND ADJUSTING THE FINANCIAL PLAN 189

Regular Reviews of Financial Goals **189**
Adapting to Life Changes **190**
Rebalancing Investment Portfolios **191**
Discussion Questions **193**

CHAPTER 20: ETHICAL AND LEGAL CONSIDERATIONS 195

Ethical Responsibilities of Financial Planners **195**
Legal Issues in Elder Financial Planning **198**
Ensuring Compliance with Financial Regulations **200**
Continuing Case—the Harmons—Ethical and Legal Considerations for the Elderly and the Importance of Monitoring and Adjusting the Financial Plan Pre- and Post-Retirement **201**
Chapter 20 Case Assignment 20.1 201

CHAPTER 21: RESOURCE MANAGEMENT FOR THE ELDERLY CASES 205

Case 1: The Retired Teacher **205**

Background: 205
Planning Process: 205
Financial Information: 206
Financial Goals: 206
Investment and Retirement Information: 207
Medical and Long-Term Care Insurance Information: 207
Estate Information: 208
Case 2: The Widow with a Complex Estate 209
Background: 209
Planning Process: 209
Financial Information: 209
Financial Goals: 210
Investment and Retirement Information: 211
Medical and Long-Term Care Insurance Information: 211
Estate Information: 212
Case 3: The Aging Couple with Long-Term Care Needs 213
Background: 213
Planning Process: 213
Financial Information: 213
Financial Goals: 214
Investment and Retirement Information: 215
Medical and Long-Term Care Insurance Information: 216
Estate Information: 216
Case 4: The Self-employed Retiree 217
Background: 217
Planning Process: 217
Financial Information: 218
Financial Goals: 219
Investment and Retirement Information: 219
Medical and Long-Term Care Insurance Information: 220
Estate Information: 221

Case 5: The Divorced Senior with Adult Children 222
Background: 222
Planning Process: 222
Financial Information: 222
Financial Goals: 224
Investment and Retirement Information: 224
Medical and Long-Term Care Insurance Information: 225
Estate Information: 225
Case 6: The Retired Veteran With Special Benefits 226
Background: 226
Planning Process: 227
Financial Information: 227
Financial Goals: 228
Investment and Retirement Information: 228
Medical and Long-Term Care Insurance Information: 229
Estate Information: 230
Case 7: The Early Retiree With Investment Income 231
Background: 231
Planning Process: 231
Financial Information: 231
Financial Goals: 232
Investment and Retirement Information: 233
Medical and Long-Term Care Insurance Information: 233
Estate Information: 234
Case 8: The Couple Planning for a Legacy 235
Background: 235
Planning Process: 235
Financial Information: 235
Financial Goals: 236
Investment and Retirement Information: 237
Medical and Long-Term Care Insurance Information: 237

Estate Information: 238
CFP Board Practice Standards for the Financial Planning Process 239
Certified Family Life Educator (CFLE) 240
Monthly Budget Example 242
Monthly Budget Worksheet 243
Net Worth Statement Example 244
Net Worth Statement Worksheet 245
Personal Statement of Cash Flows Example 247
Personal Statement of Cash Flows Worksheet 248
Estimate Your Annual Cost of Living Worksheet 250
Inflation Factor Table 251
Financial Risk Tolerance Worksheet for Elderly Clients 252
Estimating Changes in Retirement Spending Worksheet 254
Estimated Annual Cost of Living ____Years After Retirement 255
Expectation of Life by Age and Sex 256
Estimated Annual Cost of Living ____Years After Retirement 257
Large Future Irregular Expenses Worksheet 258
Age to Receive Full Social Security Benefits 259
Benefit Increases for Delayed Retirement 259
Estimated Annual Income After Retirement Worksheet 260
Monthly Cost of Living Worksheet 261
Time Value of Money (TVM) Tables 262
Basic Will Example 264
Durable Power of Attorney Example 265
Revocable Living Trust Example 266
Healthcare Proxy Example 268
Beneficiary Designation Example 270

References 271

About the Author

Lisa L. Cole Martin is a seasoned educator and financial planning expert with more than two decades of experience teaching accounting, finance, and business courses at various esteemed universities, including North Carolina A&T State University and Texas Tech University. She holds an EdD and an MS in Personal Financial Planning from Texas Tech University, an MBA. in Public Administration from the University of Findlay, and a BS in Accounting from Grambling State University.

As the author of *Cases in Family Financial Planning: A Guide for Financial Planning Analysis and Plan Preparation*, published in 2021, Lisa has demonstrated her deep commitment to advancing financial literacy. Her latest work, *Resource Management for Elderly Well-Being: A Holistic Approach to Financial Planning and Security in Retirement Years*, reflects her passion for helping individuals navigate the complexities of financial planning in their later years.

Lisa is particularly devoted to making financial planning concepts accessible to low- and middle-class individuals, empowering them to build generational wealth and secure their financial futures. She believes that everyone, regardless of their background, deserves the knowledge and tools to achieve financial security and well-being, especially in retirement.

Beyond her professional achievements, Lisa has a deep love for music and enjoys spending her free time reading, watching Marvel movies, and being with her family and friends. Her dedication to financial education is matched by her commitment to making complex financial concepts understandable and actionable for all. Through her teaching, writing, and outreach, Lisa continues to inspire and equip diverse audiences with the knowledge they need to thrive financially, particularly as they approach and navigate their retirement years.

Preface

As the global population ages, societies worldwide are confronted with unprecedented challenges in ensuring the financial security and well-being of their elderly citizens. The phenomenon, often referred to as the "Silver Tsunami," presents a complex web of economic, social, and ethical dilemmas that demand urgent attention (Flood, 2020). At the heart of this issue lies the looming specter of financial ruin for countless families who find themselves ill-prepared to navigate the financial complexities associated with aging. This textbook, *Resource Management for Elderly Well-Being: A Holistic Approach to Financial Planning and Security in Retirement Years*, is a comprehensive guide designed to equip individuals, families, caregivers, and financial professionals with the knowledge and tools necessary to confront these challenges head-on and chart a course toward financial resilience and stability in an increasingly aging world.

With the rapid advancement of medical technology, improved healthcare systems, and changing demographic trends, people are living longer than ever before. Although increased longevity brings with it the gift of more years to enjoy life, it also presents a host of financial considerations that must be carefully managed. From funding retirement to covering healthcare expenses and ensuring long-term care, the financial implications of aging are profound and far-reaching. Without proper planning and preparation, many families face the stark reality of financial ruin as they grapple with the escalating costs associated with aging. Against this backdrop, "Navigating the Silver Tsunami" serves as a beacon of hope, offering practical strategies, expert insights, and real-world examples to empower readers in safeguarding their financial future and that of their loved ones.

Drawing upon interdisciplinary expertise from fields such as finance, economics, gerontology, and social work, this textbook provides a comprehensive exploration of the multifaceted challenges posed by the aging population. Through a blend of theoretical analysis, empirical research, case studies, and practical exercises, readers will gain a deep understanding of the complex interplay between financial planning, aging, and societal dynamics. Moreover, "Navigating the Silver Tsunami" goes beyond mere diagnosis of the problem; it offers concrete solutions and actionable recommendations to help individuals and families navigate the turbulent waters of an aging society with confidence and resilience (Chambers et al., 2021). Whether you are a financial advisor seeking to better serve elderly clients, a caregiver supporting aging parents, or an individual planning for your own future, this textbook is an indispensable resource for navigating the challenges and seizing the opportunities presented by the Silver Tsunami (Flood, 2020).

1

Introduction to Resource Management for the Elderly

In the intricate tapestry of family financial planning, few threads are as vital and delicate as those concerning the elderly. As the population ages, the need for effective resource management becomes increasingly paramount, not only for the financial security of aging individuals but also for the well-being of their families. This introductory chapter lays the groundwork for understanding the unique challenges and opportunities inherent in resource management for the elderly within the context of family financial planning. By exploring the dynamics of aging, the evolving landscape of monetary responsibility, and the ethical imperatives that underpin decision-making, readers will embark on a journey toward mastering the art of safeguarding assets, ensuring dignity, and fostering resilience in the later stages of life.

The aging process is not merely a biological phenomenon but a multifaceted journey that encompasses social, psychological, and financial dimensions. As individuals transition into their golden years, they encounter a myriad of challenges, from declining health and cognitive abilities to changes in living arrangements and social networks. Amid these transitions, the management of financial resources assumes a vital role, shaping not only the quality of life for the elderly but also the stability and security of their families. Through a holistic approach to resource management, families can navigate the complexities of aging with greater confidence, enabling elderly loved ones to maintain independence, dignity, and a sense of financial well-being.

At the heart of resource management for the elderly lies the intricate interplay between financial realities and ethical considerations. The decisions made regarding the allocation and utilization of resources have far-reaching implications not only for the individuals directly involved but also for the broader familial and societal fabric. Thus, ethical awareness and sensitivity are essential compasses guiding the journey of family financial planning in the context of aging. By examining ethical dilemmas, principles of fairness, and the imperative of honoring autonomy and dignity, this chapter sets the stage for a nuanced exploration of resource management practices that uphold the values of compassion, justice, and respect for the elderly and their families.

WHAT IS RESOURCE MANAGEMENT?

Resource management for the elderly within the context of family financial planning involves the careful allocation and utilization of available resources to ensure the well-being and sustainability of older family members. It encompasses a holistic approach that considers various aspects such as income, savings, investments, healthcare costs, and estate planning. Effective resource management involves understanding the unique financial needs that arise with aging, including healthcare expenses, long-term care provisions, and potential changes in income sources such as retirement funds and pensions.

Central to this approach is proactive financial planning that anticipates the evolving needs of elderly family members. This includes assessing current financial assets and liabilities, creating budgets that accommodate both short-term and long-term expenses, and exploring options for optimizing income streams. In addition, resource management in this context emphasizes the importance of legal and estate planning to protect assets and ensure that the elderly family members' wishes are conducted effectively. By integrating these elements into a comprehensive strategy, families can navigate the complexities of elder care with greater financial security and peace of mind.

Resource management for the elderly within family financial planning involves several key components essential for ensuring their financial well-being and security. First, it begins with a thorough assessment of current financial resources. This includes evaluating income sources such as pensions, social security benefits, investments, and any other forms of regular income. Understanding the stability and growth potential of these sources is crucial for determining the available funds for immediate and future needs.

Second, effective resource management involves budgeting and expense planning tailored to the specific needs of elderly family members. This process entails identifying and categorizing essential expenses such as healthcare costs, including medical treatments, medications, and potential long-term care needs. It also involves factoring in daily living expenses, housing costs, transportation, and any other regular expenditures. By creating a detailed budget, families can ensure that resources are allocated efficiently to cover essential expenses while also preparing for unexpected costs that may arise due to health-related issues or changes in living arrangements.

Third, asset management and investment strategies play a critical role in resource management for the elderly. This includes assessing existing assets such as savings accounts, real estate, and investments like stocks or bonds. Families need to evaluate the risk tolerance of these investments and consider diversification strategies to protect against market volatility while aiming for growth. Moreover, estate planning becomes increasingly important to safeguard assets and ensure they are distributed according to the elderly family members' wishes. This involves creating wills, establishing trusts, and addressing tax implications to maximize the value of the estate for future generations.

INTERDISCIPLINARY INFLUENCES ON RESOURCE MANAGEMENT FOR THE ELDERLY

The study of resource management for the elderly within the realm of family financial planning is enriched by interdisciplinary influences that draw from various fields of knowledge. One crucial influence comes from economics, where theories and models help understand how individuals and families allocate limited financial resources across diverse needs, including healthcare, housing, and daily living expenses. Economic principles such as cost-benefit analysis and utility maximization provide frameworks for evaluating financial decisions concerning retirement savings, investment strategies, and optimizing income streams during the elder years.

Psychology also plays a significant role in shaping the study of resource management for the elderly. Behavioral economics, for instance, explores how cognitive biases and emotional factors influence financial decision-making among older adults. Understanding these psychological aspects can help financial planners and caregivers tailor strategies that align with the preferences and behaviors of elderly individuals, promoting better financial outcomes and reducing stress associated with financial decision-making.

Moreover, the field of gerontology contributes valuable insights into resource management for the elderly. Gerontologists study the aging process and its impact on health, cognition, and socioeconomic factors. Their research informs financial planning strategies by highlighting the specific needs and challenges aging individuals face, such as the rising costs of healthcare and long-term care. By integrating gerontological perspectives into financial planning, professionals can develop more personalized and effective strategies that address the unique circumstances and goals of elderly clients and their families.

These interdisciplinary influences underscore the complexity of resource management for the elderly within family financial planning. By incorporating knowledge from economics, psychology, and gerontology, practitioners can enhance their ability to provide comprehensive and tailored financial advice that supports the well-being and financial security of aging family members. This holistic approach not only addresses immediate financial needs but also prepares for the long-term challenges and opportunities associated with aging, fostering a supportive environment for elderly individuals and their families alike.

By addressing these components comprehensively, families can create a robust financial plan that not only supports the current needs of elderly relatives but also prepares for their long-term financial security and peace of mind. Effective resource management ensures that financial decisions are informed, proactive, and aligned with the evolving needs of aging family members, fostering a stable and supportive environment for all involved.

THE AGING POPULATION AND THE NEED FOR RESOURCE MANAGEMENT

Today's 65-year-old can expect to live another 20 years, according to the Social Security Administration (National Council on Aging, 2023). This statistic underscores the significance of effective financial planning for retirees to ensure their financial security throughout their extended lifespan. With longer life expectancy comes the need for a sustainable income stream that can support individuals well into their retirement years. However, the reality is that many retirees face significant financial challenges that threaten their economic well-being as they age.

According to recent studies, 80% of households with older adults—or 47 million of such households—are financially struggling today or are at risk of falling into economic insecurity as they age (National Council on Aging, 2023). This alarming statistic highlights the pervasive nature of financial vulnerability among older adults in society. Factors such as insufficient retirement savings, rising healthcare costs, and limited access to affordable housing contribute to the precarious financial position of many retirees. Without adequate support and intervention, millions of elderly individuals and their families face the prospect of financial hardship in their later years.

Considering these challenges, optimizing Social Security, accessing benefits, improving long-term care, and utilizing home equity emerge as critical strategies for retirees to maximize their savings and secure their financial future. Social Security benefits represent a significant source of income for many retirees, but navigating the complexities of the system can be daunting. By understanding the various claiming strategies, retirees can optimize their Social Security benefits to maximize their lifetime earnings and ensure financial stability throughout retirement.

Accessing benefits beyond Social Security, such as Medicare, Medicaid, and veteran's benefits, can provide additional financial support and alleviate the burden of healthcare expenses. However, many retirees may be unaware of their eligibility or unsure of how to navigate the application process. Through education and advocacy, retirees can gain access to the benefits they are entitled to and alleviate the financial strain associated with healthcare costs.

Long-term care represents another significant expense for retirees, yet it is often overlooked in financial planning discussions. By proactively planning for long-term care needs, retirees can mitigate the monetary impact of medical expenses and ensure access to quality care when needed. Strategies such as purchasing long-term care insurance or exploring alternative care options can help retirees protect their savings and maintain their financial independence in the face of health-related challenges.

In addition, leveraging home equity can provide retirees with a valuable source of funds to supplement their retirement income. Whether through downsizing, reverse mortgages, or home equity lines of credit, homeowners can tap into their home equity to cover expenses or enhance their standard of living in retirement. By carefully considering the risks and benefits associated with these options, retirees can make informed decisions that support their long-term financial goals.

In summary, today's retirees face a myriad of financial challenges that threaten their economic security as they age. However, by implementing strategies such as optimizing Social Security, accessing benefits, improving long-term care, and utilizing home equity, retirees can maximize their savings and safeguard their financial future. Through initiative-taking planning and informed decision-making, retirees can enjoy a comfortable and financially secure retirement that reflects their values and priorities.

CHALLENGES AND ISSUES IN RESOURCE MANAGEMENT FOR THE ELDERLY

Resource management for the elderly presents a myriad of challenges and issues, stemming from a complex interplay of demographic shifts, economic constraints, and societal attitudes. One significant challenge revolves around healthcare access and affordability. As the elderly population grows, the demand for healthcare services surges, placing strain on existing resources and exacerbating issues such as long wait times for appointments and shortages of specialized care providers. In addition, the rising cost of healthcare can burden elderly individuals on fixed incomes, leading to difficult choices between meeting medical needs and covering other essential expenses like housing and food.

Another pressing issue in resource management for the elderly is the inadequacy of support systems for caregivers. Many elderly individuals rely on family members or professional caregivers for assistance with daily tasks, yet these caregivers often face overwhelming demands with little to no respite. The emotional, physical, and financial toll of caregiving can be immense, leading to burnout and decreased quality of care. Moreover, the lack of comprehensive support services, such as respite care and caregiver training programs, further compounds the challenges faced by caregivers, impacting the well-being of the elderly individuals they support.

Furthermore, disparities in access to resources based on factors such as socioeconomic status, geographic location, and cultural background present significant equity issues in resource management for the elderly. Marginalized communities, including racial and ethnic minorities, individuals with disabilities, and those living in rural areas, often face barriers to accessing essential services such as transportation, affordable housing, and culturally competent healthcare. Addressing these disparities requires a multifaceted approach that includes policy interventions to improve access, increased funding for community-based services, and initiatives to promote diversity and inclusion in aging-related services and programs.

Resource management for the elderly within the context of family financial planning is fraught with unique challenges and issues. One prominent concern is the financial strain that long-term care imposes on families. The cost of assisted living facilities or in-home care services can quickly deplete savings and assets, potentially jeopardizing the financial security of both the elderly individual and their family members. Balancing the need for quality care with the reality of limited financial resources often requires families to make problematic decisions regarding care options, including relying on informal caregiving arrangements or seeking alternative sources of funding such as Medicaid or long-term care insurance.

Another significant issue is the lack of comprehensive financial literacy and planning among both elderly individuals and their families. Many older adults may not have adequately saved for retirement or planned for the possibility of increased healthcare expenses in later years. Moreover, family members may be unprepared to navigate the complex landscape of elder care financing, including understanding eligibility criteria for government assistance programs and making informed decisions about long-term care insurance coverage. This lack of financial preparedness can lead to financial instability and stress for families, exacerbating the already challenging circumstances of caregiving for aging loved ones.

In addition, intergenerational financial dynamics can introduce tensions and conflicts within families when it comes to resource management for the elderly. Siblings may disagree on the allocation of financial resources or responsibilities for caregiving, leading to strained relationships and communication breakdowns. Moreover, unequal distribution of wealth or inheritance among family members can further complicate matters, potentially fueling resentment and discord. Effective family financial planning for the elderly necessitates open and honest communication, initiative-taking decision-making, and a commitment to equitable distribution of resources to ensure the well-being of both the elderly individual and their family members.

ETHICAL CONSIDERATIONS IN RESOURCE ALLOCATION

Ethical considerations in resource allocation within the realm of family financial planning for the elderly are paramount, as they directly impact the well-being and quality of life of all involved parties. One ethical dilemma arises when determining how to allocate limited financial resources among competing needs within the family unit. For example, families may face problematic decisions regarding whether to prioritize funding for the elderly individual's long-term care needs over other financial goals such as education expenses for younger family members or saving for retirement. Balancing the immediate needs of the elderly with the long-term financial stability of the family requires careful consideration of values, priorities, and the potential consequences of different allocation strategies.

Moreover, ethical considerations come into play when evaluating the fairness and equity of resource allocation decisions within the family. In situations where multiple family members engage in caregiving or financial support for the elderly individual, ensuring equitable distribution of responsibilities and financial burdens is essential to maintaining familial harmony and avoiding resentment or feelings of injustice. Transparency, open communication, and consensus-building processes can help mitigate conflicts and promote fairness in resource allocation decisions.

Furthermore, ethical dilemmas may arise when navigating the complex landscape of long-term care financing and insurance options. Families must grapple with questions of affordability, accessibility, and the ethical implications of different care arrangements. For example, opting for less expensive care options may sacrifice quality of life for the elderly individual, whereas choosing more expensive options could strain the family's financial resources. Ethical decision-making in this context requires weighing the costs and benefits of various care alternatives while upholding principles of dignity, autonomy, and respect for the elderly individual's preferences and values.

In addition, ethical considerations extend to the broader societal implications of resource allocation decisions for the elderly within the family unit. Families must consider how their choices may impact not only their own well-being but also the welfare of vulnerable populations and the broader healthcare system. For instance, relying heavily on informal caregiving arrangements within the family may inadvertently perpetuate gender disparities in caregiving responsibilities and exacerbate socioeconomic inequalities. Ethical family financial planning entails taking a holistic view of resource allocation decisions, considering their ripple effects on individuals, families, and society, and striving to uphold principles of justice, compassion, and social responsibility.

OVERVIEW OF THE CERTIFIED FINANCIAL PLANNER FINANCIAL PLANNING PROCESS

The Certified Financial Planner (CFP) financial planning process is a structured approach designed to help individuals achieve their financial goals through comprehensive and strategic planning. It begins with establishing and defining the client–planner relationship, where the financial planner builds a foundation of trust and mutual understanding with the client. This phase involves setting clear expectations, defining the scope of services, and agreeing on the responsibilities of both parties. By establishing a strong relationship, the planner ensures that the client's specific needs and objectives are well understood and prioritized throughout the planning process (CFP Board, n.d.).

The next step is gathering client data and assessing financial **status**, which includes collecting detailed financial information and understanding the client's current situation. This involves a thorough review of financial statements, investment portfolios, income sources, expenses, and other relevant documents. The planner uses this data to conduct a comprehensive analysis, identifying the client's strengths, weaknesses, opportunities, and threats in relation to their financial goals. This analysis forms the basis for developing a tailored financial plan that aligns with the client's unique circumstances.

Developing and presenting the financial plan follows, where the financial planner creates a detailed strategy to help the client achieve their goals. This plan includes recommendations on budgeting, investments, retirement planning, tax strategies, insurance, and estate planning. The planner presents these recommendations to the client, explaining the rationale behind each suggestion and how it contributes to their overall financial objectives. The plan is designed to be actionable and realistic, considering the client's risk tolerance, time horizon, and personal preferences.

Finally, the process involves implementing the plan and monitoring progress. Once the client approves the plan, the financial planner assists in executing the recommended strategies, which may include adjusting investment allocations, setting up new accounts, or coordinating with other professionals such as accountants or attorneys. Regular reviews and monitoring are essential to ensure the plan remains aligned with the client's evolving needs and any changes in their circumstances. This ongoing oversight helps in making necessary adjustments and staying on track to meet the client's financial goals over time (CFP Board, n.d.).

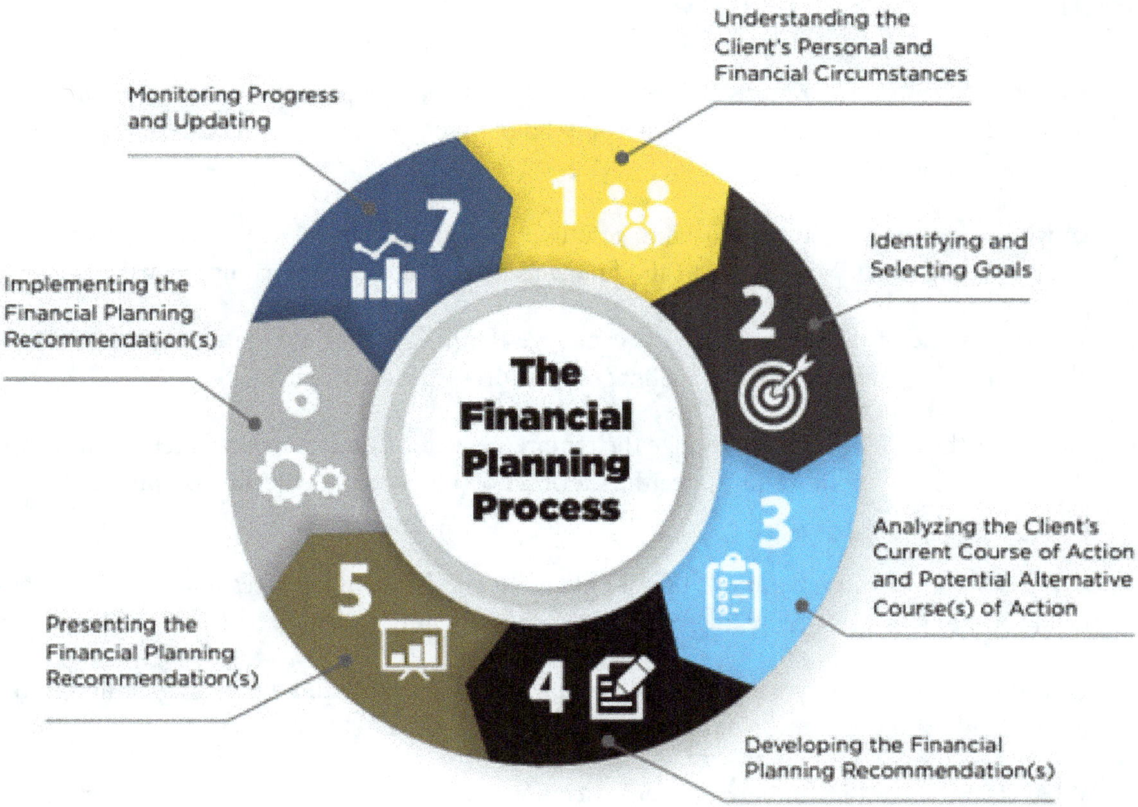

FIGURE 1.1 Seven steps in CFP financial planning process

Source: From the CFP Board (CFP Board, n.d.).

DISCUSSION QUESTIONS

1. How do ethical considerations influence the decision-making process in managing resources for the elderly within a family? Discuss examples of potential conflicts between financial needs and ethical imperatives.

2. In what ways do a holistic approach to resource management benefit the elderly? Discuss the integration of social, psychological, and financial aspects in creating a comprehensive plan.

3. What are some of the most significant challenges families face when managing resources for elderly members? How can these challenges be addressed effectively?

4. How does the process of aging change the requirements for resource management within families? Discuss the implications of health deterioration and cognitive decline on financial planning.

5. Discuss the ethical considerations that should guide the distribution of resources among elderly family members, especially in terms of fairness and equity.

6. How do interdisciplinary insights from economics, psychology, and gerontology enhance the understanding and execution of resource management for the elderly?

7. What strategies can be employed to enhance financial security and independence for elderly individuals? Consider the roles of investment, estate planning, and insurance.

8. With the changing economic landscape, such as fluctuating market conditions and new healthcare policies, how should families adapt their financial planning strategies for elderly members?

2

Establishing Client–Planner Relationships

Establishing a strong client–planner relationship is a critical first step in resource management planning for the elderly, serving as the foundation for all subsequent financial strategies and decisions. This phase is about more than just gathering information; it is about building a rapport with elderly clients, understanding their unique life stages, and addressing their specific concerns and aspirations. As elderly clients may face a range code of complex issues, from managing retirement savings to planning for long-term care, a deep level of trust and clear communication with the financial planner is essential. This relationship ensures that clients feel heard and understood, which is crucial for developing a financial plan that is both personalized and effective.

In this context, establishing the client–planner relationship involves engaging in empathetic and thorough discussions to uncover the client's financial goals, health considerations, and family dynamics. Elderly clients often require a tailored approach that considers their lifetime of experiences and evolving needs. Financial planners must navigate these conversations with sensitivity, ensuring they respect the client's preferences while also providing clear guidance. By setting clear expectations and defining the scope of services, planners can build a strong partnership that supports the elderly client through the complexities of resource management and helps secure their financial well-being for the future (CFP Board, 2019a).

BUILDING TRUST WITH ELDERLY CLIENTS

Building trust with elderly clients is a cornerstone of effective resource management planning, especially given the unique financial and emotional challenges they often face. Trust is essential for creating a collaborative environment where clients feel comfortable sharing sensitive information about their finances, health, and personal goals. Financial planners must approach these relationships with empathy and respect, recognizing that elderly clients may have experienced significant life changes such as retirement, health issues, or the loss of a spouse. Establishing trust involves active listening, showing genuine concern for their well-being, and providing reassurance that their financial future is in capable hands.

An important aspect of building trust is clear and transparent communication. Elderly clients need to understand the financial planning process and how it will address their specific needs and goals. Planners should explain complex financial concepts in simple terms, avoiding jargon that might confuse or alienate clients. Regular updates and open dialogue help demystify the planning process, making clients feel more involved and confident in the decisions being made. By ensuring that clients are fully informed and have their questions answered, planners can foster a sense of security and partnership.

Moreover, demonstrating reliability and consistency reinforces trust over time. Planners should be punctual, follow through on commitments, and be available to address concerns as they arise. Trust is further solidified when clients see that their planner is committed to their long-term success and is attentive to any changes in their circumstances. This reliability helps build a strong rapport and reassures elderly clients that their financial advisor is dedicated to navigating their unique challenges and supporting their financial stability throughout their later years (CFP Board, 2019a).

UNDERSTANDING UNIQUE NEEDS AND GOALS

Understanding the unique needs and goals of elderly clients is crucial in resource management planning, as their financial and personal circumstances often differ significantly from those of younger individuals. Elderly clients may be navigating retirement, managing fixed incomes, and dealing with the potential high costs of healthcare and long-term care. Financial planners must conduct thorough assessments to understand these specific needs, considering the client's current financial status, health conditions, family dynamics, and any other factors that could influence their financial well-being. This personalized approach ensures that the planning process is relevant and addresses the most pressing concerns of the client.

A key aspect of understanding elderly clients' goals involves recognizing their desires for retirement lifestyle, legacy planning, and financial security. Many seniors have specific aspirations, such as maintaining a certain quality of life, supporting family members, or leaving a meaningful legacy. Planners should engage in detailed discussions with clients to uncover these goals, considering both short-term needs and long-term aspirations. By aligning financial strategies with these goals, planners can develop comprehensive plans that provide not only financial stability but also emotional satisfaction and peace of mind.

In addition, understanding the unique needs of elderly clients requires a sensitivity to their evolving circumstances and potential changes over time. Health issues, changes in family structure, and shifts in personal priorities can all impact financial planning. Financial planners must remain adaptable and responsive, regularly reviewing and adjusting plans to accommodate these changes. This ongoing attention helps ensure that the financial strategies remain effective and aligned with the client's current situation and future needs, thereby reinforcing the planner's role as a trusted advisor dedicated to the client's long-term well-being.

COMMUNICATION STRATEGIES FOR EFFECTIVE PLANNING

Effective communication is pivotal in resource management planning for the elderly, as it ensures that financial strategies are clearly understood and appropriately tailored to their unique needs. To facilitate clear and productive discussions, financial planners should use simple, jargon-free language when explaining complex financial concepts. Many elderly clients may not be familiar with financial terminology or may have cognitive impairments that affect their comprehension. By breaking down information into digestible parts and using visual aids such as charts or graphs, planners can make the planning process more accessible and less intimidating for their clients.

Active listening is another crucial communication strategy. Financial planners should attentively listen to their elderly clients, validating their concerns and preferences. This involves not only hearing their words but also understanding their underlying emotions and motivations. Asking open-ended questions can help uncover deeper insights into the client's financial goals, fears, and expectations. By demonstrating empathy and attentiveness, planners can build a stronger rapport and ensure that the financial plan truly reflects the client's values and desires.

Regular and proactive communication helps maintain clarity and trust throughout the planning process. Financial planners should establish a consistent schedule for check-ins and updates, ensuring that clients are kept informed about their financial status and any necessary adjustments to their plan. Clear documentation of discussions and decisions is essential, as it provides a reference for both the planner and the client. By fostering an environment of open dialogue and ongoing support, planners can effectively address any emerging issues and ensure that the client remains confident and engaged in their financial management journey.

Table 2.1 outlines various strategies to enhance communication with clients during personal financial planning, ensuring clarity, trust, and a collaborative approach.

TABLE 2.1 Communication Strategies and Best Practices

COMMUNICATION STRATEGY	DESCRIPTION	BEST PRACTICES
Active listening	Focus fully on the client to understand their needs, goals, and concerns.	- Avoid interrupting; show empathy. - Paraphrase to confirm understanding. - Use nonverbal cues like nodding.
Clear and simple language	Explain financial concepts in a way that is easy to understand.	- Avoid jargon and technical terms. - Use analogies or stories to clarify points. - Check for understanding regularly.
Open-ended questions	Encourage clients to share more about their goals and financial situation.	- Use questions starting with "What," "How," or "Why." - Allow the client time to think and respond. - Avoid leading questions.
Personalized communication	Tailor the conversation to the client's unique circumstances and preferences.	- Adjust tone and style based on the client's personality. - Consider the client's life stage and financial knowledge.
Regular follow-ups	Maintain ongoing communication to ensure the plan stays relevant and effective.	- Schedule periodic check-ins. - Send reminders and updates on the client's plan. - Encourage clients to reach out with questions or changes.
Visual aids and tools	Use charts, graphs, and other visual tools to illustrate financial plans and concepts.	- Provide visual summaries of complex data. - Use digital tools or apps to engage clients. - Ensure visuals are clear and directly relevant.
Empathy and patience	Demonstrate understanding and patience, especially with clients who may be anxious or unsure.	- Validate the client's feelings and concerns. - Allow the client to express fears and anxieties. - Reassure and guide without pressuring.
Transparency and honesty	Be upfront about potential risks, costs, and limitations of financial plans.	- Discuss both pros and cons of financial decisions. - Provide full disclosure of fees and charges. - Admit when you do not have an immediate answer.
Setting realistic expectations	Help clients understand what they can realistically achieve with their financial plan.	- Avoid overpromising results. - Discuss potential obstacles and setbacks. - Align goals with the client's financial capacity and risk tolerance.
Documentation and summarization	Keep a written record of discussions and decisions to ensure clarity and mutual understanding.	- Provide written summaries after meetings. - Ensure all action items are clearly documented. - Share records with the client for their reference.

DISCUSSION QUESTIONS

1. How does building trust between the financial planner and the elderly client influence the effectiveness of the financial planning process? Discuss the impact of trust on both the planning and implementation phases.
2. What communication strategies are most effective when dealing with elderly clients, particularly those who may have cognitive impairments or limited financial literacy? How can financial planners ensure that they are both understood and that they fully understand their clients' needs?
3. What are some ethical challenges that might arise in the client–planner relationship when dealing with elderly clients? How should financial planners navigate these challenges to maintain professionalism and integrity?
4. How can financial planners tailor their approaches to meet the unique needs and goals of elderly clients? Provide examples of how a planner might adjust their strategy based on different client scenarios.
5. Elderly clients often face significant life transitions, such as retirement or the loss of a spouse. What role does the financial planner play in helping clients manage these transitions from a financial perspective?
6. How important is it for financial planners to set and manage expectations at the outset of the client relationship? What techniques can be used to clarify and align expectations with reality?
7. Discuss the importance of maintaining long-term relationships with elderly clients. What benefits do sustained relationships provide to both the client and the planner?
8. How should financial planners manage the involvement of family members in the planning process for elderly clients? What strategies can be used to navigate complex family dynamics while ensuring the client's wishes are prioritized?

3

Gathering and Analyzing Data

Gathering and analyzing data is a fundamental step in resource management planning for the elderly, serving as the cornerstone for creating a robust and effective financial strategy. This process begins with collecting comprehensive information about the client's financial situation, including income sources, assets, liabilities, and expenses. For elderly clients, this may also involve understanding their healthcare needs, insurance coverage, and any anticipated long-term care requirements. Accurate and thorough data collection ensures that all relevant factors are considered, providing a clear picture of the client's financial health, and enabling the planner to address their specific needs and goals.

Once the data is gathered, a detailed analysis is conducted to evaluate the client's current financial status and identify potential gaps or opportunities. This analysis involves assessing the sustainability of their income streams, evaluating investment portfolios, and examining how well their financial resources align with their retirement and long-term care needs. For elderly clients, particular attention is given to factors such as liquidity, risk tolerance, and the impact of healthcare costs on their overall financial plan. By analyzing this data, financial planners can develop tailored strategies that not only address immediate concerns but also support the client's financial stability and quality of life in the years to come.

COLLECTING FINANCIAL INFORMATION

Collecting financial information is a critical first step in resource management planning for the elderly, as it provides the foundation upon which all subsequent financial strategies are built. This process involves gathering a comprehensive array of documents and data reflecting the client's financial situation. Key elements include income sources such as Social Security benefits, pensions, and any investment returns, as well as detailed records of assets like savings accounts, real estate, and personal property. In addition, planners must collect information on liabilities, including outstanding debts, mortgages, and other financial obligations. This thorough collection of data ensures that the financial plan accurately represents the client's financial reality and forms the basis for effective decision-making.

In addition to the standard financial documents, collecting information about the client's healthcare coverage and expenses is particularly important for elderly clients. This includes details on Medicare or Medicaid coverage, long-term care insurance policies, and any out-of-pocket medical expenses. Understanding these factors is crucial, as healthcare costs can significantly impact a senior's financial stability. Planners must also consider any upcoming medical procedures or potential long-term care needs that could affect the client's budget. By integrating this information into the financial analysis, planners can develop a more comprehensive and realistic plan that accounts for both expected and unforeseen healthcare costs.

Furthermore, gathering personal and family-related information is essential for creating a well-rounded financial plan. This includes understanding the client's family structure, any dependents, and potential inheritance plans. Information about the client's estate planning documents, such as wills and trusts, is also critical. Such details help financial planners address goals related to legacy planning, tax efficiency, and the distribution of assets. By collecting and analyzing this broader spectrum of information, planners can ensure that the financial plan not only addresses immediate financial needs but also aligns with the client's long-term personal and family objectives.

ASSESSING CURRENT FINANCIAL STATUS

Assessing the current financial status of elderly clients is a crucial component of resource management planning, as it provides a comprehensive understanding of their financial health and helps identify areas that need attention. This assessment begins with a detailed review of the client's income streams, including Social Security benefits, pensions, annuities, and any other sources of regular income. Understanding the reliability and sustainability of these income sources is vital, as it influences the client's ability to cover ongoing expenses and maintain their desired standard of living. Planners must ensure that income is sufficient to meet both current and future needs, considering potential changes in financial circumstances.

Next, a thorough evaluation of the client's assets and liabilities is conducted to gauge their overall financial position. This includes analyzing savings accounts, investments, real-estate holdings, and personal property against outstanding debts such as mortgages, credit card balances, and loans. By calculating net worth and assessing asset liquidity, planners can determine how readily available resources are for immediate needs versus long-term goals. This assessment helps in identifying potential financial shortfalls and opportunities for optimizing asset allocation to better support the client's retirement and long-term care plans.

In addition, assessing current financial status involves evaluating the adequacy of existing insurance coverage and any estate planning documents. For elderly clients, this means reviewing health insurance plans, long-term care insurance, and life insurance policies to ensure they provide adequate protection against future risks. Estate planning documents, including wills and trusts, must also be examined to confirm they align with the client's wishes and legal requirements. By conducting a comprehensive assessment of these elements, financial planners can craft a well-rounded financial plan that addresses immediate financial needs, prepares for potential future expenses, and aligns with the client's broader personal and family goals.

IMPORTANCE OF A NET WORTH STATEMENT AND PERSONAL CASH FLOW STATEMENT

For elderly individuals navigating their financial future, the importance of a Net Worth Statement and Personal Cash Flow Statement cannot be overstated. These tools serve as vital compasses in understanding and managing their financial resources effectively. A Net Worth Statement provides a comprehensive snapshot of all assets and liabilities, offering clarity on their overall financial standing. This clarity enables informed decisions on investments, estate planning, and ensuring a secure financial legacy for their family. Likewise, the Personal Cash Flow Statement tracks income and expenses over time, illuminating spending patterns and identifying areas for potential savings or adjustments. This insight is crucial for elderly individuals and their families in budgeting effectively, managing retirement income, and ensuring sustainable financial health throughout their later years.

Family financial planning for the elderly hinges significantly on these statements. By maintaining an accurate Net Worth Statement, elderly individuals and their families can gauge their financial stability and plan for unforeseen expenses such as healthcare or long-term care needs. It serves as a benchmark for assessing progress toward financial goals and adjusting strategies as circumstances change. Similarly, the Personal Cash Flow Statement allows families to monitor income sources, manage retirement distributions, and plan for contingencies. This proactive approach fosters not only financial independence and security but also peace of mind for both the elderly and their loved ones. These statements empower families to make informed decisions, allocate resources wisely, and ensure a stable financial future that supports their desired quality of life during retirement years and beyond.

Net Worth Statement

A Net Worth Statement is a crucial financial document that provides a comprehensive overview of an elderly individual's financial resources and obligations. It encompasses all assets and liabilities, offering a clear picture of their overall financial health. For elderly individuals engaged in family financial planning, this statement serves as a foundational tool for assessing their current financial standing and planning for the future. By detailing assets such as savings, investments, real estate, and retirement accounts, alongside liabilities such as mortgages, loans, and credit card debt, the Net Worth Statement allows families to understand the extent of their financial resources and obligations.

For example, consider Morris and Linda Wells, both retired and managing their finances with their adult children's assistance. Their Net Worth Statement includes their home valued at $500,000, retirement accounts totaling $300,000, savings of $50,000, a checking account of $1,200, and a car worth $20,000 as assets. Liabilities include a mortgage of $100,000 and credit card debt totaling $5,000. Wells can see their financial position with a total net worth of $765,000 ($875,000 in assets minus $110,000 in liabilities). This information allows them to plan for their ongoing expenses, healthcare needs, and potential inheritance considerations for their children. By regularly updating and reviewing their Net Worth Statement, the Wells family can confidently make decisions to optimize their financial resources and ensure a stable financial future amid their retirement years.

TABLE 3.1 Wells Net Worth Statement

ASSETS	VALUE	LIABILITIES	BALANCE
Checking account	$1,200	Credit card	$50,000
Savings	$50,000	Mortgage	$100,000
Home	$500,000	Total liabilities	$150,000
Retirement accounts	$300,000		
Car	$20,000		
Total assets	$871,200	Net worth	$721,200

Personal Cash Flow Statement

A Personal Cash Flow Statement is a critical tool for elderly individuals and their families engaged in financial planning. It provides a detailed record of income and expenses over a specific period. This statement categorizes all sources of income, such as pensions, Social Security benefits, investment dividends, and any part-time earnings, alongside all expenditures, including living expenses, healthcare costs, insurance premiums, and discretionary spending. For elderly individuals, understanding their cash flow is essential for managing day-to-day finances, budgeting effectively, and planning for future expenses like long-term care or estate distributions.

For instance, consider Marly Griffin, a retired widow living with her daughter's family. Her Cash Flow Statement outlines a monthly income of $3,000 from Social Security and a small pension, with expenses totaling $2,500 for groceries, utilities, healthcare premiums, and occasional dining out. The statement also includes $500 allocated for savings and discretionary spending. By regularly updating this statement, Mrs. Griffin and her family gain insights into her financial liquidity, identifying areas where adjustments might be needed to align income with expenses and ensuring her financial stability throughout retirement. This proactive approach helps maintain a balanced budget and prepares Mrs. Griffin and her family for any unforeseen financial challenges that may arise, ensuring peace of mind and financial security in her later years.

TABLE 3.2 Griffin's Cash Flow Statement

INCOME		
Social Security		$2,000
Pension		$1,000
Total income		$3,000
Expenses		
Groceries		$300
Utilities		$800
Healthcare premiums		$300
Entertainment (dining out)		$300
Savings		$400
Home insurance		$400
Total expenses		$2,500
Net cash flow		$500

IDENTIFYING KEY FINANCIAL DOCUMENTS

Identifying key financial documents is an essential step in resource management planning for the elderly, as these documents provide critical insights into their financial landscape and facilitate informed decision-making. The primary documents to gather include bank statements, investment account statements, and records of income sources such as Social Security benefits, pensions, and annuities. These documents offer a snapshot of the client's financial assets, income streams, and investment performance. A thorough review helps planners understand the client's financial situation and identify any areas where adjustments or optimizations might be needed to ensure financial stability and growth.

In addition to income and asset documentation, it is important to collect and review documents related to liabilities and debts. This includes mortgage statements, credit card statements, personal loan agreements, and any other records of financial obligations. Understanding the client's liabilities helps planners evaluate their debt management strategies and determine how to balance debt repayment with saving and investing. This information is crucial for developing a comprehensive financial plan that ensures the client can manage their liabilities effectively while maintaining a healthy financial position.

Estate planning documents are another critical component of the financial documentation process. For elderly clients, these include wills, trusts, powers of attorney, and healthcare directives. Reviewing these documents ensures that they reflect the client's current wishes and legal requirements, and helps address issues related to legacy planning, asset distribution, and decision-making in case of incapacity. Accurate and up-to-date estate planning documents are vital for ensuring that the client's financial and personal preferences are honored and that their assets are managed according to their wishes. Collecting and analyzing these documents allows financial planners to incorporate estate planning considerations into the overall resource management strategy, providing a holistic approach to the client's financial well-being (Bajtelsmit, 2024).

Table 3.3 outlines the key documents a financial planner needs to gather a comprehensive view of a client's financial situation, enabling the development of a well-rounded and effective financial plan.

TABLE 3.3 Document Types and Their Purposes

DOCUMENT TYPE	DESCRIPTION	PURPOSE
Income documentation	Pay stubs, tax returns, and any other income statements (e.g., rental income, investment income).	To assess the client's income sources, stability, and tax obligations.
Bank statements	Statements from checking, savings, and other bank accounts.	To understand the client's cash flow, spending patterns, and liquidity.
Investment account statements	Statements from brokerage accounts, retirement accounts (401(k), IRA), and other investment accounts.	To evaluate the client's asset allocation, investment performance, and retirement savings.
Debt and liability statements	Credit card statements, mortgage documents, loan agreements, and other debt-related documents.	To assess the client's liabilities, interest rates, and debt repayment obligations.
Insurance policies	Life, health, disability, home, auto, and other insurance policy documents.	To review the client's coverage, beneficiaries, premiums, and potential risks.
Retirement plan documents	Documents related to employer-sponsored plans (e.g., 401(k), pension plans) and individual retirement plans.	To determine retirement savings, employer match details, and retirement income projections.
Estate planning documents	Wills, trusts, power of attorney, and other estate planning documents.	To ensure the client's estate plan aligns with their financial goals and to plan for wealth transfer.
Tax returns	The last two to three years of tax returns.	To analyze the client's tax situation, identify deductions, and develop tax-efficient strategies.
Budget and expense reports	Detailed reports or summaries of monthly or annual expenses.	To understand the client's spending habits and identify areas for budget adjustments.
Real estate documents	Mortgage statements, property deeds, and appraisals.	To evaluate the value, equity, and liabilities associated with real estate assets.
Employee benefits information	Details on employer-provided benefits like health insurance, retirement plans, stock options, etc.	To maximize the use of employee benefits in the client's overall financial plan.
Legal documents	Contracts, prenuptial agreements, business agreements, and other legal documents.	To ensure financial decisions comply with legal obligations and consider any potential legal risks.
Business financial statements	For business owners, profit and loss statements, balance sheets, and cash flow statements.	To assess the financial health of the client's business and its impact on their personal financial plan.
Education savings plans	Documents related to 529 plans, Coverdell ESAs, or other education savings accounts.	To plan for the client's or their dependents' education expenses.
Social Security statements	Annual Social Security statements.	To estimate future Social Security benefits and incorporate them into retirement planning.

DISCUSSION QUESTIONS

1. Why is it crucial to gather a wide range of financial, healthcare, and personal information when planning resources for elderly clients? Discuss how missing data might impact the effectiveness of a financial plan.

2. What are the key indicators of financial health that planners should focus on when assessing an elderly client's financial status? How do these indicators influence the planning process?

3. Given the significant impact of healthcare expenses on elderly finances, how should financial planners incorporate the cost of healthcare and long-term care into their clients' financial strategies?

4. Discuss the importance of analyzing the sustainability of income sources for elderly clients. What challenges might arise from fluctuating income sources such as investments or pensions?

5. How do the management of assets and liabilities differ for elderly clients compared to younger clients? What unique strategies might be employed?

6. Why are the Net Worth Statement and Personal Cash Flow Statement particularly important in the financial planning process for the elderly? How can these tools be used to make strategic decisions?

7. How does a deep understanding of an elderly client's personal and financial goals enhance the data analysis process? Provide examples of how goals might change the approach to financial planning.

8. What strategies should financial planners use to effectively communicate the results of their data analysis to elderly clients? How can planners ensure that these communications are clear and lead to actionable insights?

CONTINUING CASE STUDY: DARREN AND LISA HARMON

Introduction to the Continuing Case

The continuing case study of Darren and Lisa Harmon serves as an immersive educational simulation designed to provide students with a realistic experience in family resource management. Through this simulation, students engage with a fictitious family, allowing them to apply theoretical knowledge to practical scenarios without the risks associated with real-life interactions. This approach enables students to develop crucial professional skills, such as financial planning, budgeting, and case management, in a controlled environment that fosters learning and growth.

Objectives

The primary objective of this case study is to help students master the competencies required for the Certified Family Life Educator (CFLE) designation, particularly within the Family Resource Management domain (CFLE Credential | National Council on Family Relations, n.d.). By working through various simulated assignments, students will learn to analyze the Harmon family's financial situation, set realistic goals, and develop strategies to help them achieve financial stability and security. Each assignment is carefully crafted to build upon the previous ones, culminating in the creation of a comprehensive monthly budget sheet that reflects the family's income, expenses, and financial priorities.

As students progress through the case study, they will be expected to apply their knowledge of budgeting, financial planning, and resource management to help the Harmon family navigate their financial challenges. The assignments embedded within each chapter of the textbook will guide students in making informed decisions that align with the family's goals. By the end of the simulation, students will have gained valuable experience in managing family resources, preparing them for real-world scenarios in their future careers as family service providers.

Client Information

Ages: Both Darin and Lisa Harmon are 55 and 53 years old, respectively

Family: They have three adult children, Felicia (25), Darin Jr. (23), and Maranda (19), who is still in college.

Occupations: Darin is a tenured professor at Mellow College, whereas Lisa owns a daycare business with two locations but is planning to open two more locations in the next five years.

Financial Goals: Save for retirement in 10 years, pay off their current home, continue to fund Maranda's undergraduate and graduate education, and purchase a vacation home in which they plan to live in at retirement.

Personal and Financial Background

Darin and Lisa Harmon have ambitious financial goals, influenced by their backgrounds and current lifestyle choices. Darin's academic career provides a stable income as well as Lisa's business but like most couples in the United States today, they have faced challenges due to COVID-19, inflation, and other unpredictable events of the past few years. Lisa's decision to open the two new locations was put on hold due directly to COVID-19.

Financial Assets and Liabilities

Income: Darin earns $105,400 annually, Lisa's business averages $84,000 a year, and they have various investment incomes including dividends and capital gains.

Assets: They own real estate, including their home and the two locations that house the daycare, and investments in stocks and mutual funds.

Liabilities: They have mortgages, auto loans, and credit card debts.

Over the next year, the Harmons would like to evaluate their retirement savings plan to see if they need to change their approach as well as build an emergency fund of three times their household expenses. They also want to make sure they can continue to save to pay for Olivia's education.

In the next 5 years, the Harmons would like to buy a new car, either a BMW X5 or Volvo Xc60 for Lisa. They also want to make sure they can also pay for Olivia's graduate school. Lisa would also like to open the two new locations within the next five years. The family would also like to purchase the lake house which will be their retirement home.

In the long term, the Harmons would like to sell their current home and remodel and move to the lake house. Finally, the Harmons would like to retire in 10 years.

CLIENT INFORMATION		SPOUSE INFORMATION	
Name	Darin James Harmon Sr.	Name	Lisa Ann Harmon
Birth date	9/12/1968	Birth date	2/4/1970
Social Security no.	385-01-1658	Social Security no.	412-58-1711
Business phone	(504) 555-5800	Business phone	(985) 555-1144
Residence address	9809 Yorkshire Ave	City, state, & ZIP	Wallace, LA 78602
Residence phone	(985) 555-5187		
Wedding date	6/8/1990		

Children and Grandchildren Information

NAME	BIRTHDATE	SOCIAL SECURITY NO.	SPOUSE
Children			
Felicia Ann Harmon Phillips	8/27/1999	456-86-3291	Frank Phillips
Darin James Harmon Jr.	6/14/2001	651-12-8956	Darlene Harmon
Maranda Leigh Harmon	10/3/2016	189-34-5230	Single
Grandchildren			
Joi Ann Phillips	1/5/2021	111-25-0356	Granddaughter
John James Phillips	6/26/2023	111-26-1467	Grandson

Education Information

NAME	SCHOOL	DEGREE	YEAR RECEIVED
Darin	Floyd State University	PhD, Accounting	5/12/1991
Gina	Bland University	MEd, Educational Management	5/15/2008

Occupation Information

NAME	EMPLOYER	POSITION	YEARS
Darin	Mellow College	Assistant Professor	08/1992–Present
Lisa	Merryland Preschool & Daycare	Owner/Executive Director	01/2008–Present

Assets Information

ASSET TYPE	LOCATION	BALANCE	RATE OF INTEREST	MATURITY
Checking	First National Bank (opened 06/01/02)	$2,308.00	1.50%	N/A
Mutual fund	Citizens State Bank (opened 06/05/01)	$92,256.00	3.00%	N/A
IRA	First National Bank	$92,256.00	5.50%	5/18/2020
Cash on hand		$225.00	N/A	N/A
Pensions	Edwards Jones & Co.	$444,045.00	N/A	N/A

Note: All assets are community property.

Stocks Information

# OF SHARES	SECURITY	DATE ACQUIRED	COST OR BASIS (PER SHARE)	COST OR BASIS (TOTAL)	CURRENT VALUE (PER SHARE)	CURRENT VALUE (TOTAL)
200	Amazon Stock (MCD)	9/15/2011	$8.66	$1,732	$182.22	$36,444
200	Walmart Stock (WMT)	9/15/2013	$15.28	$3,056	$70.59	$14,118
242	Putnam New Opportunities: Class A Mutual Fund (PNOCX)	3/16/2014	$21.81	$5,278.02	$131.52	$31,827.84

Automobiles Information

YEAR	MAKE	MODEL	COST	CURRENT VALUE	MONTHLY PAY
2018	Toyota	Pathfinder	$29,500	$14,100	$431
2017	Jeep	Grand Cherokee	$29,000	$20,100	$495

Real and Personal Property Information

PROPERTY	MARKET VALUE	REPLACEMENT VALUE
House	$252,000	$275,000
Darin's mom's home	$97,000	$105,000
Daycare #1	$55,900	$70,000
Daycare #2	$65,400	$80,000
Furniture ($35,000) and Stereo and TVs ($3,000)	$38,000	$80,000
Clothing ($6,000) and Jewelry ($5,000)	$11,000	$25,000
Other–Computer equipment	$1,800	$3,000

Liabilities Information

TO WHOM OWED	ORIGINAL AMOUNT	PROPERTY	RATE	CURRENT BALANCE	PAYMENT AMOUNT	FREQUENCY	TOTAL PAYMENTS	FIRST PAYMENT
First National Bank	$29,500	Toyota	7%	$12,549	$431	Monthly	48	9/1/2015
Citizens Bank	$29,000	Jeep	12%	$16,120	$495	Monthly	48	2/1/2013
Nationwide Mortgage Co.	$150,000	House	7%	$143,728	$1,500	Monthly	300	6/1/2011

Note: All liabilities are community property debt.

Credit Card Information

TYPE	NUMBER	ANNUAL FEE	INTEREST RATE	MAXIMUM LINE OF CREDIT	OUTSTANDING BALANCE	MINIMUM MONTHLY PAYMENT	GRACE PERIOD	CALCULATION METHOD
MasterCard—Lisa	2418 1781 4615 9063	$30.00	9.00%	$15,000	$1,075	5% of balance or $20, whichever is greater	Yes	Av. daily bal.
VISA—Darin	4166 8300 1104 2760	$0.00	16.50%	$10,000	$302	10% of balance or $25, whichever is greater	Yes	Av. daily bal.
American Express (Joint)	1284 6675 8	$0.00	18.00%	$4,500	$150	10% of balance or $20, whichever is greater	Yes	Av. daily bal.

Income Information

SOURCE	GROSS INCOME
Darin's salary	$8,783
Lisa's business income	$7,000
Rental income (Darin's mom's home)	$1,200
Investment income	$300
Dividends	$100
Interest	$200

Expenses Information

EXPENSE	CASH FLOW MONTHLY
Medical/dental expenses–prescriptions	$71
House mortgage	$1,500
Home insurance	$150
Property taxes	$300
Home repairs and maintenance	$175
Food/groceries, etc.	$450
Food away from home	$200
Clothing	$300
Utilities (electricity, gas, internet, and water)	$525
Telephone	$359
Auto maintenance–gas, tires, etc.	$620
Auto loan payments	$926
Credit card payments	$1,575
College tuition for Maranda	$1,250
Entertainment and sports activities	$148
University athletic events (two season tickets)	$140
Health insurance (payroll deduction)	$440
Life insurance (paid in March)	$386
Auto insurance (paid semiannually in January and June)	$1,614
Personal care	$150
Income taxes withheld	$1,578
Social Security taxes withheld	$1,207
Charitable contributions	$250
Retirement savings	$500
Investment magazines/newsletters/software	$70
Miscellaneous	$225
Totals	$9,508

Insurance Information

INSURANCE TYPE	DETAILS	DARIN	LISA
Life insurance	Type of Life Insurance	Group Term	Group Term
	Company	New York Life	New York Life
	Face amount	$150,000	$50,000
	Beneficiary	Lisa	Darin
	Owner	Darin	Lisa
	Annual premium	$282	$104

DISABILITY INSURANCE	POLICY NUMBER	EMPLOYER GROUP POLICY
	Definition of disability	Own job for 2 years, any job educationally suited for after 2 years
	Monthly benefit	65% of gross monthly salary
	Waiting period	
	Sick	30 days
	Accident	30 days
	Benefit period	
	Sick	5 years
	Accident	5 years
	Premiums	Paid by Merryland Preschool & Daycare

AUTO INSURANCE	DESCRIPTION	(1) HONDA CIVIC	(2) JEEP GRAND CHEROKEE
	Company	U.S. Casualty	U.S. Casualty
	Policy number	156-88876-A0B6	156-88876-A0B6
	Liability	100/300/50	100/300/50
	Personal injury protection	$2,500/person	$2,500/person
	Uninsured motorist	20/40/15	20/40/15
	Collision	Actual cash value	Actual cash value
	Deductible	$500	$500
	Comprehensive	Actual cash value	Actual cash value
	Deductible	$100	$100

	Annual premium	$703	$605
	Comments	Paid semiannually in January and June	Paid semiannually in January and June

MEDICAL INSURANCE	COMPANY	BLUE CROSS / BLUE SHIELD	TRAVELERS HEALTH PLAN
	Policy number	Group #251-365-2	Group #248361
	Major medical		
	Maximum deductible	$200/person/year	$15 copayment/doctor's visit
	Emergency room	$50 copay	$50 copay
	% participation	75/25	–
	Cap on participation	$1,000/year	–
	Prescription drugs	$20 copay/prescription	$10 copay/brand prescription, $5 copay/ generic prescription
	Maternity	Covered	Covered
	Dental	Not covered	Not covered
	Monthly premiums	$225	$215

HOMEOWNERS INSURANCE	COMPANY	U.S. CASUALTY
	Policy number/type	34583-28-21888/HO-B
	Dwelling	$225,000
	Other structures	$25,000
	Personal property on premises (market value)	$65,000
	Personal property off premises	$9,500
	Additional living expenses (annual limit)	$34,000
	Comprehensive liability (per occurrence)	$150,000
	Medical payments (per person)	$1,000
	Property damage to others (per occurrence)	$500
	Deductible	$1,125
	Annual premium	$1,260

Estate Planning Information

Darin and Lisa would each like to leave all their assets to each other in case of death. They would both like Olivia to be their secondary beneficiary. In case they both died, they would like Lisa's sister, Katy Foss, to be Olivia's legal guardian.

CONTINUING CASE STUDY—THE HARMONS—CASH MANAGEMENT

Chapter 3 Case Assignment 3.1

Objective:

The goal of this exercise is to analyze the financial situation of Darin and Lisa Harmon by preparing key financial documents and calculating essential financial ratios.

Instructions:

1. **Prepare Financial Documents:**
   - **Personal Balance Sheet:**
     - Create a personal balance sheet for Darin and Lisa. List all their assets (e.g., cash, investments, property) and liabilities (e.g., mortgage, credit card debt).
     - Calculate their net worth by subtracting total liabilities from total assets.
   - **Cash Flow Statement:**
     - Prepare a Cash Flow Statement that details Darin and Lisa's income and expenses over a specific period (e.g., monthly or annually).
     - Ensure to categorize their income sources (e.g., salaries, investments) and their expenses (e.g., housing, utilities, discretionary spending).
     - Calculate their net cash flow by subtracting total expenses from total income.

2. Calculate the Debt Ratio:

- **Debt Ratio Calculation:**
  - Using the information from the balance sheet, calculate Darin and Lisa's debt ratio by dividing their total liabilities by their total assets.
  - **Formula:** Debt Ratio = Total Liabilities / Total Assets

3. Analyze the Liabilities and Net Worth Relationship:

- **Favorable Relationship Analysis:**
  - Compare Darin and Lisa's liabilities to their net worth (calculated from the balance sheet).
  - Discuss whether the relationship between their liabilities and net worth is favorable, meaning whether they have a healthy balance between what they owe and what they own.

4. Calculate the Savings Ratio:

- **Savings Ratio Calculation:**
  - Using the Cash Flow Statement, calculate Darin and Lisa's savings ratio by dividing their savings by their after-tax income.
  - **Formula:** Savings Ratio = Savings / After-Tax Income
  - Compare their savings ratio to the rule of thumb recommended by financial experts (typically, a savings rate of 15%–20% of after-tax income).
  - Discuss whether Darin and Lisa are saving enough based on this recommendation.

4

Identifying Goals and Objectives

Identifying goals and objectives is a pivotal element in resource management planning for the elderly, as it allows financial planners to tailor strategies that directly address the client's specific aspirations and needs. For elderly clients, goals might include maintaining a comfortable standard of living, managing healthcare expenses, leaving a legacy for loved ones, or ensuring financial security throughout their retirement years. By engaging in detailed discussions to uncover these personal and financial objectives, planners can create a customized financial plan that aligns with the client's vision for their later years. This process ensures that all financial decisions and strategies are purpose-driven and supportive of the client's long-term well-being.

Furthermore, setting clear and realistic goals is essential for developing a comprehensive financial plan that effectively balances immediate needs with future aspirations. Elderly clients may have diverse and evolving goals, such as funding long-term care, supporting family members, or making charitable contributions. Identifying these objectives involves understanding their priorities and any specific preferences they have regarding their financial future. By translating these goals into actionable strategies, financial planners can help clients navigate their resources more effectively, making informed decisions that optimize their financial stability and quality of life as they age.

SETTING SHORT-TERM, MID-TERM, AND LONG-TERM GOALS

Setting short-term, mid-term, and long-term goals is essential in resource management planning for the elderly, as it helps create a structured financial strategy that addresses various time horizons and needs. Short-term goals typically encompass immediate financial objectives such as covering monthly living expenses, managing healthcare costs, or addressing urgent repairs or adjustments in living arrangements. For elderly clients, these goals often focus on ensuring day-to-day financial stability and addressing any immediate concerns that could impact their quality of life. By identifying and prioritizing these short-term goals, financial planners can implement strategies that provide immediate relief and support the client's current financial situation.

Mid-term goals extend over a few years and involve more substantial financial objectives that require careful planning and resource allocation. For elderly clients, mid-term goals might include saving for potential long-term care needs, funding significant lifestyle changes, or making substantial home modifications for increased accessibility. These goals often require a more strategic approach, balancing current spending with savings and investment plans to ensure that resources are available when needed. By addressing these mid-term goals, financial planners can help clients manage their financial resources more effectively, preparing for upcoming needs without compromising their short-term financial stability.

Long-term goals focus on outcomes that extend beyond a decade, including retirement planning, legacy planning, and long-term asset management. For elderly clients, long-term goals often involve ensuring financial security throughout their remaining years, planning for the distribution of their estate, and creating a legacy for heirs or charitable causes. These goals require a comprehensive approach that considers the client's overall financial health, investment strategies, and estate planning. By setting and working toward these long-term goals, financial planners can help clients achieve sustained financial stability, align their resources with their life's objectives, and ensure that their financial legacy is preserved according to their wishes.

Let us look at the financial goals of an elderly couple, James and Margaret Willis (Table 4.1):

By setting these diverse financial goals across short-term, mid-term, and long-term timelines, James and Margaret can effectively manage their resources, enhance their financial security, and ensure they are prepared for various aspects of retirement and beyond.

TABLE 4.1 James and Margaret's Goals

TIME FRAME	GOAL	DESCRIPTION
Short-term goals (1–2 years)	Home modifications	James and Margaret aim to renovate their home to include accessibility features such as ramps, handrails, and a walk-in shower. They plan to complete these modifications within the next year to accommodate their current mobility needs and ensure a safer living environment.
	Healthcare savings fund	They intend to establish a dedicated healthcare savings fund within the next year. This fund will cover out-of-pocket medical expenses, including copayments, prescriptions, and routine checkups, ensuring they have sufficient resources to manage their health needs without impacting their regular budget.
	Travel fund	James and Margaret want to set aside funds for a memorable vacation within the next 2 years. They plan to explore destinations they have always dreamed of visiting, ensuring they can enjoy quality time together and create lasting memories while they are still active and healthy.
Mid-term goals (3–5 years)	Supplemental income stream	They aim to diversify their income sources by investing in dividend-paying stocks and bonds over the next 3–5 years. This will provide them with a reliable supplemental income to support their retirement lifestyle beyond their pensions and Social Security benefits.
	Estate planning	James and Margaret plan to work with an estate planner to update their wills, establish trusts for their grandchildren's education, and review beneficiary designations on their accounts. They aim to complete this comprehensive estate planning process within the next 4 years to ensure their assets are distributed according to their wishes and minimize tax implications.
	Downsizing decision	They will evaluate their current housing needs and consider downsizing to a smaller home or a retirement community within the next 5 years. This decision will not only reduce their living expenses but also free up equity to bolster their retirement savings and provide financial flexibility in their later years.
Long-term goals (5+ years)	Legacy planning	James and Margaret aim to establish a charitable foundation or contribute significantly to causes they care about within the next 7 years. This long-term goal reflects their desire to leave a lasting impact on their community and support initiatives that align with their values.
	Long-term care strategy	They plan to research and purchase long-term care insurance to protect their assets and ensure they have access to quality care if needed in the future. They aim to finalize this decision within the next 6 years to mitigate the financial burden of potential healthcare costs as they age.
	Family education fund	James and Margaret want to create a fund to support their grandchildren's higher education expenses. They plan to contribute regularly to this fund over the next decade, ensuring their grandchildren have access to educational opportunities without financial strain on their own children.

PRIORITIZING FINANCIAL NEEDS

Prioritizing financial needs is a critical aspect of resource management planning for the elderly, as it helps ensure that limited resources are allocated effectively to address the most pressing concerns. For elderly clients, this often involves assessing immediate necessities such as daily living expenses, health-care costs, and housing needs. By identifying and ranking these financial needs, planners can develop a budget that ensures essential expenses are covered first. This prioritization helps prevent financial shortfalls and provides a stable foundation for addressing other financial goals and aspirations.

Beyond immediate needs, prioritizing financial requirements also involves planning for mid-term and long-term expenses. This includes anticipating potential future costs such as long-term care, major home modifications, or substantial medical treatments. Financial planners must evaluate the client's current financial situation and projected income to determine how to best allocate resources to meet these anticipated needs. Prioritizing these expenses ensures that the client is prepared for future financial demands without compromising their present well-being. By creating a strategic plan that balances short-term stability with future planning, planners can help elderly clients manage their finances more effectively.

Effective prioritization also considers personal goals and preferences, which are integral to a comprehensive financial plan. Elderly clients may have specific desires, such as supporting family members, making charitable donations, or leaving a legacy. By integrating these goals into the financial planning process and ranking them according to importance, planners can create a plan that not only addresses immediate and future financial needs but also aligns with the client's personal values and aspirations. This holistic approach ensures that the financial plan supports both practical needs and personal fulfillment, enhancing the client's overall financial satisfaction and security.

Figure 4.1 shows a radar chart that visually represents the process of prioritizing financial goals and priorities. Each step in the process is plotted to show how they contribute to effective goal prioritization.

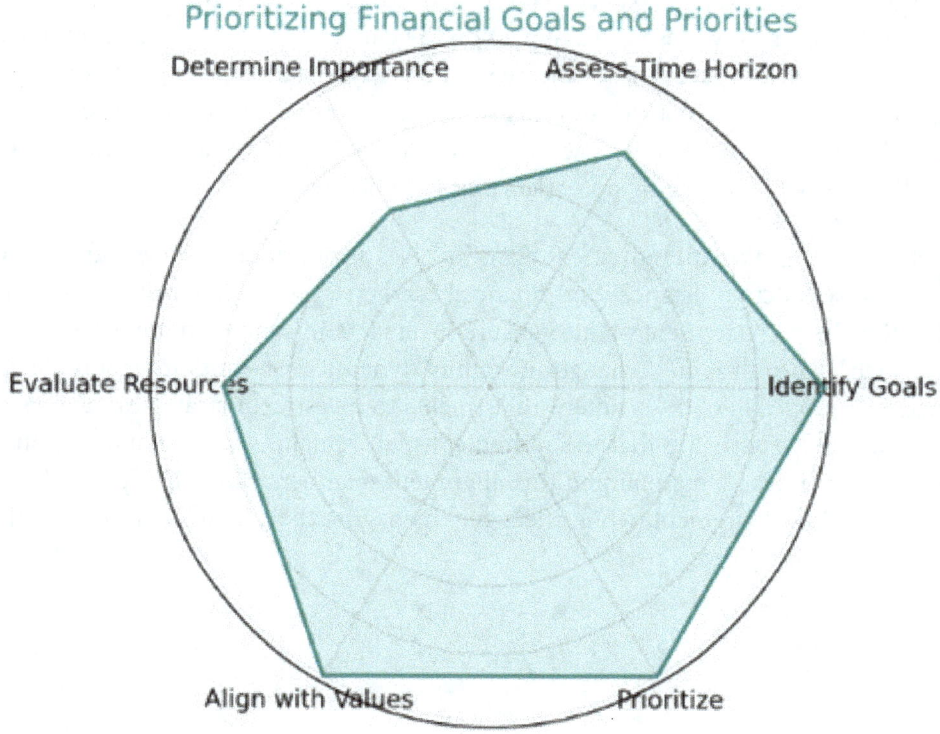

FIGURE 4.1 Financial goals and priorities

ALIGNING GOALS WITH RETIREMENT PLANS

Aligning goals with retirement plans is a crucial element of resource management planning for the elderly, ensuring that financial strategies effectively support their long-term aspirations and needs. As individuals approach retirement, their financial objectives typically shift from accumulating wealth to managing and preserving it. This transition requires a strategic approach to align retirement savings with goals such as maintaining a desired lifestyle, covering healthcare expenses, and managing debt. Financial planners must carefully evaluate the client's retirement assets, income sources, and projected expenses to develop a plan that balances these elements, providing a stable financial foundation throughout retirement.

To align goals with retirement plans, it is essential to incorporate both the client's immediate needs and long-term aspirations into the planning process. This involves setting clear retirement goals, such as desired retirement age, expected lifestyle changes, and any plans for travel or hobbies. Planners need to assess how these goals impact on the client's financial resources and determine if adjustments are needed to meet these objectives. This may include revising investment strategies, adjusting savings rates, or exploring additional income sources. By aligning retirement plans with personal goals, planners can ensure that clients have the financial means to achieve their desired retirement lifestyle while managing potential risks and uncertainties.

In addition, aligning goals with retirement plans involves a continuous review and adjustment process, as both personal circumstances and financial markets evolve. Financial planners must regularly revisit the client's retirement plan to ensure it remains in sync with any changes in goals or life events, such as health issues, changes in family dynamics, or shifts in economic conditions. This proactive approach allows for timely adjustments to investment strategies, savings plans, and expense management, ensuring that the retirement plan remains effective and responsive to the client's needs over time. By maintaining this alignment, planners can help elderly clients achieve a secure and fulfilling retirement, while effectively managing their financial resources throughout their later years.

DISCUSSION QUESTIONS

1. How does the identification of specific goals and objectives tailor financial plans to better meet the needs of elderly clients? Discuss the importance of personalized planning in achieving client satisfaction and financial stability.

2. Elderly clients often have multiple and potentially conflicting financial goals, such as maintaining lifestyle and managing healthcare costs. How can financial planners effectively balance these diverse objectives within a single comprehensive plan?

3. How does the process of setting goals with a client enhance their engagement and commitment to the financial planning process? Discuss the psychological impacts of involving clients in goal setting.

4. What criteria should financial planners use to prioritize goals, especially when resources are limited? How does prioritizing impact the overall success of financial management for the elderly?

5. How should financial planners address the challenge of balancing short-term needs with long-term objectives in planning for elderly clients? Provide examples of potential conflicts and suggested resolutions.

6. Elderly clients' goals may evolve due to changes in health, family dynamics, or financial circumstances. How should financial planners prepare for and respond to these changes to maintain alignment with the clients' current needs?

7. How can nonfinancial goals, such as leaving a legacy or supporting family members, be effectively integrated into a financial plan for elderly clients? Discuss the strategies that can be used to incorporate these broader life objectives.

8. How can success in achieving identified goals and objectives be measured and communicated to elderly clients? Discuss the importance of metrics and feedback in maintaining client trust and satisfaction.

CONTINUING CASE STUDY—THE HARMONS—SMART GOALS AND OBJECTIVES

Chapter 4 Case Assignment 4.1

Objective:

The purpose of this exercise is to help you develop clear, actionable, and measurable goals and objectives for your family's personal financial plan using the SMART criteria. SMART goals are Specific, Measurable, Achievable, Relevant, and Time-bound.

Instructions:

1. Understanding SMART Goals:

- Review the concept of SMART goals. Ensure you understand each component:
  - **Specific:** Clearly define what you want to achieve.
  - **Measurable:** Determine how you will measure progress.
  - **Achievable:** Ensure the goal is realistic given your current resources and constraints.
  - **Relevant:** Align the goal with your family's financial priorities.
  - **Time-bound:** Set a deadline or timeframe for achieving the goal.

2. Identify Family Financial Priorities:

- Discuss with your family the key financial priorities. These might include saving for a home, paying off debt, building an emergency fund, saving for education, retirement planning, etc.
- List at least three main financial priorities that are important to your family.

3. Create SMART Goals:

- For each financial priority identified, create one SMART goal.
- Ensure each goal adheres to all five SMART criteria.

- Example: Instead of "Save money for a house," a SMART goal could be "Save $30,000 for a down payment on a home within the next 3 years by setting aside $833 per month."

4. Develop Objectives:

- For each SMART goal, outline two to three specific objectives or actions that will help achieve the goal.
- These objectives should be clear steps that contribute to reaching the goal.
- Example for the goal mentioned above:
  - Objective 1: Reduce monthly discretionary spending by 20% to increase savings.
  - Objective 2: Set up an automatic transfer of $833 to a high-yield savings account each month.
  - Objective 3: Explore additional income streams, such as freelance work, to contribute to the savings goal.

5. Write a Reflection:

- Write a one-two-page reflection on the process of setting these SMART goals. Consider the following:
  - How did you determine your family's financial priorities?
  - What challenges did you encounter when setting SMART goals?
  - How do you feel these goals will impact your family's financial future?
  - What steps will you take to ensure these goals are achieved?

6. Submit Your Exercise:

- Compile your SMART goals, objectives, and reflection into a document.
- Ensure your goals are clearly labeled and organized.
- Submit your completed exercise by the due date.

5

Developing a Financial Plan

Developing a financial plan for the elderly is a pivotal step in resource management planning, aimed at creating a structured approach to managing their finances throughout retirement. This process involves synthesizing collected financial data, assessed needs, and identified goals into a cohesive strategy that addresses both immediate and long-term financial requirements. For elderly clients, the financial plan must be meticulously tailored to accommodate their unique circumstances, including managing fixed incomes, covering healthcare expenses, and preparing for potential long-term care needs. By developing a comprehensive plan, financial planners can provide clarity and direction, ensuring that resources are allocated effectively to support the client's desired lifestyle and financial security.

The development of a financial plan also requires careful consideration of various elements such as investment strategies, budgeting, and risk management. Planners must integrate the client's short-term needs with mid-term and long-term objectives, balancing current spending with future financial goals. This involves creating a detailed budget, setting up appropriate investment portfolios, and planning for unexpected expenses. The financial plan should be dynamic and adaptable, accounting for potential changes in the client's health, family situation, or economic conditions. By addressing these factors, planners can craft a plan that not only meets immediate needs but also provides a sustainable strategy for long-term financial stability and peace of mind.

CREATING A BUDGET FOR SENIORS

Creating a budget for seniors is a crucial aspect of resource management planning, designed to ensure that elderly clients can effectively manage their finances and maintain their desired quality of life. This process begins with a detailed assessment of the client's income sources, including Social Security benefits, pensions, and any other streams of revenue. Planners must then categorize and estimate all monthly expenses, such as housing costs, utilities, groceries, transportation, and healthcare. By comparing these expenses against the client's income, planners can identify any potential gaps or shortfalls and adjust the budget accordingly to ensure financial stability and avoid overspending.

In addition to managing regular monthly expenses, a senior's budget should account for irregular or annual costs that can significantly impact financial planning. These may include property taxes, insurance premiums, medical expenses, or unexpected home repairs. Creating a budget that incorporates these periodic costs requires setting aside funds in a separate savings account or creating a contingency fund to cover these expenses without disrupting the client's regular cash flow. This approach helps in avoiding financial strain and ensures that the client is prepared for both anticipated and unforeseen expenditures.

A well-structured budget for seniors also involves monitoring and adjusting spending patterns to align with changing needs and priorities. As elderly clients may experience shifts in their health, lifestyle, or living situation, their financial needs and priorities can evolve. Financial planners should encourage regular budget reviews and adjustments to accommodate these changes, ensuring that the budget remains realistic and supportive of the client's current circumstances. By maintaining flexibility and regularly updating the budget, planners can help seniors effectively manage their finances, providing a stable and secure financial environment that supports their well-being throughout retirement.

TABLE 5.1 **Monthly Household Budget Worksheet**

CATEGORY	EXPENSE	AMOUNT
Housing		
	Mortgage or rent	$850
	Property taxes	$200
	Maintenance	$50
	Phone, incl. cell phones(s), pagers, etc.	$100
	Utilities (water, gas, electricity, etc.)	$250
	Cable satellite programming	$50
	Waste removal	$30
	Total housing	$1,530

CATEGORY	EXPENSE	AMOUNT
Transportation		
	Vehicle 1 (loan payment)	$350
	Vehicle insurance	$125
	Fuel and maintenance	$100
	Total transportation	$575
Other debt		
	Credit card #1	$125
	Total other debt	$125
Personal		
	Entertainment	$175
	Household toiletries and supplies	$100
	Medical	$75
	Grooming	$50
	Clothing	$100
	Health club	$45
	Charitable contributions	$200
	Pet expenses	–
	Total personal	$745
Food		
	Groceries	$350
	Dining out	$200
	Total food	$550
Insurance		
	Home (including flood insurance)	$175
	Health (medical, dental, vision, etc.)	$275
	Life	$50
	Total insurance	$500
Saving or investments		
	Retirement account(s)	$100
	Investment account(s)	$200

CATEGORY	EXPENSE	AMOUNT
	Total savings or investments	$300
Taxes		
	Federal	$135
	State	$56
	Total taxes	$191
Total expenses		$4,516

BUDGET CATEGORIES PERCENTAGES RECOMMENDATIONS

Budget categories such as housing, transportation, entertainment, recreation, and savings are essential components of financial planning, especially for the elderly. The recommended percentage for each category ensures that spending remains balanced and manageable. For instance, allocating 0%–25% of the total budget to housing ensures that living expenses do not overwhelm other financial obligations. Similarly, keeping transportation and entertainment costs between 5%–10% helps maintain a comfortable lifestyle while preserving funds for savings. The savings category, with a recommended 0%–10%, emphasizes the importance of setting aside resources for future needs, which is crucial for financial stability and independence during retirement. Effectively managing these budget categories helps ensure that the elderly can enjoy their retirement years without financial strain.

TABLE 5.2 Budget Category Recommendations

BUDGET CATEGORY	RECOMMENDED %	CALCULATION
Housing (rent/mortgage, utilities)	0%-25%	Housing costs/total budget
Transportation	5%-10%	Transportation costs/total budget
Entertainment and recreation	5%-10%	Entertainment and recreation costs/total budget
Savings	0%-10%	Savings amount/total budget

FINANCIAL PROGRESS RATIOS

Financial progress ratios are essential tools in financial planning, particularly for the elderly, as they provide critical insights into financial stability and resource management. The debt ratio shows the relationship between liabilities and net worth; a lower ratio is preferable, indicating less debt relative to assets, which is crucial for financial security in retirement.

The current ratio and liquidity ratio are vital for assessing the ability to meet short-term obligations. A higher current ratio suggests sufficient liquid assets to cover liabilities, whereas a high liquidity ratio indicates how long living expenses can be sustained without income, both of which are key for managing unexpected expenses.

Finally, the debt payments ratio and saving ratio reflect the portion of income directed towards debt repayment and savings. Maintaining a debt payments ratio less than 20% ensures that debt does not overwhelm retirement income, whereas a saving ratio within the 5%–10% range helps in building a financial cushion for future needs. These ratios collectively ensure that the elderly can maintain financial independence and security throughout retirement.

TABLE 5.3 Financial Progress Ratios

RATIO	CALCULATION	EXAMPLE	INTERPRETATION
Debt ratio	Liabilities divided by net worth	\$25,000/\$50,000 = 0.5	Shows the relationship between debt and net worth; a low debt ratio is best.
Current ratio	Liquid assets divided by current liabilities	\$4,000/\$2,000 = 2	Indicates \$2 in liquid assets for every \$1 of current liabilities; a high current ratio is desirable to have cash available to pay bills.
Liquidity ratio	Liquid assets divided by monthly expenses	\$10,000/\$4,000 = 2.5	Indicates the number of months in which living expenses can be paid if an emergency arises; a high liquidity ratio is desirable.
Debt payments ratio	Monthly credit payments divided by take-home pay	\$540/\$3,600 = 0.15	Indicates how much of a person's earnings goes for debt payments (excluding a home mortgage); most financial advisors recommend a debt payments ratio of <20%.
Saving ratio	Amount saved each month divided by gross income	\$648/\$5,400 = 0.12	Financial experts recommend monthly savings of 5%–10%.

ALLOCATING RESOURCES FOR HEALTHCARE AND LIVING EXPENSES

Allocating resources for healthcare and living expenses is a critical component of resource management planning for the elderly, as these costs can significantly impact their financial stability and quality of life. Healthcare expenses often become a major concern for seniors, encompassing routine medical care, prescription medications, and potential long-term care needs. Financial planners must carefully evaluate these healthcare costs, including premiums for Medicare or private health insurance, out-of-pocket expenses, and the potential need for long-term care insurance. By accurately estimating these expenses and setting aside appropriate funds, planners can ensure that clients have the resources needed to cover their healthcare needs without compromising their overall financial security.

In addition to healthcare costs, it is essential to allocate resources for ongoing living expenses, which include housing costs, utilities, groceries, and other day-to-day necessities. For many elderly clients, these expenses are stable but must be carefully managed to align with their fixed or reduced income during retirement. Planners should assist clients in creating a budget that accounts for these regular expenses while also identifying areas where savings might be achieved. This might involve exploring options for downsizing their home, reducing discretionary spending, or finding cost-effective solutions for essential services. By optimizing resource allocation, planners can help ensure that living expenses are managed effectively, supporting the client's desired lifestyle and maintaining their financial well-being.

Effective allocation also involves planning for potential changes in living arrangements that may affect both healthcare and living expenses. For example, transitioning to an assisted living facility or making modifications to a current home for increased accessibility can introduce new costs. Financial planners should collaborate with clients to anticipate these potential changes and incorporate them into their resource management strategy. This proactive approach involves setting aside funds for potential future needs and adjusting the budget to accommodate any shifts in living circumstances. By planning for these possibilities, planners can help clients navigate changes smoothly and maintain financial stability throughout their retirement years.

These healthcare and medical costs should be integrated into the financial planning process to ensure that elderly clients can maintain their health and well-being without compromising their financial security.

TABLE 5.4 Healthcare Costs and Planning Considerations

HEALTHCARE COST	DESCRIPTION	PLANNING CONSIDERATIONS
Medicare premiums	Monthly premiums for Medicare Parts B and D, which cover medical services and prescriptions.	Include the costs of premiums and potential surcharges based on income levels.
Medigap insurance	Supplemental insurance covers costs not covered by Medicare, like copayments and deductibles.	Evaluate different plans and consider the client's health status and Medicare gaps.
Long-term care insurance	Insurance to cover the costs of long-term care facilities or in-home care not covered by Medicare.	Assess the likelihood of needing long-term care and the financial viability of premiums.
Out-of-pocket medical expenses	Costs for services not covered by insurance, such as certain medications, equipment, or therapies.	Estimate regular medical expenses and unexpected costs; consider a health savings account (HSA).
Home health care services	Costs for professional in-home care providers for daily living assistance or medical care.	Plan for potential in-home care needs and evaluate the duration and level of care required.
Assisted living or nursing home	Monthly fees for assisted living facilities or nursing homes.	Consider facility types, location, amenities, and the level of care provided.
Dental and vision care	Costs for dental checkups, treatments, glasses, and eye exams not covered by Medicare.	Regular dental and vision care costs can be significant; consider additional insurance.
Hearing aids	Expenses for hearing aids and related audiology services.	Include costs for purchase, maintenance, and replacement of hearing aids.
Transportation costs	Costs related to transportation for medical appointments, especially if mobility becomes restricted.	Plan for potential increased transportation costs or services like nonemergency medical transportation.
Over-the-counter medications	Regular expenses for over-the-counter drugs and health products.	Budget for ongoing and increasing costs for over-the-counter health needs.
Healthcare technology	Costs for technology that assists in monitoring and maintaining health, like blood pressure monitors.	Consider the benefits of investing in health technology that can reduce long-term healthcare costs.

PLANNING FOR UNEXPECTED COSTS

Planning for unexpected costs is a crucial aspect of resource management for the elderly, as it ensures financial stability and peace of mind amid unforeseen expenses. Seniors are particularly vulnerable to unexpected costs due to factors such as health emergencies, sudden home repairs, or unplanned travel. Financial planners should collaborate with elderly clients to establish an emergency fund specifically designed to cover these unexpected expenses. This fund should be easily accessible, typically held in a savings account or money market fund, and large enough to cover several months' worth of living expenses. By setting aside a portion of their resources for emergencies, seniors can better manage financial shocks without disrupting their long-term financial plans.

In addition to creating an emergency fund, planners should help clients evaluate and adjust their insurance coverage to mitigate the impact of unexpected costs. This includes reviewing health insurance policies to ensure they provide adequate coverage for potential medical emergencies and assessing the need for additional insurance types, such as long-term care insurance or homeowners' insurance with adequate coverage for unforeseen events. Ensuring that clients have comprehensive insurance coverage helps to reduce the financial burden of unexpected costs, providing a buffer that protects their financial stability and helps maintain their quality of life.

These unexpected costs can significantly impact on an elderly client's financial stability. A CFP should consider these when designing a flexible and robust financial plan to provide security and peace of mind.

TABLE 5.5 Unexpected Costs and Planning Considerations

UNEXPECTED COST	DESCRIPTION	PLANNING CONSIDERATIONS
Emergency medical expenses	Costs arising from sudden medical conditions or accidents.	Set aside funds in an emergency account or ensure ample liquidity to cover unexpected medical bills.
Home modifications	Costs for adapting a home to meet the needs of aging, such as ramps, grab bars, and stair lifts.	Plan for potential renovations or installations to accommodate mobility or health issues.
Major repairs	Unexpected large home repairs, such as roof replacement, plumbing issues, or heating system failures.	Maintain a reserve fund for significant home maintenance expenses.
Caregiver expenses	Costs related to hiring additional or specialized caregivers on short notice.	Consider insurance options or savings that can be allocated for sudden caregiver needs.
Legal fees	Expenses for legal advice or litigation related to estate planning, wills, or health directives.	Include potential legal costs in financial plans, especially for complex estates or family situations.
Scam and fraud losses	Financial losses due to scams, which the elderly are particularly vulnerable to.	Educate clients on common scams and invest in services that monitor and protect identities.
Transportation replacement	Costs related to the sudden need for more accessible transportation options.	Plan for changes in transportation needs, such as purchasing or modifying vehicles.
Increased utility bills	Unexpected increases in utility bills due to higher usage or price hikes.	Adjust budget forecasts to account for fluctuations in utility costs, especially with health devices.
Dental emergencies	High costs associated with urgent dental care, which is often not covered by basic health insurance.	Include a buffer for out-of-pocket expenses in dental emergencies, which are common in older age.
Change in living arrangements	Costs associated with moving to assisted living or nursing home facilities unexpectedly.	Ensure flexibility in financial plans to accommodate potential relocation or changes in care needs.
Death of a spouse	Financial implications of losing a spouse, including funeral expenses and loss of income.	Plan for the financial impact of a spouse's death, including estate settlement and income adjustment.

Furthermore, financial planners should encourage a proactive approach to managing unexpected costs by regularly reviewing and updating the client's financial plan. This includes revisiting the emergency fund's adequacy, reassessing insurance coverage, and adjusting the budget as needed. Regular check-ins allow for adjustments based on changing circumstances or new risks, ensuring that the financial plan remains robust and responsive. By maintaining flexibility and preparedness, planners can help elderly clients navigate unexpected expenses with greater confidence and minimize the potential impact on their overall financial security.

DISCUSSION QUESTIONS

1. How do financial planners integrate the collected data and identified goals into a coherent financial plan for elderly clients? Discuss the process of transforming raw data into actionable strategies.

2. Given the challenges of managing fixed incomes and rising healthcare costs, what strategies should financial planners use to ensure elderly clients can maintain their desired standard of living?

3. How do financial planners customize financial plans to accommodate the unique circumstances of elderly clients, such as long-term care needs and legacy desires?

4. Discuss the importance of creating a detailed budget within a financial plan for the elderly. How does budgeting help manage immediate and long-term financial needs?

5. What are some effective risk management strategies that can be incorporated into financial plans to protect elderly clients from potential financial shocks?

6. How can financial planners ensure that the financial plans they develop are both dynamic and adaptable to changes in an elderly client's health, family situation, or economic conditions?

7. What are the best practices for financial planners in communicating the details and benefits of the financial plan to elderly clients to ensure clarity and understanding?

8. Discuss the importance of regular evaluations and updates to financial plans for the elderly. How often should these reviews occur, and what key elements should be reassessed?

CONTINUING CASE STUDY— REATING AND EVALUATING A BUDGET

Chapter 5 Case Assignment 5.1

Objective:

The goal of this exercise is to develop a detailed budget for Darin and Lisa based on their Cash Flow Statement, categorize their income and expenses, and evaluate whether their budget aligns with typical after-tax budget allocations for their life situation. You will also identify areas where they can adjust spending or increase savings if needed.

Instructions:

1. Develop a Budget for Darin and Lisa:

- **Budget Creation:**
  - Using Darin and Lisa's Cash Flow Statement, develop a detailed budget that includes all sources of income and all planned expenses.
  - Income: Include all expected sources of income such as salaries, investments, or other regular income streams.
  - Expenses: Categorize their expenses into essential (e.g., housing, utilities, groceries) and discretionary (e.g., entertainment, dining out) categories.
  - Ensure that their total planned expenses do not exceed their total income. If their expenses exceed their income, identify areas where they can reduce spending.
- **Adjust Spending or Increase Savings:**
  - Review the budget you have created to determine if there are areas where Darin and Lisa can reduce their spending.
  - Identify opportunities to increase savings, whether by reallocating funds from discretionary spending or by other means.

2. Evaluate Budget Allocations:

- **Budget Allocation Calculation:**
  - Using the "Typical After-Tax Budget Allocations for Different Life Situations," calculate the recommended budget allocations for Darin and Lisa based on their net monthly salary (or after-tax salary).
  - These allocations typically include percentages for various categories such as housing, transportation, food, savings, and discretionary spending.
- **Comparison with Actual Budget:**
  - Compare the actual budget allocations (from the budget you created) with the recommended budget allocations.
  - Identify areas where Darin and Lisa's budget aligns with or deviates from the typical recommendations.
- **Analysis and Recommendations:**
  - Discuss whether Darin and Lisa's budget allocations are within the recommended parameters.
  - Suggest specific adjustments where necessary to help them better align their spending with recommended budget allocations.
  - Provide practical recommendations on how they can achieve a balanced budget that supports their financial goals.

6

Retirement Planning

Retirement planning is a fundamental aspect of resource management for the elderly, focusing on creating a comprehensive strategy to ensure financial stability and well-being throughout retirement. This planning involves assessing current financial resources, setting retirement goals, and developing a plan to manage income, expenses, and investments effectively. For elderly clients, retirement planning is about not just transitioning from a working career to retirement but also securing a comfortable and sustainable lifestyle. It includes evaluating how retirement savings, Social Security benefits, pensions, and other income sources will support their needs and aspirations in the years ahead.

Effective retirement planning also addresses the unique financial challenges that can arise as individuals age, such as managing healthcare costs, adjusting to fixed incomes, and planning for potential long-term care needs. By creating a tailored retirement plan, financial planners help elderly clients navigate these challenges, ensuring that their resources are allocated in a way that maximizes their financial security and quality of life. This involves strategic decisions about investments, budgeting, and risk management, all aimed at maintaining financial stability and achieving the client's retirement goals while adapting to any changes in their circumstances.

UNDERSTANDING RETIREMENT ACCOUNTS AND BENEFITS

Understanding retirement accounts and benefits is essential for effective resource management planning for the elderly, as these elements play a significant role in shaping their financial stability during retirement. Retirement accounts, such as 401(k)s, IRAs, and Roth IRAs, each have distinct features, tax implications, and withdrawal rules that impact how and when funds can be accessed. Financial planners must ensure that elderly clients are aware of the specifics of their retirement accounts, including contribution limits, required minimum distributions (RMDs), and potential tax consequences. By comprehensively understanding these factors, clients can make informed decisions about how to best utilize their retirement savings to meet their financial needs and goals.

In addition to retirement accounts, Social Security benefits represent a crucial income source for many elderly individuals. Understanding how Social Security benefits are calculated, when to begin claiming, and the potential impact of early or delayed claims is vital for optimizing this benefit. Financial planners should help clients evaluate their options, considering factors such as life expectancy, spousal benefits, and potential tax implications of Social Security income. By guiding the timing and strategy for claiming benefits, planners can help clients maximize their Social Security income and better integrate it into their overall retirement plan (Kagan, 2024).

Furthermore, it is important to consider other retirement benefits that may be available, such as pensions, annuities, or veterans' benefits. Each of these benefits comes with its own set of rules and characteristics that can affect the client's financial situation. For example, pensions may offer various payout options, such as lump sum payments or monthly annuities, which can impact long-term financial planning. Financial planners should collaborate with clients to thoroughly understand all available benefits, their features, and how they fit into the overall retirement strategy. By taking a comprehensive approach to managing retirement accounts and benefits, planners can ensure that elderly clients achieve a balanced and secure financial foundation for their retirement years.

MAXIMIZING SOCIAL SECURITY BENEFITS

Maximizing Social Security benefits is a crucial aspect of resource management planning for the elderly, as this program provides a significant and reliable source of income during retirement. To optimize Social Security benefits, it is essential to understand the factors that influence the amount received, including the age at which benefits are claimed. Social Security allows individuals to begin claiming benefits as early as age 62, but doing so results in reduced monthly payments. Conversely, delaying benefits until reaching full retirement age or beyond can significantly increase the monthly amount. Financial planners should collaborate with clients to evaluate their financial needs, health status, and life expectancy to determine the optimal age for claiming benefits and maximize the overall lifetime benefit (Social Security Administration, n.d.-b).

Another important consideration in maximizing Social Security benefits is coordinating with spousal benefits. If both spouses have worked and are eligible for benefits, they may have options to enhance their combined Social Security income. For instance, one spouse may claim benefits based on their own work record, whereas the other may claim spousal benefits or delay their own benefits to increase their future payout. Financial planners should guide clients through the various claiming strategies, such as the "file and suspend" or "restricted application" strategies, depending on their specific circumstances and changes in Social Security rules. Proper coordination of spousal benefits can lead to a more substantial cumulative income for the household.

In addition, it is crucial to consider the impact of Social Security benefits on taxes and overall retirement income planning. Social Security benefits can be subject to income taxes if the recipient's total income exceeds certain thresholds. Financial planners should help clients understand the tax implications of their Social Security income and integrate this into their overall financial strategy. By optimizing the timing and claiming strategy for Social Security benefits and considering their tax impact, planners can help elderly clients enhance their retirement income, ensuring a more secure and comfortable financial future.

PENSION PLANS AND ANNUITIES

Pension plans and annuities are integral components of resource management planning for the elderly, providing predictable income streams that can enhance financial stability during retirement. Pension plans, often provided by former employers, offer a fixed monthly income based on factors such as years of service and salary history. Understanding the specifics of a pension plan, including its payout options, vesting requirements, and survivor benefits, is essential for maximizing its benefits. Financial planners should help clients evaluate whether to take a lump sum payout or opt for monthly payments, considering factors such as their overall financial needs, life expectancy, and investment preferences to make an informed decision that best aligns with their retirement goals.

Annuities, on the other hand, are financial products purchased from insurance companies that provide a guaranteed income for a specified period or for the lifetime of the annuitant. They come in various forms, including fixed, variable, and immediate annuities, each offering different features and benefits. Fixed annuities provide predictable payments, whereas variable annuities offer the potential for higher returns based on investment performance but come with additional risk. Immediate annuities begin payments almost immediately after purchase, making them suitable for those who need immediate income. Financial planners should assist clients in selecting the right type of annuity based on their risk tolerance, income needs, and investment horizon to ensure that the annuity complements their overall retirement strategy.

Integrating pension plans and annuities into a comprehensive retirement plan involves considering their role in the broader context of the client's financial resources and goals. This includes evaluating how these income sources interact with Social Security benefits, savings, and other investments. Planners must also consider the potential impact of inflation on fixed payments and explore options for inflation protection within annuities. By carefully analyzing and incorporating pension plans and annuities into the resource management strategy, financial planners can help elderly clients achieve a balanced and secure income stream, ensuring that their financial needs are met throughout retirement.

These tools and techniques are integral to the CFP financial planning process for elderly clients, ensuring a comprehensive approach to managing retirement and associated challenges effectively.

TABLE 6.1 Retirement Tools and Techniques

RETIREMENT TOOL/ TECHNIQUE	DESCRIPTION	BENEFITS
Diversified investment portfolio	A mix of stocks, bonds, and other investments designed to balance risk and reward.	Reduces risk through diversification and potentially increases returns.
Annuities	Financial products that provide regular income payments in exchange for an initial investment.	Provides a steady stream of income for life or a specified period, helping to manage longevity risk.
Social Security optimization	Strategies to maximize Social Security benefits based on timing of claims and marital status.	Ensures maximum benefit utilization, critical for long-term financial stability.
401(k) and IRA plans	Retirement accounts with tax advantages, including traditional and Roth options.	Offers tax benefits and compound growth, with options for pretax or tax-free withdrawals.
Reverse mortgages	Loans that allow homeowners to convert part of their home equity into cash without selling the home.	Provides additional income while allowing the elderly to remain in their homes.
Long-term care insurance	Insurance coverage for long-term care needs that are not covered by regular health insurance.	Helps manage the high costs of long-term care, protecting other retirement savings.
Medicare planning	Strategies to manage healthcare costs using various parts of Medicare and supplemental plans.	Helps manage healthcare expenses, a significant part of retirement spending.
Estate planning	Tools like wills, trusts, and estate management strategies to manage and transfer wealth.	Ensures assets are distributed according to the client's wishes and can reduce estate taxes.
Budgeting and cash flow management	Techniques to plan and monitor income and expenses during retirement.	Essential for maintaining financial balance and avoiding overspending.
Tax planning	Strategies to minimize tax liabilities through withdrawals, donations, and other means.	Maximizes retirement income by reducing tax liabilities.
Inflation protection	Investments and strategies to protect savings from the eroding effects of inflation.	Helps maintain purchasing power of retirement funds over time.

DISCUSSION QUESTIONS

1. How can financial planners effectively assess a client's readiness for retirement, considering both financial resources and personal circumstances? What key indicators should be evaluated?

2. What are the implications of different Social Security claiming strategies (e.g., early claiming vs. delayed claiming), and how should financial planners guide clients in making these decisions based on their individual financial situations?

3. Given the potentially high cost of healthcare in retirement, how should financial planners incorporate healthcare planning into the overall retirement strategy? What specific financial products or strategies might be recommended?

4. How should long-term care needs be addressed in retirement planning, and what tools or insurance products are most effective in managing these risks?

5. What investment strategies are most suitable for elderly clients who are transitioning from accumulation to distribution phases in their retirement? How does risk tolerance change during this transition?

6. How can financial planners help clients structure their income streams to ensure stability and sustainability throughout retirement? What role do annuities or other fixed income products play?

CONTINUING CASE STUDY—ALLOCATING RESOURCES FOR HEALTHCARE AND LIVING EXPENSES

Chapter 6 Case Assignment 6.1

Objective:

This exercise aims to estimate your annual cost of living at the time of retirement by considering your current spending, calculating the inflation factor, and projecting the future budget needed for various living expenses. This exercise will help you understand how inflation impacts your future financial needs, especially for healthcare and other essential living expenses by completing the Estimate Your Annual Cost of Living Worksheet (in the Appendix).

Instructions:

1. Use the Estimate Your Annual Cost of Living Worksheet and Complete the Current Spending Column:

- Review your current spending in each of the categories listed below:
  - Housing
  - Household maintenance
  - Automobile/transportation
  - Food
  - Clothing
  - Personal
  - Medical/health
  - Recreation/education
  - Contributions
  - Taxes/insurance
  - Savings/investments
  - Variable essential expenses (e.g., gifts, license plates, holiday spending)

- For each category, enter the amount you currently spend annually in the "Current Spending" column of the worksheet.

2. Calculate the Inflation Factor:

- Refer to the Inflation Factor Table (in the Appendix) to calculate the inflation factor for each category.
- The inflation factor represents the increase in costs over time due to inflation.
- Enter the calculated inflation factor for each category in the "Inflation Factor" column of the worksheet. If the inflation factor is the same across all categories, you may enter the same number in each row, or calculate it individually for each category based on expected inflation.

3. Estimate Future Budget at Retirement:

- For each expense category, multiply your "Current Spending" by the corresponding "Inflation Factor" to estimate the amount you will need to budget for that category in your first year of retirement.
- Enter the resulting value in the "Future Budget at Retirement in _____ Years" column.
- Consider the number of years until retirement to choose the appropriate inflation factor.

4. Calculate the Annual Total:

- Add up all the amounts in the "Future Budget at Retirement in _____ Years" column to calculate the total income you will need during your first year of retirement.
- Enter this total in the "ANNUAL TOTAL" row at the bottom of the worksheet.

5. Reflection:

- Write a short reflection (one to two pages) on the following:
  - How does the projected future budget compare to your current spending?
  - Which categories are most affected by inflation, and how might this impact your retirement planning?
  - What strategies can you consider managing inflation's impact on your future living expenses, especially in healthcare and essential areas?

CONTINUING CASE STUDY—PLANNING FOR UNEXPECTED COSTS—LARGE FUTURE IRREGULAR EXPENSES

Chapter 6 Case Assignment 6.2

Objective:

The goal of this exercise is to help you plan for large, irregular expenses that may occur in the future. By using the worksheet provided, you will estimate the costs associated with replacing major items such as vehicles, appliances, home components, and furnishings. This exercise will assist you in budgeting for these expenses over time and ensure that you are financially prepared when these costs arise using the Large Future Irregular Expenses Worksheet (in the Appendix).

Instructions:

1. Complete the Worksheet:

- **Year Bought:** For each item listed on the worksheet (vehicles, appliances, home components, furnishings), enter the year the item was originally purchased.
- **Average Expected Years of Life:** Fill in the average expected lifespan for each item based on the guidelines provided (e.g., 12 to 13 years for a range, 15 years for a refrigerator).
- **Year to Replace:** Calculate the year when each item will need to be replaced. This can be done by adding the average expected years of life to the year the item was bought.
- **Present Replacement Price:** Research and enter the current replacement cost for each item. This is the price you would pay if you needed to replace the item today.

2. Estimate the Future Replacement Price:

- **Inflation Factor:** Choose an appropriate inflation factor based on the number of years until the replacement year. Refer to the inflation factor chart mentioned in your course materials.
- **Estimated Price in Replacement Year:** Multiply the "Present Replacement Price" by the chosen inflation factor to estimate the cost of replacing the item in the future. Enter this amount in the corresponding column on the worksheet.

3. Reflection and Planning:

- **Prioritize Replacements:** Based on the estimated replacement years and costs, prioritize which items may need attention first and plan how you will allocate resources to cover these expenses.
- **Savings Strategy:** Consider setting up a savings plan to prepare for these future costs. How much would you need to save each year to cover these expenses when they arise?
- **Emergency Fund Consideration:** Reflect on how these potential future expenses impact on your current financial planning. Should you increase your emergency fund to cover unexpected replacements?

4. Write a Summary:

- Write a summary (one to two pages) discussing your findings from completing the worksheet. Consider the following points:
  - Which items will need to be replaced first, and how do their costs compare to your current financial resources?
  - How might inflation impact your ability to replace these items when needed?
  - What steps will you take to ensure you are financially prepared for these future expenses?

7

Investment Management

Investment management is a critical aspect of resource management planning for the elderly, as it involves strategically allocating financial assets to ensure long-term stability and growth throughout retirement. For seniors, effective investment management is crucial to preserving wealth, generating income, and mitigating risks associated with market volatility. This process requires a careful balance between maintaining sufficient liquidity to cover short-term needs and investing in assets that offer potential for growth. Financial planners must tailor investment strategies to align with the client's risk tolerance, time horizon, and income requirements, providing a foundation for a secure and comfortable retirement.

As elderly clients navigate retirement, their investment priorities often shift from growth to preservation and income generation. This shift necessitates a more conservative investment approach that focuses on preserving capital and producing reliable income streams, such as through dividend-paying stocks, bonds, or annuities. Financial planners must consider factors such as the client's current financial situation, anticipated expenses, and potential healthcare costs when developing an investment strategy. By aligning investment management with these priorities, planners can help seniors achieve a balanced approach that supports their financial goals while safeguarding their assets against unexpected challenges and market fluctuations.

RISK ASSESSMENT AND TOLERANCE

Risk assessment and tolerance are crucial elements in resource management planning for the elderly, as they significantly impact how financial assets are allocated and managed throughout retirement. For seniors, understanding their risk tolerance is essential for creating a financial strategy that aligns with their comfort level regarding market fluctuations and potential losses. As individuals age, they often have a lower risk tolerance due to the need for financial stability and the reduced time horizon for recovering from potential losses. Financial planners must assess each client's risk tolerance through discussions about their investment preferences, financial goals, and psychological comfort with risk. This assessment helps in tailoring investment strategies that balance growth potential with the need for security.

Evaluating risk tolerance involves not only considering the client's personal comfort level with risk but also analyzing their financial situation and future needs. For elderly clients, this means looking at factors such as their current income sources, expenses, healthcare costs, and overall financial goals. A well-rounded risk assessment will also consider the client's investment time horizon and liquidity needs, ensuring that the investment strategy supports both short-term stability and long-term growth. By understanding these factors, financial planners can recommend appropriate asset allocations, such as more conservative investments or income-generating assets, which align with the client's risk tolerance and financial objectives.

In addition, risk management strategies must be adaptable to changing circumstances over time. As seniors' needs and priorities evolve, so should their approach to risk, too. This requires ongoing monitoring and reassessment of the client's risk tolerance, especially in response to significant life events such as health changes or shifts in financial status. Financial planners should regularly review and adjust the investment strategy to reflect these changes, ensuring that the portfolio remains aligned with the client's current risk tolerance and financial goals. By maintaining a flexible and responsive approach to risk management, planners can help elderly clients navigate the complexities of retirement planning while protecting their financial well-being against unforeseen challenges.

DIVERSIFICATION STRATEGIES

Diversification strategies are a key component of resource management planning for the elderly, serving as a fundamental approach to balancing risk and optimizing returns in a retirement portfolio. Diversification involves spreading investments across a variety of asset classes, such as stocks, bonds, real estate, and cash equivalents, to reduce the impact of any single asset's poor performance on the overall portfolio. For elderly clients, diversification helps mitigate the risk of significant losses due to market volatility, ensuring that their retirement savings are not overly exposed to any single economic or financial event. By creating a diversified portfolio, financial planners can provide a more stable and reliable source of income throughout retirement.

Implementing effective diversification strategies requires a tailored approach that considers the client's specific financial goals, risk tolerance, and investment time horizon. For seniors, this often means shifting toward more conservative investments with lower volatility, such as high-quality bonds or dividend-paying stocks, while maintaining a portion of the portfolio in growth-oriented assets to combat inflation. Diversification also involves incorporating alternative investments or income-generating assets, such as real estate or annuities, which can offer additional stability and regular income streams. Financial planners must carefully select and balance these investment options to align with the client's unique needs and financial situation.

In addition, diversification is not a one-time strategy but an ongoing process that requires regular review and adjustment. As elderly clients' financial circumstances and needs change, their investment strategy should be reevaluated to ensure continued alignment with their retirement goals. This includes periodically reviewing the asset allocation, adjusting for market conditions, and considering any shifts in the client's risk tolerance or income needs. By continuously monitoring and refining diversification strategies, financial planners can help seniors navigate the complexities of retirement investing, ensuring their portfolio remains well-positioned to support their financial stability and goals throughout their retirement years.

INVESTMENT VEHICLES FOR SENIORS

Investment vehicles for seniors play a crucial role in resource management planning, offering tailored options that align with their financial goals and risk tolerance. For elderly clients, investment vehicles such as high-quality bonds, dividend-paying stocks, and certificates of deposit (CDs) are often preferred due to their stability and income-generating potential. Bonds, particularly government and high-grade corporate bonds, provide predictable interest payments and are less volatile than equities, making them a suitable choice for preserving capital while generating steady income. Similarly, dividend-paying stocks can offer a reliable source of income through regular dividend payments, while also providing potential for modest capital appreciation.

Another important investment vehicle for seniors is annuities, which can offer guaranteed income for a specified period or for the rest of the individual's life. Immediate annuities, for instance, begin paying out almost immediately after purchase, making them ideal for those needing immediate cash flow. Fixed annuities provide a guaranteed interest rate and predictable payments, which can help in managing a fixed budget during retirement. Variable annuities, though offering the potential for higher returns based on investment performance, come with increased risk and complexity. Financial planners must carefully assess the client's needs and preferences to recommend the most suitable type of annuity that aligns with their financial goals and risk tolerance.

Last, investment vehicles such as mutual funds and exchange-traded funds (ETFs) provide diversification and professional management, which can be advantageous for seniors seeking to balance risk and return. These funds pool investments from multiple investors to purchase a diversified portfolio of assets, reducing individual investment risk. Mutual funds and ETFs can be tailored to different risk levels and investment objectives, making them flexible tools for managing retirement savings. Financial planners should help seniors select funds that align with their investment strategy, ensuring that their portfolio remains diversified and aligned with their long-term financial goals. By understanding and utilizing these investment vehicles, planners can assist elderly clients in creating a balanced and effective investment strategy that supports their financial stability throughout retirement.

These investment tools and techniques help elderly clients manage their assets effectively, focusing on income generation, capital preservation, and risk reduction, all crucial elements in the later stages of life.

TABLE 7.1 Investment Tools and Techniques

INVESTMENT TOOL/ TECHNIQUE	DESCRIPTION	BENEFITS
Diversified investment portfolio	A balanced mix of stocks, bonds, mutual funds, and ETFs designed to minimize risk and maximize potential returns.	Provides risk management through asset allocation, aiming to preserve capital and achieve stable growth.
Bonds and fixed income securities	Investments that pay regular interest income, such as government and corporate bonds.	Offers stable and predictable income, suitable for risk-averse investors.
Dividend-paying stocks	Stocks of well-established companies with a history of paying dividends.	Generates income through dividends, which can be reinvested or used as part of regular cash flow.
Annuities	Insurance products that provide guaranteed income for life or a set period.	Ensures a steady income stream, reducing the risk of outliving one's savings.
Real estate investment trusts (REITs)	Companies that own or finance income-producing real estate.	Offers a source of regular income through dividends and potential capital appreciation.
Exchange-traded funds (ETFs)	Investment funds traded on stock exchanges, much like stocks, and often focused on specific themes or sectors.	Allows for diversified investments with lower costs and flexibility in trading.
Certificate of deposits (CDs)	Time deposits at banks that offer fixed interest over a specified period.	Provides safety and a fixed interest return, ideal for conserving capital.
Managed payout funds	Mutual funds designed to provide monthly or quarterly distributions to investors.	Helps manage cash flow in retirement by delivering predictable payouts.
Tax-deferred investments	Accounts like 401(k)s and IRAs that allow taxes on returns to be paid later.	Maximizes growth potential by deferring taxes until withdrawal, often at a lower tax rate in retirement.

INVESTMENT TOOL/ TECHNIQUE	DESCRIPTION	BENEFITS
Life cycle funds	Mutual funds that automatically adjust their asset allocation based on the investor's age or a specific retirement target date.	Simplifies investment decisions and management, ensuring the investment becomes more conservative as retirement approaches.
Robo-advisors	Automated investment platforms that manage portfolios based on algorithms and the client's risk tolerance.	Offers a cost-effective and efficient way to manage investments with minimal human intervention.

CONTINUING CASE—THE HARMONS—INVESTMENT PLANNING—ADDRESSING FINANCIAL GOALS

Chapter 7 Case Assignment 7.1

Objective:

The purpose of this exercise is to create a comprehensive investment plan that addresses Darin and Lisa's financial goals across different time horizons: short range (1 year), intermediate range (1 to 5 years), and long term (more than 5 years). You will analyze their goals and develop strategies to help them achieve these goals, prioritizing the most important financial objective: opening two new daycare locations.

Instructions:

1. Analyze the Financial Goals:

Short-Range Goals (1 Year):

- Start a more aggressive savings plan for retirement.
- Build an emergency fund.
- Save and continue to pay for Olivia's education.

Intermediate-Range Goals (1 to 5 Years):

- Buy a new car.

- Save for Olivia's education.
- Open the two new daycare locations.

Long-Term Goals (More than 5 Years):

- Sell their current home and move to the lake house.
- Remodel the lake house for use as their primary residence.
- Retire comfortably in 10 years.

Most Important Financial Objective:

- Opening the two new daycare locations is identified as their single most important financial objective currently.

2. Develop an Investment Strategy for Each Goal:

Short-Range Goals (1 Year):

- Identify the best investment vehicles for aggressive retirement savings within a one-year timeframe. Consider options like high-yield savings accounts, short-term bonds, or other low-risk investments.
- Develop a plan to build an emergency fund. Consider how much they should save monthly to reach their desired emergency fund goal by the end of the year.
- Outline a strategy for continuing to save and pay for Olivia's education. This might involve setting aside a specific portion of income or utilizing specific education savings plans.

Intermediate-Range Goals (1 to 5 Years):

- Explore investment options that align with the goal of buying a new car within 1 to 5 years. Consider short-term bonds, CDs, or a separate savings account dedicated to this purpose.
- Propose a savings plan for Olivia's education over the next 5 years. This might include contributing to a 529 plan or other tax-advantaged education savings accounts.
- Develop a detailed investment plan to fund the opening of the two new daycare locations. Consider the capital required, potential loan options, and the possibility of redirecting current investments to meet this objective.

Long-Term Goals (More than 5 Years):

- Create a strategy for selling their current home and purchasing the lake house, including timing the sale, and managing the proceeds for the lake house purchase.
- Outline the steps for remodeling the lake house, including budgeting, and potentially using long-term investments to fund the remodel.
- Develop a comprehensive retirement plan that includes the projected retirement savings needed and the investment vehicles that will help them retire comfortably in 10 years.

3. Prioritize the Most Important Financial Objective:

- Provide a focused plan on how Darin and Lisa can achieve their most important financial objective: opening the two new daycare locations.
- Analyze potential funding sources, including reallocating current investments, taking on business loans, or finding investors.
- Outline the steps they need to take over the next 1 to 5 years to ensure this goal is met, including any adjustments to their other financial goals if necessary.

4. Write a Comprehensive Investment Plan:

- Prepare a comprehensive investment plan (three to five pages) that addresses all the financial goals outlined above.
- A summary of Darin and Lisa's financial goals.
- Detailed investment strategies for each goal, including specific investment products, savings plans, and timelines.
- A prioritized action plan for achieving the most important financial objective: opening the two new daycare locations.
- Recommendations for adjustments to their current financial strategy to ensure all goals are met.

CONTINUING CASE—THE HARMONS—RETIREMENT PLANNING AND RETIREMENT INCOME FORECASTING

Chapter 7 Case Assignment 7.2

Objective:

The purpose of this exercise is to assess Darin and Lisa's retirement readiness by forecasting their retirement income, identifying any potential shortfalls, and developing a comprehensive retirement income strategy that will allow them to sustain their desired lifestyle post-retirement. You will use the provided financial data to determine the necessary actions they need to take before retirement.

Instructions:

1. Calculate Current Monthly Expenses:

- Fixed Expenses: $4,500/month
- Variable Expenses: $2,400/month
- Calculate the total current monthly expenses for Darin and Lisa by adding fixed and variable expenses.
- Multiply the total monthly expenses by 12 to determine their annual expenses.

2. Determine Retirement Expense Goal:

- Darin and Lisa anticipate being able to live comfortably with 80% of their current expenses during retirement.
- Calculate the target annual expenses during retirement by multiplying their current annual expenses by 0.8.

3. Estimate Retirement Income:

- Social Security income: $2,550/month
- IRA withdrawal: $250/month
- Other investments: $33,900/year

- Calculate the total monthly retirement income by adding Social Security and IRA withdrawal amounts.
- Multiply the monthly retirement income by 12 to determine the total annual income from these sources.
- Add the annual income from other investments to find the total estimated annual retirement income.

4. Identify the Income Shortfall:

- Compare the target annual expenses during retirement with the total estimated annual retirement income.
- Determine the annual income shortfall (if any) by subtracting the total estimated retirement income from the target annual retirement expenses.

5. Calculate the Required Annual Deposit Until Retirement:

- Use the following assumptions:
  - Current IRA balance: $83,000
  - Rate of return until retirement: 5%
  - Rate of return after retirement: 4%
- Determine the number of years until Darin and Lisa retire at age 65.
- Calculate the amount of additional annual deposits they need to make to their retirement accounts to cover the identified income shortfall.
- Consider the rate of return on their investments in your calculation.

6. Develop a Comprehensive Retirement Income Strategy:

- Based on your calculations, develop a strategy that will enable Darin and Lisa to meet their retirement income goals.
- Consider the following elements in your strategy:
  - Adjustments to current spending and savings habits.

- Increasing contributions to retirement accounts.
- Adjustments to the expected lifestyle during retirement.
- Diversifying or reallocating investments to maximize returns while managing risk.

- Provide specific recommendations for each element of your strategy.

7. Write a Summary Report:

- Prepare a summary report (two to three pages) that includes:
  - An overview of Darin and Lisa's current financial situation.
  - The calculations and findings from the steps above.
  - A detailed explanation of the recommended retirement income strategy.
  - Any additional considerations or advice for Darin and Lisa as they approach retirement.

8

Estate Planning

Estate planning is a critical component of resource management for the elderly, focusing on the strategic arrangement of assets and legal documents to ensure that a person's wishes are honored after their passing. For seniors, estate planning involves not only the distribution of assets but also considerations regarding healthcare directives, guardianship, and minimizing estate taxes. Effective estate planning helps to protect the individual's legacy, provide for loved ones, and reduce the potential for conflicts or complications among heirs. By proactively addressing these aspects, financial planners can help elderly clients create a comprehensive plan that secures their assets and ensures their wishes are conducted according to their preferences.

Moreover, estate planning also includes the preparation of key documents such as wills, trusts, and powers of attorney. These documents are essential for guiding the distribution of assets, managing affairs in case of incapacitation, and ensuring that financial and healthcare decisions align with the individual's desires. Establishing trusts can help in avoiding probate, reducing estate taxes, and providing for specific bequests. Powers of attorney and living wills provide instructions for decision-making in the event of incapacitation. By integrating these elements into a cohesive estate plan, financial planners can offer elderly clients' peace of mind, knowing that their financial and personal affairs are well-managed and protected.

WILLS AND TRUSTS

Wills and trusts are foundational elements of estate planning, offering critical tools for managing the distribution of assets and ensuring that an individual's wishes are conducted after their passing. For the elderly, a will serves as a legal document that specifies how their assets, including property, investments, and personal belongings, should be distributed among beneficiaries. A well-crafted will provides clarity and direction, helping to prevent disputes and confusion among heirs. It also allows individuals to designate guardians for minor children or dependents, ensuring that their care is managed according to their preferences. Financial planners must assist elderly clients in drafting a comprehensive will that accurately reflects their wishes and adheres to legal requirements, providing a clear plan for the transfer of assets.

Table 8.1 provides an overview of the various types of wills, their specific purposes, and guidance on when and how to apply each type effectively.

TABLE 8.1 Types of Wills

TYPE OF WILL	PURPOSE	HOW TO APPLY
Simple will	Straightforwardly distributes assets, typically for uncomplicated estates.	Best suited for individuals with modest estates and clear distribution wishes.
Living will	Specifies medical treatment preferences if incapacitated or terminally ill.	Used to guide healthcare providers and loved ones on your medical care preferences.
Testamentary trust will	Establishes a trust upon death to manage and distribute assets to beneficiaries over time.	Ideal for those wanting to provide for minor children or beneficiaries who need asset management.
Joint will	A single will made by two people, usually spouses, to distribute their combined estate.	Appropriate for couples with shared assets who want to make mutual decisions about asset distribution.
Holographic will	A handwritten will without witnesses, valid in some jurisdictions.	Can be used in emergencies or when legal formalities cannot be met but should be validated legally.
Pour-over will	Transfers any remaining assets into an existing trust upon the testator's death.	Effective when used in conjunction with a living trust to ensure all assets are effectively managed.
Nuncupative will	An oral will, often used in emergencies, valid in limited circumstances and jurisdictions.	Typically applied in situations of imminent death but should be followed by legal documentation.

Trusts, on the other hand, offer additional benefits beyond those provided by a will. A trust is a legal arrangement where a trustee manages assets on behalf of the beneficiaries according to the terms set forth in the trust document. Trusts can help avoid the lengthy and costly probate process, allowing for a more efficient transfer of assets. They also offer flexibility in managing and distributing assets, particularly for complex estates or specific bequests. Seniors commonly use revocable living trusts to manage assets during their lifetime and provide for their distribution upon death. By establishing a trust, elderly clients can maintain control over their assets, provide for loved ones, and potentially reduce estate taxes.

Table 8.2 provides an overview of several types of trusts commonly used for estate planning, asset protection, charitable giving, and other specific purposes. Each type of trust has unique features and benefits, depending on the goals and circumstances of the grantor and beneficiaries.

TABLE 8.2 Types of Trusts

TYPE OF TRUST	DESCRIPTION	KEY FEATURES
Revocable living trust	A trust created during the grantor's lifetime that can be modified or revoked by the grantor.	- Grantor retains control. - Avoids probate. - Can be used for incapacity planning.
Irrevocable trust	A trust that cannot be modified or revoked once established; typically used for asset protection, estate tax planning, or Medicaid planning.	- Assets transferred out of the grantor's estate. - Offers protection from creditors. - May have tax benefits.
Charitable trust	A trust established for charitable purposes, with the charity as the beneficiary.	- Provides tax benefits for grantors. - Allows for philanthropic goals to be fulfilled.
Special needs trust	A trust designed to provide for a beneficiary with special needs without affecting their eligibility for government benefits.	- Enhances quality of life without jeopardizing benefits. - Managed by trustee on behalf of beneficiary.
Asset protection trust	A trust created to shield assets from creditors and legal judgments, often established in jurisdictions with favorable trust laws.	- Protects assets from lawsuits and creditors. - May require compliance with specific jurisdictional laws and regulations.
Generation-skipping trust	A trust designed to transfer assets to grandchildren (skip persons) while avoiding estate taxes that would apply if the assets were transferred directly to the children.	- Helps minimize estate taxes over multiple generations. - Requires careful tax planning and compliance with generation-skipping transfer tax rules.
Testamentary trust	A trust established through the terms of a will, taking effect upon the death of the grantor.	- Created under terms of a will. - Can be used for minor children or beneficiaries who are not ready to manage their inheritance.
Bypass trust	A trust that allows a surviving spouse to use the deceased spouse's exemption from estate taxes, thus maximizing the use of both spouses' exemptions.	- Utilizes estate tax exemptions of both spouses. - Common in estate planning for couples with significant assets.
Life insurance trust	A trust specifically designed to hold life insurance policies, removing the proceeds from the insured's estate for tax purposes.	- Keeps life insurance proceeds out of the insured's estate. - Manages and distributes funds according to trust terms.

Incorporating both wills and trusts into an estate plan requires careful consideration of the client's financial situation, goals, and family dynamics. Financial planners should collaborate with elderly clients to evaluate the benefits of each instrument and determine how they can be used in conjunction to achieve their estate planning objectives. This may involve deciding which assets should be placed in a trust and which should be addressed in a will, as well as considering any tax implications or legal requirements. By providing a well-rounded estate planning strategy that includes both wills and trusts, planners can help ensure that elderly clients' assets are managed and distributed according to their wishes while minimizing potential legal and financial challenges for their heirs.

FIGURE 8.1 Will example

Last Will and Testament of Miles Dunn and Harriet Dunn

We, Miles Dunn and Harriet Dunn, residing at 1525 First Street, Wallace, LA 12345, being of sound mind and memory, declare this to be our Last Will and Testament, revoking all prior wills and codicils.

1. Appointment of Executors: We appoint our children, Millie Dunn Williams and Matthew Dunn, as co-executors of our estate. If either of them is unable or unwilling to function as executor, we appoint Harry Miller as the alternate executor.

2. Bequests and Distributions:

To Our Children: We leave our entire estate, including all real and personal property, to be divided equally among our children, Millie Dunn Williams and Matthew Dunn, share, and share alike.

To Our Grandchildren: We leave 100% of our estate in equal shares to our grandchildren: Mackenzie Dunn, Mark Dunn, Wendy Williams, and Wallace Williams

Business and Investments: Our small business, Well Wishes LLC, shall be transferred to Millie Dunn Williams on the condition that they manage it according to their best judgment. Our investments shall be distributed equally between our children.

3. Guardianship of Minor Children: As all our children are adults, this clause does not apply.

4. Powers of Executors: Our executors shall have full authority to manage, invest, and distribute our estate in accordance with the terms of this will, paying all just debts, expenses, and taxes from our estate.

5. Miscellaneous Provisions:

We request that our executors consult with our financial advisor, [Advisor's Name], regarding the management and distribution of our investments.

We authorize our executors to sell any real property if necessary to conduct the terms of this will.

We waive the requirement of surety on the bond of our executors.

6. Revocation Clause: We declare that this will expresses our wishes regarding the disposition of our estate and supersedes any prior wills and codicils made by us.

In witness whereof, we have hereunto set our hands and seals this 21st day of March 2024.

Signed, sealed, published, and declared by John Doe and Mary Doe as their Last Will and Testament, in the presence of us, who, at their request, in their presence, and in the presence of each other, have subscribed our names as witnesses.

Witnesses:

Morris Hill *Morris Hill* Address: 2244 Warren Avenue, Wallace, LA 12345

Tracy Garrett *Tracy Garrett* Address: 4422 Morris Drive, Wallace LA 12345

POWERS OF ATTORNEY AND HEALTHCARE DIRECTIVES

Powers of Attorney and healthcare directives are essential components of estate and resource management planning for the elderly, providing mechanisms to ensure that personal and financial decisions are made according to their preferences in the event of incapacitation. A Power of Attorney (POA) is a legal document that designates an individual, known as an attorney-in-fact or agent, to make financial or legal decisions on behalf of the principal if they become unable to do so themselves. This can include managing bank accounts, paying bills, and handling investments. By establishing a POA, elderly clients can ensure that their financial matters are managed by a trusted person who can act on their behalf, thereby maintaining control and minimizing potential disruptions to their financial stability.

Healthcare directives, including living wills and medical powers of attorney, are crucial for managing medical decisions and end-of-life care. A living will outlines an individual's preferences for medical treatment in the event they are unable to communicate their wishes, such as whether they wish to receive life-sustaining treatments or be placed on a ventilator. Meanwhile, a medical POA designates a person to make healthcare decisions on the individual's behalf if they are incapacitated. These directives ensure that medical care aligns with the individual's values and wishes, reducing the burden on family members to make difficult decisions and preventing potential conflicts among loved ones regarding treatment preferences.

Integrating POAs and healthcare directives into resource management planning involves a thorough review of the client's personal preferences and family dynamics. Financial planners should guide elderly clients in selecting trusted individuals for these roles and in drafting documents that clearly articulate their wishes. Regularly reviewing and updating these documents is also important to reflect any changes in the client's circumstances or preferences. By carefully managing these legal instruments, planners can help ensure that elderly clients' financial and healthcare decisions are made by their desires, providing peace of mind and protecting their interests in all aspects of their lives.

Table 8.3 provides an overview of several types of POA commonly used for legal, financial, medical, and other specific purposes. Each type serves a distinct role in granting authority to an agent to act on behalf of the principal under specific circumstances or needs.

TABLE 8.3 Types of Power of Attorney

TYPE OF POWER OF ATTORNEY	DESCRIPTION	KEY FEATURES
General power of attorney	Grants broad authority to an agent (attorney-in-fact) to act on behalf of the principal in various legal and financial matters.	- Typically used for managing financial affairs. - Can be revoked by the principal at any time or upon incapacity.
Limited (special) power of attorney	Grants specific powers to an agent for a limited purpose or period, often used for a single transaction or specific task.	- Limited scope and duration. - Often used for real estate transactions, banking, or other specific legal matters.
Durable power of attorney	Remains effective even if the principal becomes incapacitated or unable to make decisions.	- Continues beyond the principal's incapacity. - Requires specific language indicating durability.
Springing power of attorney	Becomes effective only upon the occurrence of a specific event, typically the principal's incapacity.	- Provides a safeguard until incapacity occurs. - Requires documentation or certification of incapacity to activate.
Health care power of attorney	Authorizes an agent (healthcare proxy) to make medical decisions on behalf of the principal if they are unable to do so.	- Covers medical treatment decisions. - May include end-of-life decisions if specified.
Financial power of attorney	Specifically grants authority to oversee financial matters on behalf of the principal, separate from medical decisions.	- Focuses on managing financial affairs and assets. - Can be general or limited in scope depending on the principal's needs.
Special power of attorney for real estate	Grants authority to oversee specific real estate transactions or manage real estate assets on behalf of the principal.	- Often used for buying or selling property, managing rental properties, or overseeing mortgage transactions.
Military power of attorney	Designed for military personnel to appoint an agent to oversee their legal and financial affairs during deployment or other military service.	- Allows for management of financial matters, legal affairs, and other issues related to military service.
Tax power of attorney	Authorizes an agent to represent the principal before tax authorities and handle tax-related matters, such as filing tax returns and negotiating with the IRS.	- Specific authority limited to tax matters. - Can be general or limited depending on the principal's needs and circumstances.
Guardianship power of attorney	Appoints an agent to care for minor children or adults who are unable to care for themselves due to incapacity or disability.	- Provides legal authority to make decisions for the person in need of care. - Often used in conjunction with legal guardianship proceedings.

MINIMIZING ESTATE TAXES

Minimizing estate taxes is a crucial aspect of resource management planning for the elderly, as it helps to preserve wealth and ensure that more of an individual's assets are passed on to their heirs rather than being consumed by taxes. Estate taxes can significantly impact the value of an estate, especially for those with substantial assets, making it essential to implement strategies to reduce their liability. Financial planners can assist elderly clients by exploring various tax-saving strategies, such as utilizing gifting strategies to transfer assets before death, which can help reduce the taxable value of the estate. By gifting assets to beneficiaries within the annual gift tax exclusion limits, clients can decrease the overall size of their estate and potentially avoid or lower estate taxes.

Another effective strategy for minimizing estate taxes involves the use of trusts. Trusts, particularly irrevocable trusts, can be employed to transfer assets out of the estate, thereby reducing their taxable value. For instance, placing assets in a charitable remainder trust allows clients to provide for charitable organizations while receiving a tax deduction and potentially reducing estate taxes. In addition, utilizing irrevocable life insurance trusts (ILITs) can help remove life insurance proceeds from the taxable estate, providing a tax-efficient way to provide for beneficiaries. Financial planners should collaborate closely with elderly clients to evaluate the most appropriate type of trust and other estate planning tools to align with their financial goals and minimize estate tax liability.

Proper estate planning also involves staying informed about changes in tax laws and regulations, as these can impact the effectiveness of various strategies. Regular reviews of the estate plan, in consultation with tax professionals and estate attorneys, are essential to ensure that the plan remains effective and compliant with current laws. Financial planners should keep clients updated on any tax law changes and adjust strategies accordingly to optimize tax savings. By proactively addressing estate tax issues and implementing well-considered strategies, planners can help elderly clients preserve their wealth, achieve their estate planning goals, and provide for their loved ones in a financially efficient manner.

These tools and techniques are essential in the CFP financial planning process for elderly clients, helping to manage the complexities of estate distribution, tax implications, and ensuring that the client's wishes are honored effectively.

TABLE 8.4 Estate Planning Tools and Techniques

ESTATE PLANNING TOOL/TECHNIQUE	DESCRIPTION	BENEFITS
Wills	Legal documents that dictate how a person's assets will be distributed upon their death.	Ensures that personal wishes are fulfilled and assets are distributed according to the individual's desires.
Trusts	Legal arrangements where assets are held by a third party for the benefit of another party or parties.	Provides more control over how and when assets are distributed and can also offer tax benefits and privacy.
Durable power of attorney	A legal document that grants an individual the power to act on behalf of another in financial matters.	Ensures financial matters can be managed if the person becomes incapacitated.
Healthcare power of attorney	A document that appoints someone to make medical decisions if the individual becomes unable to do so.	Ensures that healthcare preferences are followed when one cannot make decisions for themselves.
Living wills	Documents that outline desired medical treatments and interventions in various scenarios.	Provides clear instructions for medical care, relieving family members from making tough decisions.
Beneficiary designations	Designations on financial accounts and insurance policies that specify who will receive the assets.	Allows for the direct transfer of assets outside of probate, ensuring faster access to benefits.
Gifts	The transfer of assets during one's lifetime to reduce the taxable estate.	Can reduce estate size and potential taxes, while benefiting heirs during the donor's lifetime.
Life insurance	Policies that provide a death benefit to designated beneficiaries upon the policyholder's death.	Offers financial support to beneficiaries and can be used to pay estate taxes or other expenses.
Joint ownership	Ownership of property by two or more parties, often with the right of survivorship.	Allows property to pass automatically to the co-owner, bypassing probate.
Family limited partnerships (FLPs)	Business entities that hold assets that family members own shares of.	Helps in managing family assets, providing control to senior family members, and reducing estate taxes.
Charitable trusts	Trusts are designed to benefit a charity or the public and offer tax benefits to the donor.	Provides tax benefits and fulfills philanthropic goals.

MINIMIZING ESTATE TAXES AND MAXIMIZING WEALTH TRANSFER

Minimizing estate taxes and maximizing wealth transfer are key objectives in estate planning, particularly for families aiming to preserve their financial legacy for future generations. Effective estate tax planning involves strategic use of various financial instruments and legal structures to reduce the taxable value of an estate. One common approach is the use of gifting during an individual's lifetime, taking advantage of annual gift tax exclusions and lifetime exemption amounts. By transferring assets to heirs gradually, families can reduce the overall size of the estate subject to taxation. In addition, establishing irrevocable trusts can remove assets from the taxable estate while still providing for beneficiaries, ensuring that more wealth is preserved and passed on.

Another critical strategy in minimizing estate taxes is leveraging marital deductions and exemptions. The unlimited marital deduction allows spouses to transfer assets to each other without incurring estate taxes, effectively deferring taxation until the death of the surviving spouse. Combining this with the portability of the estate tax exemption, where the unused portion of a deceased spouse's exemption can be transferred to the surviving spouse, families can significantly enhance their tax planning efficiency. This coordinated approach ensures that couples can fully utilize both exemptions, maximizing the amount of wealth that can be transferred to heirs tax-free.

Advanced estate planning techniques, such as charitable giving and the establishment of family limited partnerships (FLPs), further enhance the ability to minimize estate taxes. Charitable donations, whether through direct gifts or the creation of charitable remainder trusts, can reduce the taxable estate while supporting causes that reflect the family's values. FLPs, on the other hand, allow families to transfer business interests or other assets to heirs at a reduced tax cost by taking advantage of valuation discounts for minority interests and lack of marketability. By integrating these sophisticated strategies into their estate planning, families can ensure that a greater portion of their wealth is preserved for future generations, supporting both financial stability and the continued pursuit of family goals and aspirations.

TYPES OF ADVANCED ESTATE PLANNING TECHNIQUES

Table 8.5 outlines advanced estate planning techniques that individuals and families may consider for minimizing estate taxes, transferring wealth efficiently, and preserving assets for future generations. Each technique offers unique benefits depending on specific financial goals, family dynamics, and estate planning objectives.

TABLE 8.5 Advanced Estate Planning Techniques: Descriptions and Key Benefits

TECHNIQUE	DESCRIPTION	KEY BENEFITS
Irrevocable life insurance trust (ILIT)	A trust designed to hold life insurance policies outside of the insured's estate, minimizing estate taxes and providing liquidity for estate settlement.	- Removes life insurance proceeds from taxable estate. - Provides funds for estate expenses and liquidity needs.
Grantor retained annuity trust (GRAT)	A trust allowing the grantor to transfer assets with potential appreciation to beneficiaries, while retaining an annuity payment for a specified period.	- Transfers assets with potential growth to beneficiaries at reduced gift tax cost. - Minimizes estate and gift taxes if assets appreciate significantly.
Charitable remainder trust (CRT)	A trust that allows the grantor to donate assets to charity while retaining an income stream for beneficiaries, reducing income and estate taxes.	- Provides income to beneficiaries for a specified period or life. - Generates charitable income tax deduction for the grantor.
Qualified personal residence trust (QPRT)	A trust enabling the grantor to transfer a personal residence or vacation home to beneficiaries at a reduced gift tax value, while retaining the right to use the property for a specified term.	- Reduces gift tax on transfer of property with potential future appreciation. - Allows continued use of the residence or vacation home for a specified period.
Family limited partnership (FLP)	A partnership that holds family assets, allowing for centralized management and potential estate tax savings through discounted asset valuation.	- Provides centralized management of family assets. - Facilitates tax-efficient transfer of assets to future generations.
Dynasty trust	A long-term trust designed to transfer wealth across multiple generations while minimizing transfer taxes, such as estate and gift taxes.	- Shields assets from estate taxes for multiple generations. - Allows for wealth accumulation and management over time.
Intentionally defective grantor trust (IDGT)	A trust intentionally designed to be disregarded for income tax purposes but effective for estate tax purposes, allowing the grantor to transfer assets with potential appreciation tax-free.	- Freezes asset values for estate tax purposes while transferring appreciation tax-free. - Allows grantor to pay income taxes on trust income, reducing overall estate size for tax purposes.
Crummey trust	A trust that allows annual exclusion gifts to beneficiaries, providing them with withdrawal rights to the trust contributions for a limited time.	- Utilizes annual gift tax exclusion for transfers to beneficiaries. - Provides liquidity and access to trust assets for beneficiaries.
Installment sale to grantor trust	A strategy where the grantor sells assets to a grantor trust in exchange for a promissory note, freezing asset values for estate tax purposes while transferring future appreciation tax-efficiently.	- Freezes asset values for estate tax purposes while transferring future appreciation tax-efficiently. - Allows grantor to pay income taxes on trust income, reducing overall estate size for tax purposes.

DISCUSSION QUESTIONS

1. What are the essential components of a comprehensive estate plan for elderly clients, and why is each component critical for ensuring their wishes are honored effectively?
2. Discuss the different types of trusts available for estate planning. How do these trusts help in asset protection, tax minimization, and the provision of long-term support for beneficiaries?
3. How do powers of attorney and healthcare directives complement an estate plan, and what specific situations are they designed to address for elderly individuals?
4. How can a well-drafted will prevent potential conflicts among heirs, and what strategies can financial planners use to ensure that a will reflects the true intentions of the client?
5. What are the most effective strategies for minimizing estate taxes, and how can these strategies be tailored to fit different sizes and types of estates?
6. Considering the potential changes in law and family dynamics, how often should estate plans be reviewed and updated? What key factors should trigger a review of an estate plan?

CONTINUING CASE—THE HARMONS EVALUATING AND UPDATING THE ESTATE PLAN

Chapter 8 Case Assignment 8.1

Objective:

The goal of this exercise is to evaluate and update the estate plan of Darin and Lisa Harmon to ensure that their assets are transferred according to their wishes, protected from unnecessary taxation, and preserved for future generations. This exercise will involve reviewing and updating their wills, establishing appropriate trusts, reviewing beneficiary designations, and incorporating advanced estate planning techniques to achieve their goals.

Instructions:

1. Review and Update Wills:

- Current Will Assessment:
  - Review the current wills of Darin and Lisa Harmon. Identify any changes in their family situation, financial circumstances, or goals that may require updates to their wills.
  - Ensure that their wills accurately reflect their current wishes regarding the distribution of assets, guardianship of any dependents, and the appointment of executors.
- Updating the Wills:
  - Outline the steps Darin and Lisa should take to update their wills, such as adding new assets, removing outdated provisions, or making changes to the distribution of their estate.
  - Recommend consulting with an estate planning attorney to finalize any updates to ensure that the wills comply with current legal requirements.

2. Establish Trusts to Protect Assets:

- Trust Options Overview:
  - Explain the benefits of establishing a revocable trust versus other types of trusts, considering Darin and Lisa's goals for asset protection, tax minimization, and estate management.

- Provide recommendations for the best trust options to achieve their specific goals. For example:
    - Revocable Trust: Provides flexibility and control over assets while living and simplifies asset transfer after death.
    - Irrevocable Life Insurance Trust (ILIT): Protects life insurance proceeds from estate taxes.
    - Grantor Retained Annuity Trust (GRAT): Allows for tax-efficient transfer of appreciating assets to beneficiaries.
    - Qualified Personal Residence Trust (QPRT): Protects a primary residence or vacation home from high gift taxes.

- Implementation Steps:
    - Outline the steps required to establish the recommended trusts, including selecting a trustee, drafting trust documents, and transferring assets into the trust.
    - Discuss ongoing management strategies to ensure that the trust remains effective over time.

3. Review and Update Beneficiary Designations:

- Current Beneficiary Review:
    - Instruct Darin and Lisa to review the beneficiary designations on all their accounts, including retirement accounts, bank accounts, and life insurance policies.
    - Identify any accounts or policies where the beneficiary designations may need updating to reflect current wishes.
- Updating Beneficiary Designations:
    - Provide guidance on how to update beneficiary designations to ensure they align with their current estate planning goals.
    - Discuss the importance of coordinating beneficiary designations with the provisions in their wills and trusts to avoid conflicts or unintended consequences.

4. Incorporate Advanced Estate Planning Techniques:

- Evaluate Advanced Estate Planning Techniques:
    - Review the advanced estate planning techniques outlined in Table 8.5. Determine which techniques are most applicable to Darin and Lisa's financial situation and goals.

  - Techniques to consider may include:
    - Irrevocable Life Insurance Trust (ILIT): To protect life insurance proceeds from estate taxes and provide liquidity for estate settlement.
    - Grantor Retained Annuity Trust (GRAT): For tax-efficient transfer of appreciating assets.
    - Charitable Remainder Trust (CRT): To donate assets to charity while retaining income for beneficiaries.
    - Dynasty Trust: To transfer wealth across generations while minimizing estate taxes.
    - Installment Sale to Grantor Trust: To freeze asset values for estate tax purposes while transferring future appreciation tax-efficiently.
- Recommendations for Implementation:
  - Provide specific recommendations for incorporating these advanced techniques into the Harmons' estate plan, explaining how each technique will benefit their estate planning objectives.
  - Outline any potential drawbacks or considerations that should be considered when implementing these techniques.

5. **Write a Comprehensive Estate Plan Review Report**:
- Report Content:
  - Prepare a comprehensive report (four to six pages) that includes:
    - An assessment of the current estate plan, including gaps or areas that need updating.
    - Detailed recommendations for updating wills, establishing trusts, and reviewing beneficiary designations.
    - An evaluation of the advanced estate planning techniques and recommendations for incorporating them into the Harmons' estate plan.
    - A step-by-step action plan for implementing the recommended updates and ensuring the estate plan meets Darin and Lisa's goals.
- Action Plan:
  - Include a timeline for each recommended action, prioritizing steps that should be taken immediately versus those that can be addressed over time.
  - Suggest regular reviews of the estate plan to ensure it continues to reflect their wishes as circumstances change.

9

Tax Planning

Tax planning is a vital component of resource management for the elderly, focusing on strategies to optimize tax efficiency and minimize tax liabilities as individuals navigate retirement. For seniors, managing taxes effectively involves understanding how various sources of income, such as Social Security benefits, pensions, and retirement account withdrawals, are taxed and planning accordingly to avoid unexpected tax burdens. By developing a comprehensive tax strategy, financial planners can help elderly clients manage their income in a way that maximizes their after-tax wealth and ensures that their retirement resources are utilized efficiently.

Effective tax planning for the elderly also requires a thorough understanding of the tax implications of estate planning and investment decisions. This includes strategies to minimize estate taxes, manage required minimum distributions (RMDs) from retirement accounts, and take advantage of tax deductions and credits. Financial planners play a crucial role in guiding clients through these complex tax considerations, helping them make informed decisions that align with their overall financial goals and enhance their long-term financial stability. By incorporating proactive tax planning into resource management, seniors can better manage their resources and secure a more comfortable retirement.

UNDERSTANDING TAX IMPLICATIONS FOR SENIORS

Understanding tax implications is a crucial aspect of resource management planning for seniors, as it helps in effectively managing income and preserving wealth throughout retirement. For elderly individuals, various sources of income, such as Social Security benefits, pensions, retirement account withdrawals, and investment income, can have different tax consequences. Social Security benefits, for example, may be partially taxable depending on the recipient's total income, which includes other sources of income like pensions and investment returns. Financial planners must help clients understand how these income sources interact and influence their overall tax liability, ensuring that they can anticipate and plan for their tax obligations.

Retirement accounts, such as 401(k)s and IRAs, also have significant tax implications. Withdrawals from traditional retirement accounts are subject to income tax, which can impact the client's tax bracket and overall tax liability. RMDs, which mandate that individuals begin withdrawing a certain amount from their retirement accounts starting at age 73, can further complicate tax planning. Financial planners need to assist clients in strategizing their withdrawals in a way that minimizes their tax impact while meeting RMD requirements. This might involve coordinating withdrawals from different accounts or considering conversions to Roth IRAs, which offer tax-free withdrawals.

Investment income, including dividends, interest, and capital gains, also affects a senior's tax situation. Investment income is typically taxable and can push individuals into higher tax brackets if not managed properly. Financial planners should help clients understand the tax implications of their investment choices, such as the benefits of holding assets in tax-advantaged accounts or strategically timing the sale of investments to manage capital gains taxes. By addressing these tax considerations, planners can help seniors optimize their investment strategy, minimize their tax liabilities, and ensure that their resource management plan supports their long-term financial goals.

TAX-EFFICIENT WITHDRAWAL STRATEGIES

Tax-efficient withdrawal strategies are a key element of resource management planning for the elderly, aimed at minimizing tax liabilities while optimizing the longevity of retirement savings. One fundamental approach is to strategically plan withdrawals from different types of accounts, such as taxable accounts, tax-deferred accounts (like traditional IRAs and 401(k)s), and tax-exempt accounts (like Roth IRAs). Typically, it is beneficial to withdraw from taxable accounts first, as these do not incur taxes upon withdrawal and help preserve the tax-advantaged accounts for future use. This strategy allows for the deferral of taxable income, reducing the immediate tax impact and potentially lowering the overall tax burden over time.

Another effective strategy involves managing the timing and amount of withdrawals to optimize tax brackets. By carefully planning withdrawals, seniors can avoid significant spikes in taxable income that might push them into a higher tax bracket. For example, taking smaller withdrawals from tax-deferred accounts over several years can help maintain a lower taxable income, whereas taking larger withdrawals in a single year could result in a higher tax rate. Financial planners should collaborate with clients to protect their future income needs and tax implications, ensuring that withdrawals are timed and sized to minimize tax impact and align with the client's overall financial plan.

In addition, considering the role of RMDs is crucial in tax-efficient withdrawal planning. Since RMDs from traditional retirement accounts are mandated by law and are taxable, it is important to plan withdrawals in a manner that optimally balances these required distributions with other financial needs. Converting portions of tax-deferred accounts to Roth IRAs before reaching the age for RMDs can also be a strategic move, as Roth IRAs offer tax-free withdrawals and are not subject to RMDs during the account holder's lifetime. By integrating these strategies into the retirement plan, financial planners can help seniors manage their tax liabilities effectively, ensuring a more sustainable and tax-efficient use of their retirement resources.

UTILIZING TAX CREDITS AND DEDUCTIONS

Utilizing tax credits and deductions is an essential aspect of resource management planning for the elderly, as it can significantly reduce their overall tax liability and enhance their financial stability during retirement. Tax credits directly reduce the amount of tax owed and can provide substantial savings. For seniors, credits such as the Credit for the Elderly or Disabled, which offers tax relief based on age and income, and the Child and Dependent Care Credit, which helps offset the cost of caregiving, can be particularly valuable. Financial planners should ensure that elderly clients are aware of and take advantage of all applicable credits, helping them to effectively lower their tax bills and maximize their after-tax income.

In addition to credits, deductions play a critical role in reducing taxable income. Seniors may benefit from various deductions, including those for medical and dental expenses, which can be significant for those with high healthcare costs. The deduction for medical expenses is available if the total exceeds a certain percentage of the taxpayer's adjusted gross income (AGI). Furthermore, deductions for charitable contributions can be beneficial for seniors who are philanthropically inclined, as these can reduce taxable income while supporting their favorite causes. Financial planners should help clients identify and maximize deductions relevant to their situation, ensuring that they fully leverage available opportunities to lower their tax burden.

Moreover, seniors should also be aware of potential deductions related to retirement account contributions and investment losses. Although contributions to traditional IRAs may be limited after age 70½, seniors who are still earning income might benefit from making the maximum allowable contributions. In addition, if seniors have experienced investment losses, they can use these losses to offset capital gains or up to $3,000 of other income per year. Financial planners play a vital role in guiding clients through these opportunities, ensuring that they effectively utilize tax credits and deductions to optimize their financial situation and support a more secure retirement.

TABLE 9.1 Tax Deductions, Credits, and Exemptions for the Elderly

TAX BENEFIT	DESCRIPTION	ELIGIBILITY CRITERIA
Standard deduction	A set amount that reduces the amount of income subject to tax, available to all taxpayers, including elderly individuals.	Age 65 or older by the end of the tax year (for the tax year 2023, born before January 2, 1958).
Additional standard deduction	Higher standard deduction amounts available to elderly taxpayers and those who are blind.	Age 65 or older by the end of the tax year, or blind as defined by IRS rules.
Credit for the elderly or disabled	A tax credit available to elderly or disabled taxpayers with low to moderate incomes, providing a direct reduction of tax liability.	Age 65 or older by the end of the tax year or retired on permanent and total disability.
Medical and dental expenses deduction	Allows taxpayers to deduct qualifying medical and dental expenses that exceed a certain percentage of adjusted gross income (AGI).	Any age, expenses must exceed 7.5% of AGI for tax years 2021 and 2022; 10% of AGI for tax year 2023 and beyond.
Property tax exemption	Some states offer property tax exemptions or reductions for elderly homeowners based on income, age, or disability status.	Age 65 or older, meet state-specific income and residency requirements.
IRA contributions deduction	Allows taxpayers to deduct contributions made to traditional individual retirement accounts (IRAs), subject to certain income limits and eligibility rules.	No age limit, must have earned income to contribute to an IRA, and subject to IRS contribution limits.
Social Security income exclusion	Excludes a portion of Social Security income from taxable income, depending on the taxpayer's total income and filing status.	Any age, portion of Social Security benefits may be taxable depending on total income.
Retirement savings contributions credit	Also known as the Saver's Credit, provides a tax credit for low- to moderate-income individuals who contribute to retirement savings plans (e.g., IRA, 401(k)).	Age 18 or older, not a full-time student, meet income eligibility requirements.
Exemption from required minimum distributions (RMDs)	Exemption for certain retirement account holders from taking mandatory withdrawals after reaching age 72 (for those born on or after July 1, 1949).	At age 72 (for those born on or after July 1, 1949), certain retirement accounts (e.g., Roth IRAs) are exempt from RMDs.
Estate tax exemption	Exempts a certain amount of an individual's estate from federal estate taxes upon death, providing relief for heirs from tax liabilities.	Any age, exemption amount adjusted annually (as of 2023, $12.06 million per individual).

DISCUSSION QUESTIONS

1. How do various income sources for seniors, such as Social Security benefits, pensions, and retirement account withdrawals, interact to affect their overall tax liabilities? What strategies can financial planners employ to optimize these interactions?

2. Discuss the tax implications of required minimum distributions from retirement accounts for elderly clients. How can financial planners develop strategies to manage RMDs effectively to minimize their clients' tax burdens?

3. Considering the significant health expenses that many seniors face, what are the most effective ways to incorporate medical deductions into tax planning? How can maximizing these deductions impact the financial well-being of elderly clients?

4. How does tax planning intersect with estate planning for the elderly? Discuss the role of tax-efficient gifting and the use of specific trusts to minimize estate taxes.

5. Explore the various tax credits and deductions specifically available to seniors. How can financial planners ensure their elderly clients are fully benefiting from these opportunities?

6. Tax laws frequently change, impacting strategies for tax planning. What processes should financial planners have in place to stay informed about these changes and adapt plans accordingly to protect and benefit their elderly clients?

CONTINUING CASE— THE HARMONS—ELDERLY RELATED TAX PLANNING

Chapter 9 Case Assignment 9.1

Objective:

The purpose of this exercise is to create a comprehensive tax planning strategy for Darin and Lisa Harmon as they approach retirement. This strategy will incorporate tax benefits, deductions, and exemptions available to elderly individuals, ensuring they maximize their tax savings and plan effectively for their financial future.

Instructions:

1. Understand Tax Benefits for the Elderly:

- **Review the Tax Benefits:**
  - Familiarize yourself with the following tax benefits and deductions available to elderly individuals:
    - Standard deduction
    - Additional standard deduction
    - Credit for the elderly or disabled
    - Medical and dental expenses deduction
    - Property tax exemption
    - IRA contributions deduction
    - Social Security income exclusion
    - Retirement savings contributions credit
    - Exemption from RMDs
    - Estate tax exemption
  - Understand the description, eligibility criteria, and potential impact of each tax benefit.

2. Evaluate the Harmons' Eligibility:

- **Eligibility Assessment:**
  - Evaluate Darin and Lisa's current financial and personal situation to determine their eligibility for each of the tax benefits listed above.
  - Consider their age, income, retirement plans, and any specific circumstances that may affect their eligibility for certain deductions, credits, or exemptions.
- **Calculation of Potential Tax Savings:**
  - Calculate the potential tax savings that Darin and Lisa could achieve by taking advantage of these benefits.
  - For example, estimate how much they could save through the additional standard deduction, medical and dental expense deductions, or property tax exemptions.
  - Consider the impact of excluding a portion of their Social Security income from taxation based on their total income and filing status.

3. Develop a Tax Planning Strategy:

- **Tax Strategy Outline:**
  - Based on your assessment of their eligibility, outline a tax planning strategy that incorporates the relevant tax benefits for Darin and Lisa.
  - Include specific recommendations on how they can maximize their tax savings, such as:
    - Contributing to an IRA to take advantage of the IRA contributions deduction.
    - Timing the sale of assets or withdrawals from retirement accounts to minimize tax liability.
    - Exploring state-specific property tax exemptions or reductions.
    - Utilizing the Credit for the elderly or disabled if eligible.
- **Consideration of RMDs:**
  - Explain how RMDs will impact their tax situation after they reach age 72 (for those born on or after July 1, 1949).

  - Provide recommendations on managing RMDs, including whether to delay distributions if possible or convert traditional IRAs to Roth IRAs to avoid RMDs.

- **Estate Tax Planning:**
  - Discuss the importance of estate tax planning in their overall strategy.
  - Explain how the Estate tax exemption could protect a portion of their estate from federal estate taxes and provide recommendations for structuring their estate to minimize tax liabilities for their heirs.

4. Write a Comprehensive Tax Planning Report:

- **Report Content:**
  - Prepare a comprehensive report (four to six pages) that includes:
    - An overview of the tax benefits available to the elderly and how they apply to Darin and Lisa.
    - Detailed calculations of potential tax savings for each relevant benefit.
    - A step-by-step tax planning strategy tailored to the Harmons' specific situation.
    - Recommendations for ongoing tax management and estate planning to ensure they continue to maximize their tax savings as they age.
- **Action Plan:**
  - Include a timeline for implementing each part of the tax strategy, such as when to make IRA contributions, when to take RMDs, and when to update estate plans.
  - Suggest regular reviews of their tax plan to adjust for changes in tax laws, financial circumstances, or personal goals.

10

Government Benefits and Entitlement Programs

Government benefits and entitlement programs play a crucial role in supporting families with their financial planning needs. These programs are designed to aid individuals and families who may be facing financial challenges, ensuring they have access to essential services and resources. By understanding and utilizing these programs effectively, families can better navigate their financial circumstances and improve their overall well-being.

One key aspect of government benefits is that they offer a safety net for families during times of hardship or unexpected circumstances. Programs such as Social Security, unemployment benefits, and Supplemental Nutrition Assistance Program (SNAP) can help families meet their basic needs when faced with job loss, disability, or other financial setbacks. By tapping into these resources, families can avoid financial strain and maintain stability in their daily lives.

In addition, government benefits and entitlement programs can also provide long-term financial security for families. Programs such as Medicare and Medicaid help families access affordable healthcare, whereas Social Security benefits ensure a steady stream of income for retirees. By incorporating these benefits into their financial planning strategies, families can build a more secure future and safeguard against unexpected costs or emergencies. Understanding the eligibility criteria and application process for these programs is essential for families to maximize their benefits and plan for their long-term financial well-being.

These government benefits and entitlement programs aim to provide financial, healthcare, nutritional, and supportive services to help improve the quality of life for elderly individuals and their families in the United States.

TABLE 10.1 Government Benefits and Entitlement Programs for the Elderly

GOVERNMENT PROGRAM	DESCRIPTION	ELIGIBILITY CRITERIA
Social Security Retirement Benefits	Provides monthly income to retired workers based on their earnings history and age at retirement.	Age 62 or older, worked and paid Social Security taxes for a required number of years (credits), or spouse of a worker.
Supplemental Security Income (SSI)	Provides cash assistance to low-income individuals aged 65 and older (as well as disabled individuals) to meet basic needs for food, clothing, and shelter.	Age 65 or older, limited income and resourc-es, U.S. citizen or eligible noncitizen.
Medicare	Federal health insurance program primarily for people aged 65 and older, covering hospi-tal stays, medical services, and prescription drugs.	Age 65 or older, or below 65 with certain disabilities, U.S. citizen or permanent resident who has lived in the United States for at least 5 years.
Medicaid	Joint federal and state programs providing health coverage to low-income individuals, including long-term care services for the elderly who meet eligibility criteria.	Age 65 or older, low income and limited resources, varies by state residency and Medicaid expansion eligibility.
(Supplemental Nutrition Assis-tance Program (SNAP)	Formerly known as Food Stamps, provides nutrition assistance to low-income individuals and families, including elderly persons with limited income.	Age 60 or older, low income, U.S. citizen or eligible noncitizen.
Low Income Home Energy Assis-tance Program (LIHEAP)	Assists eligible households, including elderly persons, with heating and cooling costs to ensure safe and healthy living conditions.	Age 60 or older, low income based on household size and income, U.S. citizen or eligible noncitizen.
Veterans Pension (Aid and Attendance)	Provides financial support to wartime veter-ans and their surviving spouses who require assistance with daily living activities and have limited income and assets.	Veteran who served during a qualifying period of war, or surviving spouse, meet income and asset limits, require assistance with daily living, or are housebound.
Senior Farmers' Market Nutri-tion Program	Provides low-income seniors with coupons to purchase fresh fruits, vegetables, and herbs from farmers' markets, roadside stands, and community-supported agriculture programs.	Age 60 or older, income eligibility based on federal poverty guidelines, reside in an area served by the program.
Older Americans Act (OAA) Programs	Supports a range of services and programs, including congregate and home-delivered meals, transportation, caregiver support, and legal assistance for older adults.	Age 60 or older, in need of services, often targeting low-income individuals and those with disabilities.

Eligibility Criteria: Specific eligibility requirements may vary based on income, assets, residency, military service, and other factors. Programs often have income limits adjusted annually.

Application Process: Applications for these programs typically require documentation of income, assets, citizenship or residency status, and sometimes medical conditions.

Consultation: Eligibility and benefits may differ by state or locality. It is advisable to consult with local agencies or organizations specializing in elderly services for personalized assistance and guidance.

SOCIAL SECURITY, MEDICARE, AND MEDICAID

Social Security, Medicare, and Medicaid are three vital government programs that play a significant role in family financial planning. Social Security provides a crucial source of income for retirees, survivors, and individuals with disabilities, offering a safety net for families to rely on during times of need. Understanding how to optimize Social Security benefits, such as timing retirement and spousal benefits, can help families maximize their financial resources and secure their retirement years.

Medicare is another essential program that supports family financial planning by providing affordable healthcare coverage for individuals aged 65 and older, as well as certain younger individuals with disabilities. As healthcare costs continue to rise, having access to Medicare can alleviate a significant financial burden for families facing medical expenses. By strategizing on enrollment timelines, coverage options, and supplemental insurance plans, families can effectively plan for their healthcare needs and protect their financial well-being.

Medicaid, on the other hand, serves as a critical safety net for low-income families by offering access to healthcare coverage and long-term care services. Understanding the eligibility requirements for Medicaid and planning accordingly can help families navigate complex healthcare systems and avoid financial strain when faced with medical emergencies. By incorporating Medicaid benefits into their financial planning strategies, families can ensure they have the necessary resources to safeguard their health and financial stability for the long term (Social Security Administration, 2024).

This table helps distinguish between these three critical government programs, outlining their purpose, who they serve, and what benefits they provide, essential for comprehensive financial planning.

TABLE 10.2 **Overview of Major Government Programs for Health and Financial Support**

PROGRAM	DEFINITION	ELIGIBILITY	BENEFITS
Social Security	A federal program that provides retirement, disability, and survivor benefits to eligible beneficiaries, funded through payroll taxes.	Typically, eligible to retirees 62 years and older, disabled individuals, and families of deceased workers.	Provides monthly financial benefits based on earnings history, helping cover living expenses after retirement or disability.
Medicare	A federal health insurance program for people aged 65 and older, some younger individuals with disabilities, and people with End-stage renal disease (ESRD).	Must be 65 years or older, younger with certain disabilities, or any age with ESRD.	Covers hospital care (Part A), medical services (Part B), prescription drugs (Part D), and optional managed care (Part C).
Medicaid	A state and federal program that provides health coverage to eligible low-income adults, children, pregnant women, elderly adults, and people with disabilities.	Based on income level, family size, and disability status, varies by state.	Offers a broad range of health services, including doctor visits, hospital care, long-term care services, and mental health treatment.

VETERANS' BENEFITS AND OTHER GOVERNMENT PROGRAMS

Veterans' benefits and other government programs play a crucial role in family financial planning, offering support to military service members and their families. Veterans' benefits, such as healthcare, disability compensation, education assistance, and home loans, provide an array of resources to help veterans and their families achieve financial security. By leveraging these benefits effectively, families can boost their financial stability and access specialized services that cater to their unique needs.

Other government programs, such as the SNAP, Temporary Assistance for Needy Families (TANF), and the Women, Infants, and Children (WIC) program, also contribute to family financial planning by aiding with basic needs like food, cash support, and healthcare. These programs serve as a vital support system for low-income families, offering temporary relief during times of financial hardship. By understanding the eligibility criteria and available resources of these programs, families can create a more robust financial plan that addresses their immediate needs while working toward long-term stability.

Furthermore, programs like the Earned Income Tax Credit (EITC) and the Child Tax Credit (CTC) offer tax benefits specifically designed to assist working families with children. By taking advantage of these tax credits, families can reduce their tax liability, increase their disposable income, and create opportunities to save for their future. Incorporating these government programs into their financial planning can help families optimize their resources, reduce financial stress, and build a stronger foundation for their children's well-being.

Table 10.3 provides a concise overview of various government programs designed to assist different segments of the population, highlighting how each serves its eligible members with specific benefits.

TABLE 10.3 Government Programs for the Elderly

PROGRAM	DEFINITION	ELIGIBILITY	BENEFITS
Veterans' Benefits	Programs administered by the Department of Veterans Affairs (VA) to provide compensation, pension, healthcare, education, and housing assistance to eligible veterans.	Service in the United States Armed Forces and discharge under conditions other than dishonorable.	Includes healthcare, disability compensation, pensions for disabled or elderly veterans, education benefits, and home loans.
Social Security	A federal program that provides retirement, disability, and survivors' benefits. Funded through payroll taxes.	Eligibility for retirement benefits starts at age 62, with disability benefits and survivors' benefits available under specific conditions.	Provides monthly financial support for retired workers, disabled individuals, and families of deceased workers.
Medicare	A federal health insurance program primarily for people aged 65 and older, but also available to younger people with certain disabilities and diseases like ESRD.	People aged 65 or above, people below 65 with certain disabilities, and people of any age with ESRD.	Covers hospital care (Part A), medical services (Part B), and prescription drugs (Part D), with optional managed care (Part C).
Medicaid	Joint federal and state program providing health coverage to low-income individuals and families.	Eligibility based on income, family size, disability, and other factors; varies by state.	Provides comprehensive health coverage including doctor visits, hospital care, long-term care services, and more.
Supplemental Security Income (SSI)	A federal program providing financial aid to elderly, blind, or disabled individuals with limited income and resources.	Must be aged 65 or older, blind, or disabled with limited income and resources.	Offers monthly cash assistance to meet basic needs for food, clothing, and shelter.
Temporary Assistance for Needy Families (TANF)	A federal assistance program that provides temporary financial aid and support services to low-income families with dependent children.	Low-income families with dependent children; eligibility requirements vary by state.	Provides financial assistance for a limited time, work opportunities, and support services such as childcare and job training.

ELIGIBILITY CRITERIA AND APPLICATION PROCESSES

Understanding the eligibility criteria and application processes for government programs is essential for family financial planning. Each program has specific requirements that determine who qualify for benefits, making it crucial for families to research and assess their eligibility before applying. By familiarizing themselves with the criteria, families can determine which programs align with their needs and create a more effective financial plan that maximizes available resources.

The application processes for government programs vary in complexity, with some requiring extensive documentation and verification of income, whereas others may have simpler procedures. It is important for families to gather all necessary information beforehand to streamline the application process and avoid delays in receiving assistance. By being initiative-taking and organizing in preparing their applications, families can increase their chances of qualifying for benefits and accessing the support they need to improve their financial situation.

Moreover, seeking guidance from financial advisors or community organizations can help families navigate the eligibility criteria and application processes more effectively. These professionals can provide valuable insights, assistance with paperwork, and guidance on maximizing available benefits. By leveraging external resources and expertise, families can enhance their financial planning efforts and make informed decisions that lead to a more secure financial future for themselves and their loved ones.

INTERACTION BETWEEN GOVERNMENT BENEFITS AND FINANCIAL RESOURCES

The interaction between government benefits and family financial resources plays a crucial role in shaping a family's overall financial planning strategy. Understanding how these benefits impact available resources is key to optimizing financial stability and security. By carefully analyzing the eligibility criteria and application processes for government programs, families can identify opportunities to leverage benefits to supplement their existing financial resources and improve their overall financial well-being.

Government benefits can serve as a vital safety net for families facing financial hardships, aiding with essential needs such as housing, healthcare, food, and education. By incorporating these benefits into their financial planning strategy, families can allocate resources more strategically, freeing up funds for other critical expenses or savings goals. In addition, leveraging government benefits can help families build a more robust financial cushion, providing a buffer against unforeseen emergencies or economic downturns.

However, it is important for families to consider the potential impact of government benefits on their overall financial picture, including taxes, eligibility for other programs, and long-term financial goals. Some benefits may be taxable or could affect eligibility for certain tax credits or programs, requiring careful planning to minimize adverse consequences. By evaluating the implications of government benefits on their financial resources holistically, families can make informed decisions that optimize their financial outcomes and support their long-term financial well-being.

DISCUSSION QUESTIONS

1. How can financial planners integrate government benefits like Social Security, Medicare, and Medicaid into the broader financial plans of elderly clients to enhance their long-term financial stability?

2. Discuss the role that government benefits can play in supporting family financial planning during crises such as job loss, disability, or sudden healthcare needs.

3. What strategies can families employ to adapt their financial planning when facing reductions or changes in government benefits due to policy shifts or economic downturns?

4. How do programs like Medicare and Medicaid contribute to long-term financial security for the elderly, and what are the potential gaps that families need to plan for?

5. Considering the varying needs of different family structures, how can government entitlement programs be best utilized to meet specific familial challenges, such as caring for elderly parents or disabled family members?

6. What approaches can be taken to improve awareness and understanding among families about the eligibility criteria and application processes for government benefits to ensure they are fully utilized?

CONTINUING CASE—THE HARMONS—GOVERNMENT BENEFITS AND ENTITLEMENT PROGRAMS ANALYSIS

Chapter 10 Case Assignment 10.1

Objective:

Evaluate the potential impact and optimization of government benefits and entitlement programs for the Harmon family, focusing on their long-term financial stability and healthcare needs.

Instructions:

1. **Research Phase**:

- Investigate the eligibility requirements and benefits of the following government programs: Social Security Retirement Benefits, Medicare, Medicaid, and the Veterans Pension (Aid and Attendance) as Darren is a retired veteran.
- Understand how these programs can integrate with the Harmons' current financial situation, including their retirement savings, healthcare needs, and family dynamics.

2. **Analysis Phase**:

- Social Security Optimization: Assess the best timing for the Harmons to start taking their Social Security benefits considering their financial needs, health status, and the benefits of delaying retirement.
- Medicare Planning: Develop a plan for transitioning from private health insurance to Medicare, including considerations for supplemental coverage (Medigap) and potential impacts on their long-term healthcare costs.
- Medicaid Eligibility: Evaluate the possibility of qualifying for Medicaid for long-term care, especially considering Lisa's recent health issues and potential future needs.
- Veterans Benefits Utilization: Discuss how Darren can utilize Veterans benefits, focusing on healthcare, and the Aid and Attendance benefit, which could assist if either Darren or Lisa requires daily aid and attendance of another person.

3. **Application Process Guidance:**

- Detail the application processes for each relevant program, including necessary documentation and timelines. Provide a step-by-step guide tailored to the Harmons' situation.

4. **Financial Impact Report:**

- Create a comprehensive report analyzing how each benefit could affect the Harmons' overall financial plan, tax implications, and potential for reducing out-of-pocket healthcare expenses.
- Include a forecast model showing the financial impact over the next 10–20 years with and without the utilization of these government benefits.

5. **Recommendation Plan:**

- Based on the analysis, recommend an integrated approach to utilizing government benefits that aligns with the Harmons' financial goals, healthcare needs, and estate planning considerations.
- Address any potential risks or areas of concern that could affect their long-term financial health.

11

Healthcare and Long-Term Care Planning

Healthcare and long-term care planning are essential elements of resource management for the elderly, reflecting the need to address significant aspects of well-being and financial stability in retirement. As individuals age, the likelihood of requiring medical services and long-term care increases, making it crucial to incorporate these needs into a comprehensive financial plan. Effective planning involves understanding the potential costs of healthcare services, including routine medical care, prescription medications, and the possibility of extended long-term care, such as assisted living or nursing home care. By proactively addressing these aspects, financial planners can help seniors manage their resources to ensure they can access necessary care without jeopardizing their financial security.

Integrating healthcare and long-term care planning into resource management requires careful consideration of various financial products and strategies designed to cover these expenses. Options such as long-term care insurance, health savings accounts (HSAs), and Medicare supplemental plans play a pivotal role in mitigating the financial impact of healthcare needs. Financial planners must guide elderly clients in evaluating these options and determining the most suitable approach based on their health status, financial situation, and personal preferences. By developing a well-rounded plan that addresses both immediate and future healthcare needs, planners can help seniors maintain their quality of life and financial stability throughout their retirement years.

MEDICARE AND MEDICAID OVERVIEW

Medicare and Medicaid are crucial components of resource management planning for the elderly, providing essential healthcare coverage and financial support for medical expenses. Medicare is a federal health insurance program primarily for individuals aged 65 and older, though it also serves younger individuals with certain disabilities. It consists of different parts: Part A covers hospital insurance, Part B covers outpatient services, Part C (Medicare Advantage) offers an alternative to Original Medicare with additional benefits, and Part D provides prescription drug coverage. Understanding the various parts of Medicare, including their coverage limits and associated costs, is vital for financial planners to help elderly clients manage their healthcare expenses effectively and make informed choices about their insurance options.

Medicaid, on the other hand, is a joint federal and state program that provides health coverage to low-income individuals, including many elderly people. Unlike Medicare, Medicaid eligibility is based on financial need rather than age. It offers a broader range of benefits, including long-term care services such as nursing home care and personal care services, which Medicare does not typically cover. Financial planners must assist elderly clients in navigating Medicaid eligibility requirements, which can be complex and involve assessing income and asset limits. In addition, planners should help clients understand how Medicaid can work in conjunction with Medicare to cover gaps in healthcare services and manage long-term care costs.

Both Medicare and Medicaid have significant implications for resource management planning, as they affect out-of-pocket costs and the need for additional insurance or savings. Seniors should be guided in understanding how Medicare's coverage interacts with Medicaid and other insurance plans, as well as strategies for managing costs not covered by these programs. Planners may also advise on how to optimize Medicare benefits, such as through supplemental insurance plans (Medigap) and exploring Medicaid planning options to protect assets while qualifying for coverage. By addressing these aspects, financial planners can help seniors develop a comprehensive healthcare strategy that supports their overall financial well-being and ensures access to necessary medical care throughout their retirement (Social Security Administration, 2024).

LONG-TERM CARE INSURANCE

Long-term care insurance is a vital component of resource management planning for the elderly, offering financial protection against the high costs of extended care services that Medicare and standard health insurance typically do not cover. This type of insurance is designed to help cover expenses associated with long-term care needs, such as assisted living facilities, nursing homes, and in-home care. As individuals age, the likelihood of requiring such care increases, making it essential to plan for these potential costs to avoid depleting retirement savings or relying on Medicaid. Financial planners must assist elderly clients in evaluating long-term care insurance options, helping them understand the policy features, benefits, and limitations to ensure the coverage aligns with their needs and financial goals.

Selecting the right long-term care insurance policy involves assessing various factors, including the type of care covered, the duration of coverage, and the benefit amounts. Policies can vary widely in terms of their coverage options and cost, so it is important for clients to carefully review these aspects to choose a plan that provides adequate protection without overextending their budget. For instance, some policies offer coverage for in-home care, whereas others may only cover institutional care. In addition, the waiting period before benefits kick in and the inflation protection options are crucial elements to consider. Financial planners should guide clients through these considerations, helping them balance the cost of premiums with the anticipated benefits to make an informed decision.

Furthermore, long-term care insurance planning should be integrated into a broader financial strategy that includes evaluating other resources, such as savings, investments, and government programs like Medicaid. Planners can help clients understand how long-term care insurance fits within their overall resource management plan and how it can complement other financial protections. This involves reviewing existing policies, adjusting coverage as needed, and ensuring that the client's plan is flexible enough to adapt to changing circumstances. By incorporating long-term care insurance into a comprehensive financial strategy, planners can help elderly clients safeguard their financial stability and ensure they are prepared for potential long-term care needs in a manner that aligns with their personal preferences and financial situation.

Types of Long-Term Care

Understanding long-term care services and costs is crucial for individuals and families preparing for potential future care needs. Proper planning can help mitigate financial strain and ensure quality care tailored to individual preferences and health requirements.

TABLE 11.1 Overview of Types of Long-Term Care Services

TYPE OF SERVICE	DESCRIPTION	COSTS
Home health care	Care provided at home by licensed healthcare professionals, including skilled nursing care, physical therapy, and assistance with daily activities.	Costs vary widely depending on the level of care needed and geographic location. On average, home health aides can cost $20–$30 per hour, whereas skilled nursing care can be significantly higher.
Assisted living facilities	Residential facilities offering personal care services, such as meals, medication management, housekeeping, and assistance with activities of daily living (ADLs).	Monthly costs typically range from $3,000 to $7,000, depending on the location, level of care provided, and amenities.
Nursing homes (skilled nursing facilities)	Facilities providing 24-hour skilled nursing care, rehabilitation services, and assistance with ADLs for individuals with complex medical needs.	Costs can vary widely based on location and the level of care required. Semiprivate rooms average around $7,000 to $8,000 per month, whereas private rooms can exceed $10,000 per month.
Memory care facilities	Specialized facilities providing care for individuals with Alzheimer's disease, dementia, or other cognitive impairments, offering structured routines and specialized care.	Like assisted living or nursing homes, costs vary based on location and level of care, typically ranging from $4,000 to $9,000 per month.
Factors affecting long-term care costs:		
Location: Costs can vary significantly by region, with urban areas having higher costs than rural areas.		
Level of care: More intensive medical care and specialized services increase costs.		
Type of facility: Assisted living facilities are less expensive than nursing homes or memory care facilities.		
Duration of care: Long-term care costs accumulate over time, impacting overall expenses.		

LONG-TERM CARE INSURANCE AND OTHER FINANCING OPTIONS

Long-term care insurance (LTCI) is a critical component of family financial planning, providing a means to cover the substantial costs associated with extended healthcare services for elderly family members. LTCI policies typically cover a range of services, including in-home care, assisted living, and nursing home care, ensuring that individuals receive the necessary support without depleting their family's financial resources. When considering LTCI, it is essential to evaluate the policy's coverage limits, waiting periods, and inflation protection to ensure it meets the specific needs of the family. By investing in LTCI, families can safeguard their assets, reduce the financial burden on loved ones, and have peace of mind that long-term care needs will be met.

Beyond LTCI, families have several other financing options to consider for covering the costs of extended care. One option is Medicaid, a government program that provides financial assistance for long-term care services to individuals who meet specific income and asset requirements. To qualify for Medicaid, families often need to engage in strategic planning, such as asset reallocation or establishing certain types of trusts to meet eligibility criteria. Medicaid can be a valuable resource for those with limited financial means, but it requires careful and early planning to navigate the complex eligibility rules and ensure access to needed care.

Another financing option is the use of reverse mortgages, which allows homeowners aged 62 and older to convert part of their home equity into cash without having to sell their home. This option can provide a significant source of funds to cover long-term care expenses while enabling the individual to remain in their home. In addition, families can explore the possibility of setting up HSAs or dedicated savings plans specifically for future care needs. By incorporating a combination of these financing strategies into their overall financial plan, families can better manage the excessive costs of long-term care, ensuring that their loved ones receive the necessary support while preserving their financial stability and achieving their long-term financial goals.

TABLE 11.2 Payment Options and Planning Strategies for Long-Term Care

PAYMENT OPTION	DESCRIPTION
Private funds	Individuals or families pay out-of-pocket using personal savings, investments, or retirement funds.
Long-term care insurance	Insurance policies are specifically designed to cover long-term care services, providing financial assistance for eligible services.
Medicare and Medicaid	Limited coverage for skilled nursing care under Medicare, with Medicaid providing more comprehensive coverage for eligible low-income individuals.
Veterans benefits	Veterans and their spouses may qualify for long-term care benefits through the Department of Veterans Affairs.

PLANNING FOR LONG-TERM CARE STRATEGY	DESCRIPTION
Early planning	Start planning for long-term care needs well in advance to explore options, understand costs, and make informed decisions.
Legal and financial planning	Establishing powers of attorney, healthcare directives, and reviewing estate plans can ensure wishes are followed and assets are protected.
Consultation	Seek guidance from financial advisors, elder law attorneys, and healthcare professionals to navigate long-term care decisions effectively.

MANAGING OUT-OF-POCKET HEALTHCARE COSTS

Managing out-of-pocket healthcare costs is a crucial aspect of resource management planning for the elderly, given the increasing expense of medical care as individuals age. Out-of-pocket costs can include deductibles, copayments, coinsurance, and expenses for services not covered by insurance. These costs can accumulate significantly over time, impacting the individual's overall financial stability. Financial planners must help elderly clients develop strategies to manage these costs effectively, which may include budgeting for regular medical expenses, setting up emergency funds specifically for healthcare needs, and exploring supplemental insurance options to cover gaps in primary health insurance coverage.

One effective strategy for managing out-of-pocket costs is to utilize HSAs or flexible spending accounts (FSAs), which offer tax advantages and can be used to cover qualified medical expenses. For clients who are eligible, contributing to an HSA provides a way to save money on a tax-deferred basis, and withdrawals for medical expenses are tax-free. FSAs, on the other hand, allow for pretax contributions to cover out-of-pocket healthcare costs within a given year. By incorporating these accounts into the financial plan, elderly clients can better manage and reduce their immediate healthcare expenses while benefiting from tax savings.

In addition, reviewing and optimizing insurance coverage is essential for managing out-of-pocket healthcare costs. Financial planners should assist clients in evaluating their Medicare plans and supplemental insurance options, such as Medigap policies or Medicare Advantage plans, to ensure they provide adequate coverage for their needs. Comparing different plans and understanding their coverage limits, as well as the potential for additional out-of-pocket costs, can help clients choose the most cost-effective options. Regularly reassessing insurance coverage considering changing health needs and costs can also prevent unexpected financial strain and ensure that clients are prepared for any healthcare expenses that may arise. By adopting a proactive approach to managing out-of-pocket healthcare costs, seniors can maintain their financial health and access the care they need without jeopardizing their retirement savings.

These tools and techniques are essential for CFPs to understand and incorporate into the financial planning process for elderly clients, assisting them in navigating the complexities of healthcare needs and insurance as they age.

TABLE 11.3 HEALTHCARE AND INSURANCE PLANNING TOOLS AND TECHNIQUES

TOOL/TECHNIQUE	DESCRIPTION	BENEFITS
Medicare planning	Strategic enrollment in Medicare Parts A, B, C, and D to cover hospital, medical, and prescription drug needs.	Ensures comprehensive health coverage, manages costs, and leverages available Medicare benefits.
Medigap policies	Supplemental insurance policies that cover costs not covered by standard Medicare, such as copayments.	Reduces out-of-pocket expenses and provides predictability in healthcare spending.
Long-term care insurance	Insurance products that cover the cost of long-term care services, which are not covered by Medicare.	Protects assets from the high costs of long-term care, preserving financial stability.
Health savings accounts (HSAs)	Tax-advantaged savings accounts used to pay for eligible medical expenses, particularly useful with high-deductible health plans.	Offers tax savings and a way to fund healthcare expenses in retirement, providing financial flexibility.
Dual eligibility planning	Coordination of Medicare and Medicaid benefits for those who qualify for both, covering a broad range of healthcare services.	Maximizes coverage while minimizing out-of-pocket costs, ideal for low-income seniors.
Special needs trusts	Trusts designed to manage resources for a person with disabilities without jeopardizing eligibility for public benefits like Medicaid.	Allows individuals to maintain eligibility for government healthcare benefits while using trust assets for other expenses.
Discount prescription programs	Programs and cards that offer discounts on prescription medications.	Helps reduce the cost of medications not fully covered by insurance.
Annual insurance review	Regular reviews of health, long-term care, and life insurance policies to adjust coverage as health needs change.	Ensures that insurance coverage remains aligned with changing health needs and financial situations.
Chronic care management	Programs designed to manage chronic diseases such as diabetes or heart disease, often covered under Medicare or private insurance.	Provides coordinated care to manage chronic conditions, potentially reducing complications and costs.
Asset protection strategies	Techniques used to safeguard assets from being depleted due to high medical and long-term care costs.	Helps preserve wealth for future generations while ensuring care needs are met.

DISCUSSION QUESTIONS

1. What are the key differences between Medicare and Medicaid in terms of eligibility, coverage, and benefits for the elderly? How should financial planners advise their clients to integrate both programs into their healthcare planning?

2. How can long-term care insurance mitigate the financial risks associated with prolonged healthcare needs in old age? Discuss the factors that should be considered when choosing a long-term care insurance policy.

3. Evaluate the role of HSAs and FSAs in managing out-of-pocket healthcare expenses for the elderly. What are the benefits and limitations of each in terms of healthcare planning?

4. Discuss the impact of the RMDs from retirement accounts on the tax implications for elderly clients receiving Medicare. How can financial planners help their clients strategically manage withdrawals to minimize tax liability and maximize healthcare benefits?

5. How does the type of long-term care (e.g., home health care, assisted living, nursing homes) influence the financial planning needs of elderly clients? Consider factors such as cost, quality of care, and personal preferences in your discussion.

6. Analyze the potential financial and social benefits of integrating Veterans' Benefits with other government programs like Medicare or Medicaid in the context of long-term care planning. What strategic considerations should financial planners keep in mind when advising clients who are eligible for these benefits?

CONTINUING CASE—THE HARMONS—ANALYZING THE INTERACTION BETWEEN GOVERNMENT BENEFITS AND FINANCIAL RESOURCES FOR RETIREMENT

Chapter 11 Case Assignment 11.1

Objective:

The goal of this exercise is to evaluate how the interaction between government benefits (such as Social Security, Medicare, and other potential benefits) and the Harmons' financial resources will impact their finances in retirement. You will analyze the potential effects on their overall financial stability, consider strategies to maximize their benefits, and assess how these benefits should be integrated into their retirement planning.

Instructions:

1. Review Government Benefits Available to the Harmons:

- **Social Security Benefits:**
  - Calculate the expected Social Security benefits for Darin and Lisa based on their earnings history, age at retirement, and the impact of claiming benefits at different ages (e.g., at full retirement age vs. early retirement).
  - Discuss the factors that may influence their decision on when to begin claiming Social Security benefits, including the impact on their overall retirement income.
- **Medicare:**
  - Explain the different parts of Medicare (Part A, Part B, Part C, and Part D) and how they will affect the Harmons' healthcare costs in retirement.
  - Analyze the impact of Medicare premiums, deductibles, and out-of-pocket costs on their retirement budget.
  - Consider whether they should purchase supplemental insurance (Medigap) or enroll in a Medicare Advantage plan to cover additional healthcare expenses.

- **Other Government Benefits:**
  - Identify any other potential government benefits or programs that the Harmons may be eligible for in retirement, such as veterans' benefits, state-specific programs, or low-income subsidies.
  - Evaluate how these benefits could contribute to their financial security in retirement.

2. Assess the Interaction Between Government Benefits and the Harmons' Financial Resources:

- **Impact on Income and Taxes:**
  - Calculate the combined income from Social Security and other government benefits alongside the Harmons' personal financial resources, such as IRAs, pensions, and investment income.
  - Assess the tax implications of receiving Social Security benefits and how it interacts with other income sources. Consider how much of their Social Security benefits may be taxable based on their total income.
  - Explore strategies to minimize taxes in retirement, such as adjusting withdrawal strategies from retirement accounts.
- **Budgeting for Retirement:**
  - Develop a retirement budget that includes income from both government benefits and personal financial resources.
  - Analyze how fluctuations in government benefits, such as changes in Medicare premiums or Social Security cost-of-living adjustments (COLAs), may affect their budget and financial planning.
- **Longevity and Inflation Considerations:**
  - Discuss the potential impact of longevity and inflation on the value of government benefits over time.
  - Consider strategies to protect against the erosion of purchasing power, such as investing in inflation-protected securities or diversifying income streams.

3. Develop a Retirement Income Strategy:

- **Maximizing Government Benefits:**
  - Provide recommendations on how Darin and Lisa can maximize their Social Security benefits, including the optimal age to claim benefits and the potential benefits of delaying retirement.
  - Suggest ways to manage healthcare costs effectively, including the best Medicare options and supplemental insurance strategies.
- **Integrating Financial Resources:**
  - Develop a strategy for integrating the Harmons' financial resources with their government benefits to ensure a stable and sustainable retirement income.
  - Discuss the best order for withdrawing from various retirement accounts to maximize income and minimize taxes.
- **Contingency Planning:**
  - Outline contingency plans for unexpected changes in government benefits or personal financial resources, such as a significant increase in healthcare costs or changes in Social Security regulations.
  - Provide recommendations for building a financial buffer, such as maintaining an emergency fund or adjusting investment strategies.

4. Draft a Comprehensive Report:

- **Report Content:**
  - Prepare a comprehensive report (four to six pages) that includes:
    - A detailed analysis of the government benefits available to the Harmons and how they interact with their financial resources.
    - An assessment of the tax implications and budgetary considerations related to their government benefits and retirement income.
    - A retirement income strategy that maximizes government benefits while integrating their financial resources effectively.
    - Contingency plans and recommendations for managing potential risks.

- **Action Plan:**
  - Include a timeline for implementing each part of the retirement income strategy, such as when to begin claiming Social Security benefits or when to make specific healthcare decisions.
  - Suggest regular reviews of their retirement plan to adjust for changes in benefits, income, or personal circumstances.

12

Insurance Planning

Insurance planning is a fundamental aspect of resource management for the elderly, playing a critical role in safeguarding financial stability and ensuring access to essential services throughout retirement. As individuals age, their risk profile changes, and the likelihood of encountering health issues or unexpected events increases. Proper insurance planning involves evaluating and selecting appropriate insurance coverage to protect against various risks, such as health-related expenses, long-term care needs, and potential financial losses. By integrating insurance planning into their resource management strategy, elderly individuals can mitigate the financial impact of unforeseen events and maintain greater control over their financial future.

For seniors, insurance planning encompasses a range of products, including health insurance, long-term care insurance, life insurance, and property insurance. Each type of insurance addresses different aspects of financial risk and provides varying levels of protection. Health insurance, such as Medicare and supplemental plans, helps cover medical expenses that can otherwise deplete retirement savings. Long-term care insurance offers financial support for extended care services, reducing the potential burden on personal assets. Life insurance can provide financial security for loved ones and cover estate taxes or final expenses. By carefully assessing and selecting the right combination of insurance products, financial planners can help elderly clients create a robust safety net that supports their overall resource management plan and enhances their quality of life in retirement.

TYPES OF INSURANCE FOR SENIORS

Insurance plays a vital role in resource management for seniors, offering protection against various financial risks that arise in retirement. One of the primary types of insurance for elderly individuals is health insurance, including Medicare and its supplemental plans. Medicare, a federal program available to those aged 65 and older, provides essential coverage for hospital stays (Part A), outpatient services (Part B), and prescription drugs (Part D). Seniors may also consider Medicare Advantage (Part C) plans, which often include additional benefits beyond standard Medicare coverage. Supplemental insurance, known as Medigap, can help cover costs that Medicare does not, such as copayments, coinsurance, and deductibles. Evaluating and selecting the right health insurance options is crucial for managing out-of-pocket healthcare costs and ensuring access to necessary medical services.

Long-term care insurance is another important type of insurance for seniors, addressing the costs associated with extended care services that Medicare typically does not cover. This includes care provided in nursing homes, assisted living facilities, or through in-home services. Long-term care insurance can help alleviate the financial burden of these services, which can be substantial, and protect personal savings from being depleted. When planning for long-term care insurance, it is essential to consider factors such as coverage limits, elimination periods, and benefit amounts to ensure the policy aligns with individual needs and financial circumstances.

Life insurance is also a significant consideration in resource management planning for the elderly. It provides financial security for beneficiaries by offering a death benefit that can be used to cover final expenses, pay off debts, or leave a financial legacy. There are different types of life insurance policies, including term life insurance, which provides coverage for a specified period, and whole life or universal life insurance, which offers lifelong coverage and may accumulate cash value over time. Selecting the appropriate type of life insurance depends on individual goals, such as providing for dependents or managing estate taxes. By incorporating life insurance into their overall financial plan, seniors can ensure that their loved ones are financially protected and that their estate planning goals are met.

These tools and techniques are integral for CFPs when crafting comprehensive financial plans for elderly clients, addressing the unique risks and requirements that arise with age, and ensuring that they are adequately protected against various financial challenges.

TABLE 12.1 Insurance Planning Tools and Techniques

TOOL/TECHNIQUE	DESCRIPTION	BENEFITS
Medicare Supplement Insurance (Medigap)	Policies that cover healthcare costs not covered by Medicare, such as deductibles, copayments, and coinsurance.	Reduces out-of-pocket healthcare expenses, providing financial predictability and stability.
Long-term care insurance	Insurance products designed to cover the costs of long-term care services, which Medicare does not cover.	Protects assets from the high costs of long-term care and ensures access to quality care when needed.
Life insurance evaluation	Review and adjustment of life insurance policies to fit current needs, including converting or downsizing policies.	Ensures that life insurance coverage is appropriate for current life stage and financial goals.
Annuities	Financial products that can be structured to provide income for life, which helps manage longevity risk.	Provides a guaranteed income stream, which can be critical in managing retirement finances.
Disability insurance review	Assessment of current disability coverage to ensure it meets the needs as conditions change with age.	Provides income replacement in case of disability, securing financial stability.
Critical illness insurance	Insurance that provides a lump sum payment if diagnosed with a specific major illness listed in the policy.	Helps manage high costs associated with severe illnesses, protecting savings and investments.
Estate liquidity planning	Using life insurance and other financial instruments to provide cash for settling estate taxes and other expenses without selling assets.	Facilitates the smooth transfer of assets to beneficiaries, avoiding the need to liquidate other investments.
Health savings accounts (HSAs)	Tax-advantaged accounts that can be used to pay for qualified medical expenses, compatible with high-deductible health plans.	Provides a way to fund healthcare costs in retirement with pretax dollars, reducing taxable income.
Insurance trusts	Trusts that hold life insurance policies to remove them from the taxable estate, potentially avoiding estate taxes.	Allows for the tax-efficient transfer of large life insurance benefits to heirs.
Gap insurance for Medicare	Additional insurance that covers services and costs not covered by Medicare, such as vision, dental, and hearing aids.	Enhances medical coverage, reducing unexpected out-of-pocket healthcare expenses.

EVALUATING EXISTING INSURANCE POLICIES

Evaluating existing insurance policies is a critical aspect of resource management planning for the elderly, as it ensures that current coverage aligns with changing needs and financial goals. As individuals age, their healthcare needs and financial circumstances evolve, which can necessitate adjustments in their insurance coverage. Regularly reviewing existing policies helps identify any gaps in coverage or areas where policies may no longer be cost-effective. For example, seniors might find that their current health insurance plan no longer adequately covers new medical needs or that their long-term care insurance does not provide sufficient benefits for the type of care they anticipate needing. Financial planners play a key role in guiding clients through this evaluation process to ensure their insurance coverage remains appropriate and effective.

In addition to assessing coverage adequacy, evaluating existing insurance policies involves scrutinizing the cost of premiums and benefits relative to the client's current financial situation. Seniors should assess whether they can afford ongoing premiums and if the benefits provided are worth the cost. This evaluation may lead to decisions such as adjusting coverage levels, switching to more affordable plans, or even canceling policies that no longer serve a practical purpose. For instance, an older individual might decide to downsize their life insurance policy if their financial situation has improved or if they no longer need as much coverage. By carefully reviewing and managing insurance costs, seniors can better allocate their resources and ensure they are not overspending on unnecessary coverage.

Finally, evaluating existing insurance policies also includes understanding how changes in personal circumstances, such as health status or living situation, impact insurance needs. As health conditions change or the need for long-term care increases, existing policies might need to be updated or supplemented to provide adequate protection. In addition, life events such as retirement or the loss of a spouse can alter insurance needs. Financial planners should help elderly clients navigate these changes by recommending appropriate adjustments to their insurance coverage, ensuring that their plans remain aligned with their current needs and long-term objectives. By maintaining up-to-date and relevant insurance coverage, seniors can better manage their financial risks and maintain greater control over their resource management strategy.

MAKING INFORMED INSURANCE DECISIONS

Making informed insurance decisions is a cornerstone of effective resource management planning for the elderly, ensuring that individuals are adequately protected while optimizing their financial resources. As seniors navigate their retirement years, the decision-making process involves evaluating various types of insurance and understanding how each policy aligns with their specific needs. This includes assessing health insurance options, such as Medicare and supplemental plans, long-term care insurance, and life insurance. Financial planners must help elderly clients weigh the benefits, costs, and coverage details of each option, ensuring that their choices provide comprehensive protection without straining their financial resources.

Informed insurance decisions require a thorough understanding of policy details and the potential impact on overall financial health. Seniors should carefully review policy terms, such as coverage limits, exclusions, deductibles, and premiums, to ensure they meet their needs and budget. For instance, when considering long-term care insurance, it is essential to understand factors such as the benefit amount, waiting periods, and coverage duration. Financial planners should guide clients through this process, helping them compare different policies, interpret complex insurance jargon, and select options that offer the best value and protection. This approach helps seniors avoid costly mistakes and ensures their insurance choices support their long-term financial goals.

In addition, making informed insurance decisions involves staying updated on changes in insurance products and regulations. Insurance needs and available options can evolve over time due to changes in health status, advancements in healthcare, and shifts in regulatory policies. Financial planners should monitor these changes and advise clients on how they might affect their current coverage and future needs. Regularly revisiting insurance plans and adjusting based on updated information and personal circumstances ensures that seniors remain well-protected and financially secure. By fostering a proactive and informed approach to insurance planning, seniors can better manage their resources and enhance their overall quality of life in retirement.

DISCUSSION QUESTIONS

1. How do different types of insurance (e.g., health, long-term care, life, property) address the specific risks associated with aging, and how should they be prioritized in a financial plan for the elderly?

2. Discuss the impact of Medicare and supplemental health plans on the financial stability of elderly clients. How should financial planners assist clients in navigating the complexities of Medicare options to optimize their healthcare coverage and financial outcomes?

3. Evaluate the importance of long-term care insurance in managing the potential costs associated with aging. What key factors should be considered when advising elderly clients on whether to purchase long-term care insurance?

4. Life insurance can be a tool for estate planning as well as financial security for dependents. Discuss the considerations that need to be made when choosing the type of life insurance (term, whole, universal) for an elderly client.

5. Assess the role of property insurance in safeguarding the assets of elderly individuals. What unique considerations should financial planners keep in mind due to the vulnerabilities associated with aging?

6. How should elderly clients be guided to evaluate and potentially adjust their existing insurance policies to reflect changes in their health, lifestyle, or financial situation? What process should financial planners follow to ensure these insurance policies remain aligned with the clients' needs?

CONTINUING CASE—THE HARMONS—HEALTHCARE AND COMPARING LONG-TERM CARE POLICIES OPTIONS

Chapter 12 Case Assignment 12.1

Objective:

The objective of this exercise is to evaluate and compare different long-term care insurance policies for a hypothetical 55-year-old couple, assessing their benefits, costs, and suitability for future needs. You will research various policies, analyze their features, and provide recommendations based on a comprehensive assessment.

Scenario:

Darin and Lisa Harmon, both aged 55, are planning for their retirement and considering various long-term care insurance options. They aim to review and compare policies to understand the coverage, benefits, and financial implications associated with each option.

Exercise Tasks:

1. Research and Selection:

- Research Long-Term Care Policies:
  - Research at least three different long-term care insurance policies offered by reputable insurance providers.
  - Choose policies that vary in terms of coverage options, premium costs, elimination periods, and additional benefits.
  - Focus on policies that would be applicable for a couple in their mid-50s with average health status.

2. Policy Comparison:

- **Create a Comparative Table:**
  - Develop a comparative table that outlines the key features of each policy. Your table should include the following columns:
    - **Insurance Provider:** Name of the insurance company offering the policy.

- **Coverage Details:** Include the daily benefit amount, coverage period, and types of long-term care services covered (e.g., nursing home care, home health care).
- **Premium Costs:** List the annual or monthly premiums for both individuals (Darin and Lisa).
- **Elimination Period:** State the waiting period before benefits start to be paid.
- **Additional Benefits:** Note any supplemental benefits included, such as inflation protection, caregiver training, or return of premium.

3. Analysis and Recommendations:

- **Analyze the Policies:**
  - Analyze the strengths and weaknesses of each policy based on the information provided in your comparative table.
  - Consider Darin and Lisa's financial situation, health status, and long-term care preferences in your evaluation. For example, if they prefer aging in place, a policy with strong home care benefits may be prioritized.
  - Discuss how each policy aligns or does not align with their needs.
- **Provide Recommendations:**
  - Provide a recommendation on which policy you believe best meets their needs and explain why.
  - Justify your choice by referencing specific features of the policy that align with Darin and Lisa's priorities and financial situation.

4. Financial Impact Assessment:

- **Calculate Total Annual Premium Costs:**
  - Calculate the total annual premium costs for each policy based on the premiums listed in the comparative table.
- **Discuss Financial Impact:**
  - Discuss the potential financial impact of purchasing long-term care insurance on Darin and Lisa's retirement savings and budget.

- Consider how the premiums might affect their overall retirement plan, including whether they may need to adjust other expenses or savings goals to accommodate the cost of the insurance.

5. Conclusion:

- **Summarize Findings and Recommendations:**
  - Summarize your findings and recommendations in a brief report format.
  - Highlight the most important factors that influenced your recommendation.
- **Include Additional Considerations:**
  - Mention any additional factors or considerations that may influence Darin and Lisa's decision-making process, such as future changes in health, the potential need for other types of insurance, or the desire to leave a financial legacy.

CONTINUING CASE—THE HARMONS—INSURANCE PLANNING FOR RETIREMENT

Chapter 12 Case Assignment 12.2

Objective:

The purpose of this exercise is to evaluate Darin and Lisa Harmon's existing insurance policies and explore additional insurance tools and techniques that can help protect their financial resources as they age. You will assess the adequacy of their current coverage, identify any gaps, and recommend appropriate adjustments or additional policies to align with their current and future needs.

Instructions:

1. Evaluate Existing Insurance Policies:

- **Review Current Policies:**
  - Begin by reviewing Darin and Lisa's existing insurance policies, including life insurance, health insurance, long-term care insurance, and any other relevant coverage they currently hold.

- Assess whether these policies provide adequate coverage for their current stage of life and financial goals. Consider factors such as coverage amounts, premium costs, and whether the policies align with their evolving needs as they approach retirement.

- **Analyze Coverage Adequacy:**
  - Identify any gaps in coverage or areas where their current policies may no longer be cost-effective or appropriate.
  - Consider their healthcare needs, long-term care preferences, and overall financial situation when evaluating the adequacy of their existing coverage.
  - Discuss the potential need to adjust coverage levels, switch to more affordable plans, or downsize policies that no longer serve a practical purpose.

2. Explore Additional Insurance Tools and Techniques:

- **Medicare Supplement Insurance (Medigap):**
  - Research and explain how Medigap policies can complement Medicare by covering healthcare costs not covered by Medicare, such as deductibles, copayments, and coinsurance.
  - Evaluate whether a Medigap policy would be beneficial for the Harmons, considering their expected healthcare needs and desire for financial stability.
- **Long-Term Care Insurance:**
  - Reassess their existing long-term care insurance (if any) or explore the benefits of purchasing long-term care insurance to protect against the high costs of long-term care services.
  - Provide recommendations on whether the Harmons should maintain, adjust, or purchase long-term care insurance based on their financial goals and preferences for care in later years.
- **Life Insurance Evaluation:**
  - Review and adjust their life insurance policies to ensure they align with their current needs and financial goals.
  - Consider options such as converting, downsizing, or maintaining their existing policies, and discuss how these decisions will impact their estate planning and legacy goals.

- **Annuities:**
  - Explain the role of annuities in providing a guaranteed income stream for life, helping to manage longevity risk.
  - Evaluate whether annuities would be a suitable addition to the Harmons' retirement plan, considering their need for stable income in retirement.
- **Critical Illness Insurance:**
  - Assess the potential benefits of critical illness insurance, which provides a lump sum payment if diagnosed with a specific major illness.
  - Determine whether this type of insurance is necessary for the Harmons, given their health status and financial situation.
- **Estate Liquidity Planning:**
  - Discuss the importance of estate liquidity planning and how life insurance and other financial instruments can provide cash for settling estate taxes and other expenses without selling assets.
  - Recommend strategies for ensuring the Harmons' estate has sufficient liquidity to meet their estate planning objectives.
- **Health Savings Accounts (HSAs):**
  - Evaluate the benefits of HSAs as a tax-advantaged way to fund healthcare costs in retirement.
  - Consider whether the Harmons should utilize HSAs in their financial planning to reduce taxable income and save for future medical expenses.
- **Insurance Trusts:**
  - Explore the use of insurance trusts to hold life insurance policies, potentially removing them from the taxable estate and avoiding estate taxes.
  - Determine if establishing an insurance trust would be beneficial for the Harmons' estate planning and wealth transfer goals.
- **Gap Insurance for Medicare:**
  - Consider the benefits of gap insurance that covers services and costs not covered by Medicare, such as vision, dental, and hearing aids.

- Recommend whether the Harmons should purchase gap insurance to enhance their medical coverage and reduce unexpected out-of-pocket expenses.

3. Financial Impact and Recommendations:

- **Calculate Costs and Benefits:**
  - For each recommended insurance tool or technique, calculate the potential costs (e.g., premiums) and benefits (e.g., coverage, protection, tax advantages).
  - Discuss the financial impact of implementing these recommendations on the Harmons' overall retirement plan and budget.
- **Provide Recommendations:**
  - Based on your analysis, provide a comprehensive set of recommendations for the Harmons. This should include adjustments to existing policies, the purchase of new insurance products, and strategies for integrating these tools into their broader financial plan.
  - Justify your recommendations by referencing how each tool or technique aligns with the Harmons' needs, goals, and financial situation.

4. Write a Comprehensive Insurance Planning Report:

- **Report Content:**
  - Prepare a comprehensive report (five to seven pages) that includes:
    - An evaluation of the Harmons' existing insurance policies.
    - An exploration of additional insurance tools and techniques.
    - A financial impact assessment and detailed recommendations.
    - Any additional considerations or strategies for maintaining appropriate coverage as they age.
- **Action Plan:**
  - Include a timeline for implementing the recommended changes, prioritizing steps that should be taken immediately versus those that can be addressed over time.
  - Suggest regular reviews of their insurance planning to adjust for changes in health, financial circumstances, or insurance market conditions.

13

Social Security and Pension Analysis

Social Security and pension analysis are crucial components of resource management planning for the elderly, playing a significant role in ensuring a stable and reliable income stream throughout retirement. Social Security benefits, a federal program designed to provide financial support to retirees, disabled individuals, and survivors, form a foundational aspect of many seniors' income plans. Understanding the intricacies of Social Security, including benefit calculations, claiming strategies, and potential impacts on taxes, is essential for optimizing this source of income. In addition, pension plans, which may be available through former employers or as part of a retirement package, provide another vital income stream. Analyzing these pensions involves evaluating their terms, such as payout options, vesting schedules, and survivorship benefits, to ensure they effectively support long-term financial stability.

Effective resource management for the elderly requires a comprehensive analysis of both Social Security and pension benefits to maximize income and enhance financial security. Financial planners must assist clients in understanding the best time to start claiming Social Security benefits, considering factors such as life expectancy, health status, and other income sources. Similarly, evaluating pension plans involves analyzing the specific features and benefits of each plan to determine the most advantageous way to receive these funds. By integrating Social Security and pension analysis into a broader financial plan, planners can help seniors make informed decisions that align with their retirement goals, ensuring a steady income flow and long-term financial well-being.

SOCIAL SECURITY BENEFITS OVERVIEW

Social Security benefits are a foundational element of resource management planning for the elderly, providing a reliable source of income that supports financial stability throughout retirement. The

Social Security program, managed by the U.S. Social Security Administration (SSA), offers monthly payments to retirees based on their earnings history and the number of credits they have earned over their working years. Understanding the formula used to calculate benefits, which considers the highest-earning 35 years of work, is essential for retirees to estimate their potential income accurately. Financial planners must help clients comprehend how their benefit amounts are determined and how different factors, such as delayed claiming or early retirement, can impact their monthly payments.

A key consideration in Social Security benefits planning is the timing of claims. Seniors can begin receiving benefits as early as age 62, but doing so can result in reduced monthly payments compared to waiting until full retirement age (FRA) or even age 70. Full retirement age varies depending on the year of birth, and delaying benefits can increase the monthly amount due to delayed retirement credits. Financial planners should guide clients in evaluating their personal circumstances, including health, financial needs, and expected longevity, to determine the optimal age for claiming Social Security benefits. This strategic decision can have a significant impact on overall retirement income and financial well-being.

In addition, Social Security benefits can be subject to taxation based on the recipient's total income, including other sources of retirement income such as pensions and investments. Financial planners need to help seniors understand the tax implications of their Social Security benefits and how to manage their overall income to minimize tax liabilities. Strategies may include managing withdrawals from retirement accounts, timing income sources, or exploring tax-efficient investment options. By incorporating Social Security benefits into a comprehensive financial plan and addressing potential tax impacts, planners can help seniors maximize their retirement income and maintain greater financial stability throughout their retirement years (Kagan, 2024).

TABLE 13.1 Age to Receive Full Social Security Benefits

YEAR OF BIRTH	FULL RETIREMENT AGE	MONTHS BETWEEN AGE 62 AND FULL RETIREMENT AGE	AT AGE 62: $1000 RETIREMENT BENEFIT REDUCED TO	BENEFIT REDUCTION	AT AGE 62: $500 SPOUSE'S BENEFIT REDUCED TO	SPOUSE'S BENEFIT REDUCTION
1943-1954	66	48	$750	25.00%	$350	30.00%
1955	66 and 2 months	50	$741	25.83%	$345	30.83%
1956	66 and 4 months	52	$733	26.67%	$341	31.67%
1957	66 and 6 months	54	$725	27.50%	$337	32.50%
1958	66 and 8 months	56	$716	28.33%	$333	33.33%
1959	66 and 10 months	58	$708	29.17%	$329	34.17%
1960 and later	67	60	$700	30.00%	$325	35.00%

Notes: If you were born on January 1st you should refer to the previous year. If born on the 1st of any month benefits are calculated as if your birthday was in the previous month. You must be 62 for the entire month to receive benefits. All percentages are approximate due to rounding.

Source: Social Security Administration (n.d.-a).

STRATEGIES FOR MAXIMIZING BENEFITS

Strategies for maximizing Social Security benefits are essential for resource management planning for the elderly, as these benefits often represent a significant portion of retirement income. One effective strategy is to delay claiming benefits until reaching FRA or even age 70. Although individuals can start receiving benefits as early as age 62, doing so results in reduced monthly payments. Conversely, delaying benefits increases the monthly amount due to delayed retirement credits, which can significantly enhance overall lifetime benefits, especially for those in good health with a longer life expectancy. Financial planners should help clients evaluate their personal health, financial situation, and anticipated longevity to determine the optimal claiming age that maximizes their Social Security benefits.

Another crucial strategy involves coordinating Social Security benefits with other sources of retirement income. By strategically managing withdrawals from retirement accounts, such as 401(k)s and IRAs, clients can potentially lower their taxable income, which might reduce the portion of Social Security benefits subject to taxation. In addition, coordinating the timing of Social Security claims with the start of pension benefits or other income sources can help manage overall tax liabilities and enhance the efficiency of retirement income. Financial planners should assist clients in developing a comprehensive income strategy that considers all sources of retirement funds and their interactions, optimizing overall financial outcomes.

Couples can also benefit from strategic Social Security planning by considering the options available for maximizing combined benefits. For married couples, one strategy is to have one spouse delay claiming benefits to maximize their monthly payment, whereas the other spouse begins benefits earlier. This approach can help ensure that at least one spouse receives a higher benefit amount, which can be especially advantageous if the higher earning spouse has a longer life expectancy. In addition, the Social Security spousal benefit allows one spouse to receive a portion of the other spouse's benefit if it is higher, which can provide additional financial support. Financial planners should guide couples in evaluating their specific situations and considering various claiming strategies to enhance their overall Social Security benefits and improve their retirement income planning .(Social Security Administration, n.d.-a).

TABLE 13.2 Rate of Increase for Delayed Retirement by Year of Birth

YEAR OF BIRTH	12-MONTH RATE OF INCREASE	MONTHLY RATE OF INCREASE
1933–1934	5.5%	11/24 of 1%
1935–1936	6.0%	1/2 of 1%
1937–1938	6.5%	13/24 of 1%
1939–1940	7.0%	7/12 of 1%
1941–1942	7.5%	5/8 of 1%
1943 or later	8.0%	2/3 of 1%

Note: Percentages and fractions are approximations and apply to benefits delayed past full retirement age.

Source: U.S. Department of Health and Human Services Washington D.C.: Retirement Benefits. Retrieved August 2006 from www.ssa.gov/retire2/delayret.htm

PENSION OPTIONS AND DECISIONS

Pension options and decisions are pivotal elements of resource management planning for the elderly, as they directly impact retirement income stability and financial security. When evaluating pension options, seniors must consider the type of pension plan they have, such as defined benefit plans, which provide a predetermined monthly payout based on factors like years of service and salary, or defined contribution plans, which depend on the accumulated value of the account. Each type of plan comes with its own set of benefits and considerations, and understanding these can help retirees make informed decisions about their income strategy. Financial planners play a crucial role in helping clients navigate these options and choose the one that best aligns with their retirement goals and financial needs.

One key decision in managing pension benefits involves selecting the appropriate payout option. Pension plans often offer different distribution choices, such as a lump sum payment, a single-life annuity, or a joint-and-survivor annuity. Each option has implications for long-term financial security and should be carefully evaluated. A lump sum payment provides immediate access to a large amount of money but may require careful investment and management to ensure long-term stability. On the other hand, annuity options offer predictable, regular payments for life or for a set period but might be less flexible. Financial planners need to help clients assess these options based on their longevity expectations, overall financial situation, and the need for ongoing income for themselves or their beneficiaries.

In addition, understanding the tax implications of pension withdrawals is essential for effective resource management. Pension income is subject to income tax, and the way withdrawals are structured can impact the overall tax burden. For instance, withdrawing a large sum in a single year can push an individual into a higher tax bracket, whereas spreading out withdrawals may result in a lower tax rate. Financial planners should assist clients in devising a strategy that minimizes tax liabilities while optimizing pension benefits. This includes exploring opportunities for tax-efficient withdrawals and integrating pension income with other sources of retirement funds to create a comprehensive and tax-efficient financial plan. By carefully evaluating pension options and making informed decisions, seniors can enhance their financial stability and better manage their resources throughout retirement.

These techniques are critical in the financial planning process for elderly clients, helping them to navigate complex decisions regarding Social Security and pension benefits effectively.

TABLE 13.3 Analysis Tools and Techniques for Social Security and Pension Planning

TOOL/TECHNIQUE	DESCRIPTION	BENEFITS
Social Security optimization	Techniques to maximize Social Security benefits by analyzing the best age to begin claiming benefits.	Maximizes lifetime benefits, potentially increasing retirement income by analyzing various claiming strategies.
Pension valuation	Assessing the value of pension benefits, including both defined benefit and defined contribution plans.	Helps clients understand the value of their pensions in current terms and plans for future income needs.
Pension payout analysis	Comparison of different pension payout options, such as lump sum versus annuity payments.	Assists clients in choosing the payout option that best suits their financial and tax situation.
Break-even analysis for Social Security	Calculation to determine the age at which the total benefits received begin to outweigh the benefits of delaying Social Security.	Informs decision-making on when to start taking Social Security benefits based on longevity and financial needs.
Coordination of benefits	Strategies for coordinating Social Security with other retirement income sources, such as pensions and IRAs.	Optimizes total retirement income by effectively timing and combining different income streams.
Survivor benefit analysis	Evaluation of the impact of various decisions on the survivor benefits for a spouse.	Ensures that surviving spouses are financially protected with optimal benefits planning.
Inflation impact assessment	Analysis of how inflation could affect the purchasing power of fixed pension and Social Security payments.	Helps clients plan for cost-of-living adjustments and maintain their standard of living.
Tax efficiency planning	Strategies to minimize taxes on Social Security and pension income to maximize net retirement income.	Reduces tax liability, increasing the amount of spendable income during retirement.
Risk assessment	Evaluation of the risk of pension plan underfunding or changes in Social Security policy affecting benefits.	Prepares clients for potential risks and changes in their expected retirement income.

DISCUSSION QUESTIONS

1. How can financial planners assist clients in determining the optimal age to begin claiming Social Security benefits, considering factors such as health, life expectancy, and other income sources?

2. Discuss the pros and cons of various pension payout options, such as lump sum versus annuity. What are the key considerations for retirees when choosing how to receive their pension benefits?

3. Evaluate the impact of delayed Social Security claiming on a retiree's overall financial stability. What scenarios might justify taking benefits at full retirement age or delaying until age 70?

4. How can pension and Social Security benefits be coordinated to maximize retirement income while minimizing tax liabilities? Provide examples of effective strategies for different types of retirees.

5. Discuss the importance of including survivor benefits in the planning of Social Security and pensions. How should financial planners address the needs of the surviving spouse in their strategies?

6. What are the key challenges and considerations when dealing with pensions from multiple employers, including public and private sources? How can retirees integrate these into a cohesive retirement plan?

CONTINUING CASE—THE HARMONS—EVALUATING SOCIAL SECURITY AND PENSION PLANNING

Chapter 13 Case Assignment 13.1

Objective:

The goal of this exercise is to evaluate Darin and Lisa Harmon's Social Security and pension options to help them make informed decisions that maximize their retirement income. You will use various techniques to analyze their benefits, consider the impact of inflation and taxes, and develop strategies for coordinating these income streams with other retirement resources.

Instructions:

1. Social Security Optimization:

- **Analyze Claiming Strategies:**
  - Use Social Security optimization techniques to evaluate the best age for Darin and Lisa to begin claiming their Social Security benefits.
  - Consider different scenarios, such as claiming benefits at the earliest age (62), FRA, and delaying benefits until age 70.
  - Calculate the potential lifetime benefits for each scenario and identify the strategy that maximizes their Social Security income.

2. Pension Valuation:

- **Assess Pension Value:**
  - Evaluate the current value of Darin and Lisa's pension benefits, including both defined benefits and defined contribution plans.
  - Calculate the present value of their pension income streams and compare them to their expected retirement needs.
  - Consider factors such as the guaranteed income provided by a defined benefit plan and the investment growth potential of a defined contribution plan.

3. Pension Payout Analysis:

- **Compare Payout Options:**
  - Analyze the different payout options available to Darin and Lisa for their pension benefits, such as lump sum payments versus annuity payments.
  - Evaluate the financial and tax implications of each option, considering their overall retirement strategy, life expectancy, and income needs.
  - Provide a recommendation on which payout option may be most beneficial for them based on their financial situation.

4. Break-Even Analysis for Social Security:

- **Conduct Break-Even Analysis:**
  - Perform a break-even analysis to determine the age at which the total Social Security benefits received begin to outweigh the benefits of delaying.
  - Use this analysis to inform the decision-making process on when Darin and Lisa should start taking Social Security benefits, considering their health, life expectancy, and financial needs.

5. Coordination of Benefits:

- **Strategize Income Coordination:**
  - Develop a strategy for coordinating Social Security benefits with other retirement income sources, such as pensions, IRAs, and investment income.
  - Consider the timing and combination of income streams to optimize their total retirement income.
  - Discuss how coordinating these benefits can help smooth income throughout retirement and reduce the risk of outliving their resources.

6. Survivor Benefit Analysis:

- **Evaluate Survivor Benefits:**
  - Assess the impact of various Social Security and pension decisions on survivor benefits for the remaining spouse.

- Ensure that the surviving spouse is financially protected by optimizing the decisions that affect survivor benefits.
- Provide recommendations for the best strategies to maximize survivor benefits and ensure long-term financial security.

7. Inflation Impact Assessment:

- **Analyze Inflation Impact:**
  - Evaluate how inflation could affect the purchasing power of fixed pension and Social Security payments over time.
  - Discuss the importance of cost-of-living adjustments (COLAs) in maintaining their standard of living during retirement.
  - Recommend strategies to mitigate the impact of inflation, such as investing in inflation-protected securities or diversifying income streams.

8. Tax Efficiency Planning:

- **Plan for Tax Efficiency:**
  - Develop strategies to minimize taxes on Social Security and pension income, maximizing the net retirement income for the Harmons.
  - Consider the impact of different withdrawal strategies from tax-deferred accounts, Roth conversions, and the timing of income recognition on their overall tax liability.
  - Provide recommendations for tax-efficient retirement planning, including the use of tax-advantaged accounts and strategic income timing.

9. Risk Assessment:

- **Evaluate Risks:**
  - Assess the potential risks associated with Darin and Lisa's pension plan, including the risk of underfunding or changes in Social Security policy that could affect their benefits.
  - Discuss the importance of diversification and risk management in their overall retirement strategy.

- Recommend strategies to protect against these risks, such as maintaining an emergency fund, diversifying income sources, or purchasing additional insurance products.

10. Write a Comprehensive Social Security and Pension Analysis Report:

- **Report Content:**
  - Prepare a comprehensive report (five to seven pages) that includes:
    - An analysis of Social Security optimization and pension valuation.
    - A comparison of pension payout options and break-even analysis for Social Security.
    - Coordination of benefits, survivor benefit analysis, and inflation impact assessment.
    - Tax efficiency planning and risk assessment.
    - A detailed set of recommendations for maximizing retirement income and protecting against potential risks.
- **Action Plan:**
  - Include a timeline for implementing the recommended strategies, prioritizing steps that should be taken immediately versus those that can be addressed over time.
  - Suggest regular reviews of their Social Security and pension plans to adjust for changes in personal circumstances, financial goals, or policy changes.

14

Housing and Living Arrangements

Housing and living arrangements are integral components of resource management planning for the elderly, significantly impacting both financial stability and quality of life in retirement. As individuals age, their housing needs often change, and planning for these changes involves evaluating various living options that align with their health, financial situation, and personal preferences. Whether considering modifications to their current home, downsizing to a more manageable property, or moving to an assisted living facility, elderly individuals need to carefully assess how these choices will affect their long-term financial resources and overall well-being. Effective resource management includes planning for housing expenses, such as maintenance, property taxes, and utility costs, as well as ensuring that living arrangements support their health and safety needs.

When evaluating housing and living arrangements, financial planners must help clients consider the costs associated with different options and how these fit into their broader financial plan. This includes analyzing the affordability of staying in their current home versus the financial implications of moving to a new property or facility. Seniors may need to factor in the costs of home modifications for accessibility, moving expenses, and the potential impact on their retirement savings. In addition, exploring options such as independent living communities, assisted living, or nursing homes requires a thorough understanding of the associated costs, services provided, and how these align with the client's health needs and lifestyle preferences. By integrating housing and living arrangements into resource management planning, seniors can make informed decisions that enhance their quality of life while maintaining financial stability throughout their retirement years.

ASSESSING HOUSING NEEDS

Assessing housing needs is a fundamental aspect of resource management planning for the elderly, as it involves evaluating how current and future living arrangements align with an individual's health, mobility, and financial situation. As people age, their ability to maintain a large home or navigate complex living environments may diminish, necessitating a reassessment of their housing requirements. This assessment should consider factors such as accessibility, maintenance needs, and the suitability of the home for any physical limitations. Financial planners should collaborate with clients to evaluate whether their current home can be adapted to meet their changing needs or if relocating to a more accessible and manageable living space might be a better solution.

In addition to physical accessibility, evaluating housing needs involves considering the costs associated with different living arrangements. Seniors must weigh the expenses of modifying their existing home, such as installing ramps or grab bars, against the potential savings from downsizing to a smaller, more manageable property. In addition, moving to a retirement community or assisted living facility comes with its own set of costs, including monthly fees and additional services. Financial planners should assist clients in understanding these costs and how they impact their overall financial plan, ensuring that any housing decision aligns with their budget and long-term financial goals.

Furthermore, assessing housing needs should account for the social and emotional aspects of living arrangements. Maintaining social connections and having access to community resources can impact an elderly individual's quality of life. Housing options such as retirement communities or independent living facilities often offer social activities and support services that can enhance well-being and reduce feelings of isolation. Financial planners should help clients consider not only the financial implications of different housing options but also how these choices affect their overall happiness and social engagement. By addressing both practical and emotional factors in housing assessments, seniors can make well-rounded decisions that support their long-term quality of life and financial stability.

FINANCIAL CONSIDERATIONS FOR DOWNSIZING

Financial considerations for downsizing are crucial elements of resource management planning for the elderly, as this decision can significantly impact both immediate finances and long-term financial stability. Downsizing typically involves moving to a smaller, more manageable property, which can reduce ongoing costs such as property taxes, utility bills, and maintenance expenses. The sale of a larger home can also provide a substantial amount of cash, which can be redirected into retirement savings, invested to generate additional income, or used to cover other expenses. Financial planners should help clients evaluate the potential financial benefits of downsizing, including how the proceeds from the sale will affect their overall financial situation and what adjustments might be needed to their retirement plan.

Another important consideration in the downsizing process is the cost of moving and purchasing a new property. Expenses related to selling a home, such as real estate agent commissions, closing costs, and repairs to make the home market-ready, can add up quickly. In addition, buying a new property may involve new costs, including closing costs, moving expenses, and potential renovations or modifications to accommodate any specific needs. Financial planners should assist clients in estimating these costs and understanding how they will impact on their finances. By accurately calculating both the costs and benefits of downsizing, clients can make more informed decisions and avoid financial surprises.

Finally, seniors must consider the impact of downsizing on their lifestyle and future expenses. Although moving to a smaller home can reduce monthly expenses, it is important to assess how the new living situation aligns with their long-term needs, including healthcare and accessibility requirements. In addition, the decision to downsize should be evaluated in the context of future potential needs, such as assisted living or long-term care. Financial planners should help clients balance the immediate financial benefits of downsizing with their long-term goals and potential future costs. This comprehensive approach ensures that downsizing not only supports current financial stability but also aligns with future needs and retirement objectives.

EXPLORING SENIOR LIVING COMMUNITIES

Exploring senior living communities is an important aspect of resource management planning for the elderly, as these communities offer various levels of care and amenities tailored to meet the needs of aging individuals. Senior living options, such as independent living, assisted living, and continuing care retirement communities (CCRCs), provide different levels of support and services based on an individual's health, lifestyle, and financial situation. Independent living communities are designed for seniors who can manage daily activities independently but seek a community with social opportunities and minimal maintenance responsibilities. Assisted living facilities offer additional support with daily activities such as bathing, dressing, and medication management. CCRCs provide a continuum of care, allowing individuals to transition from independent living to higher levels of care as their needs change. Evaluating these options helps seniors find a community that aligns with their current and future needs, enhancing their overall quality of life.

Financial planners play a key role in helping clients navigate the costs associated with senior living communities, which can vary widely depending on the level of care and amenities provided. Costs can include monthly rent or fees, which may cover services such as meals, housekeeping, and transportation, as well as additional charges for personal care services. It is crucial to understand the full scope of what is included in the monthly fee and any potential additional costs that may arise. Planners should assist clients in comparing different communities, factoring in both the cost and the services provided, and determining how these expenses fit into their overall retirement budget. By analyzing the financial implications of various senior living options, clients can make informed decisions that align with their financial goals and ensure long-term stability.

In addition, exploring senior living communities involves assessing the nonfinancial benefits and services that impact overall well-being. These communities often offer social activities, fitness programs, and wellness services that can significantly enhance quality of life. Access to on-site medical care, emergency assistance, and a supportive community environment can also contribute to a higher level of comfort and security. Financial planners should help clients evaluate how these nonfinancial factors align with their personal preferences and health needs. By considering both the financial and lifestyle aspects of senior living communities, seniors can make a well-rounded decision that supports their overall well-being and long-term financial health.

Each of these options has different financial implications, and the suitability of each will depend on the individual's health needs, financial situation, and personal preferences. A CFP must consider these factors to provide recommendations that align with the client's long-term goals and circumstances.

TABLE 14.1 Housing and Living Options for Seniors: Descriptions and Financial Considerations

HOUSING/LIVING OPTION	DESCRIPTION	FINANCIAL CONSIDERATIONS
Aging in place	Remaining in one's own home with modifications and support services as needed.	Cost of home modifications, in-home care services, and potential for reverse mortgage funding.
Independent living communities	Housing designed for seniors that offers community engagement without medical support.	Monthly fees for housing and amenities, upfront community fees, cost of moving.
Assisted living facilities	Residential options that provide personal care and health services for those who need assistance.	Monthly fees that cover room, board, and care; entrance fees; insurance coverage.
Nursing homes	Facilities that provide a higher level of medical care and personal assistance.	High cost for extensive care, often including medical and personal care services.
Continuing care retirement communities (CCRCs)	Communities that offer a range of housing options, from independent living to nursing care, as residents age.	Entry fees and monthly charges based on the level of care and services provided.
Memory care facilities	Specialized facilities for individuals with Alzheimer's, dementia, or other memory issues.	Typically, more expensive than standard assisted living due to specialized care and security.
Shared housing	Living arrangements where seniors share a residence with peers or younger individuals.	Reduced housing costs through shared expenses; potential income if renting out space.
Accessory dwelling units (ADUs)	Small homes or apartments that are on the same property as a larger home, often used for family members.	Construction or conversion costs, potential rental income if used as a rental property.
Co-housing communities	Planned communities consisting of private homes supplemented by shared facilities and common areas.	Costs like home ownership, with additional fees for community maintenance and activities.
Home equity conversion mortgages (HECMs)	Reverse mortgage programs insured by the federal government, allow seniors to convert part of their home equity into cash.	Can provide funds for living expenses, healthcare, or other needs without monthly payments, but decreases estate value.

DISCUSSION QUESTIONS

1. How should elderly individuals evaluate the cost-benefit trade-offs of staying in their current home versus moving to a senior living community? Consider both financial and nonfinancial factors in your discussion.

2. What financial planning strategies should seniors implement when considering a move from a large family home to a more manageable living environment like an independent living community or an assisted living facility?

3. How do different housing options, such as aging in place versus moving to a nursing home or assisted living facility, affect the quality of life and social connections for elderly individuals?

4. Discuss the role of a financial planner in helping elderly clients navigate the complex decisions associated with choosing the right type of housing. What key financial and personal factors should be considered?

5. How should changes in health and mobility influence the decision-making process regarding elderly housing? Consider the implications of requiring home modifications or the need for proximity to medical facilities.

6. How can elderly individuals plan for potential future needs, such as the transition to higher levels of care within CCRCs? What financial preparations are necessary to accommodate such transitions?

CONTINUING CASE—THE HARMONS—EVALUATING HOUSING AND LIVING ARRANGEMENTS IN RETIREMENT

Chapter 14 Case Assignment 14.1

Objective:

The purpose of this exercise is to evaluate Darin and Lisa Harmon's housing and living arrangements as they approach retirement. This will involve assessing their housing needs, considering the financial implications of downsizing, exploring senior living communities, and analyzing their goal of transitioning to the lake house they plan to buy and remodel.

Instructions:

1. Assessing Housing Needs:

- **Current Housing Situation:**
  - Begin by evaluating Darin and Lisa's current housing situation. Consider the size, location, maintenance requirements, and suitability of their current home for aging in place.
  - Discuss whether their current home meets their needs as they enter retirement, or if there are challenges related to mobility, maintenance, or accessibility that should be addressed.
- **Future Housing Preferences:**
  - Identify their preferences for future housing arrangements, considering factors such as proximity to family, healthcare facilities, and social activities.
  - Discuss how their lifestyle goals, such as traveling, spending time with grandchildren, or pursuing hobbies, might influence their housing needs.
- **Aging in Place versus Moving:**
  - Evaluate the pros and cons of aging in place in their current home versus moving to a new location. Consider factors such as health, community support, accessibility, and potential need for home modifications.

2. Financial Considerations for Downsizing:

- **Downsizing Analysis:**
  - Analyze the financial implications of downsizing to a smaller home or condominium. Consider potential savings on mortgage payments, property taxes, utilities, and maintenance costs.
  - Calculate the expected proceeds from selling their current home and how those funds could be used to purchase a smaller home or supplement their retirement savings.
- **Cost Comparison:**
  - Compare the costs of maintaining their current home versus the costs associated with downsizing. Include considerations such as moving expenses, renovation costs for the new home, and any potential impact on their lifestyle.
  - Discuss how downsizing could free up capital for other retirement goals, such as travel, hobbies, or healthcare.
- **Tax Implications:**
  - Consider any tax implications of selling their current home, including potential capital gains taxes and how to minimize them.
  - Explore the tax benefits of purchasing a smaller home or condominium, such as property tax reductions or homestead exemptions.

3. Exploring Senior Living Communities:

- **Research Senior Living Options:**
  - Research and compare diverse types of senior living communities, including independent living, assisted living, and CCRCs.
  - Evaluate the benefits and drawbacks of each option, considering factors such as cost, level of care, amenities, and social opportunities.
- **Suitability Assessment:**
  - Assess whether moving to a senior living community aligns with Darin and Lisa's lifestyle goals, health needs, and financial situation.

  - Discuss the potential advantages of living in a community with access to healthcare, social activities, and a supportive environment.

- **Cost Analysis:**
  - Analyze the costs associated with senior living communities, including entrance fees, monthly fees, and additional services. Compare these costs to the expenses of maintaining their current home or downsizing.
  - Provide recommendations on whether a senior living community is a viable option for the Harmons, either now or in the future.

4. Transitioning to the Lake House:

- **Lake House Goals:**
  - Discuss Darin and Lisa's goal of purchasing and remodeling a lake house to use as their primary residence in retirement.
  - Evaluate how this goal aligns with their overall retirement plan, including lifestyle preferences, family considerations, and financial resources.
- **Financial Feasibility:**
  - Analyze the financial feasibility of purchasing and remodeling the lake house. Consider the cost of the home, renovation expenses, ongoing maintenance, and property taxes.
  - Compare these costs to their current financial situation and retirement budget. Discuss whether they can comfortably afford this transition without compromising other retirement goals.
- **Remodeling Considerations:**
  - Discuss the necessary modifications to make the lake house suitable for aging in place, such as accessibility features, energy efficiency upgrades, and maintenance considerations.
  - Provide recommendations on how to approach the remodeling process, including setting a budget, hiring contractors, and prioritizing essential upgrades.
- **Lifestyle Impact:**
  - Consider the lifestyle impact of transitioning to the lake house, including proximity to family and healthcare, access to social activities, and the overall quality of life.

  - Discuss how this move aligns with their long-term goals and whether it supports their vision of an enjoyable and fulfilling retirement.

5. Write a Comprehensive Housing and Living Arrangements Report:

- **Report Content:**
  - Prepare a comprehensive report (five to seven pages) that includes:
    - An assessment of Darin and Lisa's current and future housing needs.
    - A financial analysis of downsizing and its implications for their retirement plan.
    - An evaluation of senior living communities as an alternative or future option.
    - A detailed analysis of their goal to transition to the lake house, including financial feasibility, remodeling considerations, and lifestyle impact.
    - Recommendations for the best housing and living arrangements based on their needs, preferences, and financial situation.
- **Action Plan:**
  - Include a timeline for implementing the recommended housing strategies, prioritizing steps that should be taken immediately versus those that can be addressed over time.
  - Suggest regular reviews of their housing plan to adjust for changes in health, financial circumstances, or personal goals.

15

Income and Cash Flow Management

Income and cash flow management are critical components of resource management planning for the elderly, as they directly influence financial stability and the ability to meet ongoing living expenses throughout retirement. Effective management of income and cash flow ensures that seniors can maintain their desired lifestyle, cover necessary expenses, and avoid financial stress. This involves carefully planning and monitoring all sources of income, including Social Security benefits, pensions, retirement account withdrawals, and any other income streams. By creating a comprehensive cash flow plan, elderly individuals can balance their income with expenditures, ensuring that their financial resources are utilized efficiently and sustainably over the long term.

In addition to managing income, cash flow management encompasses the strategic allocation of funds to meet both short-term and long-term needs. This includes budgeting for regular expenses such as housing, healthcare, and daily living costs, as well as planning for occasional or unexpected expenses. Financial planners play a crucial role in helping seniors develop and implement effective cash flow strategies, including setting up appropriate savings accounts, managing debt, and making informed investment decisions. By integrating income and cash flow management into their overall resource management plan, elderly individuals can achieve greater financial security, enhance their quality of life, and better prepare for any future financial challenges.

MANAGING MONTHLY INCOME

Managing monthly income is a crucial aspect of resource management planning for the elderly, as it directly affects their ability to meet ongoing living expenses and maintain financial stability throughout retirement. Effective management involves creating a detailed budget that accounts for all sources of income, such as Social Security benefits, pensions, annuities, and any other sources of retirement funds. By establishing a clear understanding of monthly income, seniors can allocate funds to cover essential expenses such as housing, utilities, groceries, and healthcare, while also setting aside money for discretionary spending and savings. This structured approach helps ensure that income is sufficient to cover regular expenses without depleting savings or relying on credit.

In addition to budgeting for regular expenses, managing monthly income involves planning for variability and unexpected costs. Seniors may encounter fluctuating expenses, such as seasonal utility bills or unplanned medical costs, which can strain their monthly budget. To address these variations, financial planners recommend setting up an emergency fund to cover unexpected expenses and incorporating flexibility into the budget to accommodate occasional changes. By proactively planning for these potential fluctuations, seniors can avoid financial stress and ensure that their monthly income is effectively utilized to maintain a stable and comfortable lifestyle.

Moreover, managing monthly income requires ongoing monitoring and adjustment to adapt to changing financial circumstances. As individuals age, their income sources may shift, and their expenses may evolve, necessitating periodic reviews of their financial plan. For instance, a change in Social Security benefits or pension amounts, adjustments in living expenses, or shifts in health needs can all impact monthly income management. Financial planners should collaborate with clients to regularly reassess their budgets, make necessary adjustments, and ensure that their income management strategies remain aligned with their current financial situation and long-term goals. This dynamic approach to managing monthly income helps seniors maintain financial stability and adapt to any changes in their retirement years.

CASH FLOW STRATEGIES FOR STABILITY

Cash flow strategies for stability are essential to effective resource management planning for the elderly, ensuring that retirees can meet their financial needs and maintain their standard of living throughout retirement. One key strategy involves creating a detailed budget that categorizes income and expenses, providing a clear overview of cash flow. This budget should account for fixed expenses such as housing, utilities, and insurance, as well as variable costs like groceries, transportation, and discretionary spending. By meticulously tracking income and expenses, seniors can identify areas where they might reduce spending, optimize their use of resources, and prevent financial shortfalls.

Another important cash flow strategy is to establish and maintain an emergency fund. This reserve of readily accessible funds acts as a financial buffer to cover unexpected expenses, such as medical emergencies or urgent home repairs, without disrupting the regular cash flow. Financial planners typically recommend setting aside at least three to six months' worth of living expenses in a liquid savings account. By having an emergency fund in place, seniors can manage unexpected costs without resorting to high-interest debt or depleting their retirement savings, thereby ensuring greater financial stability and peace of mind.

In addition, managing cash flow effectively involves regular monitoring and adjusting of financial plans in response to changing circumstances. As seniors' financial situations evolve due to shifts in income sources, health needs, or lifestyle changes, it is crucial to periodically review and update the budget and cash flow strategies. This might include adjusting spending plans, revising savings goals, or reallocating resources to better align with current needs. Financial planners should collaborate with clients to evaluate their cash flow regularly and make necessary adjustments to ensure that their financial plans remain robust and responsive to their evolving needs, thereby maintaining stability and supporting long-term financial well-being.

PLANNING FOR VARIABLE INCOME

Planning for variable income is a critical aspect of resource management planning for the elderly, as fluctuations in income can significantly impact financial stability and daily living. For retirees who rely on sources of income that may vary, such as investment returns, rental income, or part-time work, it is essential to develop a strategy that accommodates these uncertainties. Financial planners should help clients create a budget that reflects both their stable and variable income sources, ensuring that essential expenses are covered even during periods of lower income. This often involves setting up a system to manage income variability, such as using a conservative estimate for income levels and maintaining a buffer to cover any shortfalls.

To address the challenges of variable income, building an emergency fund becomes even more important. This reserve should be sufficient to cover several months of expenses during times when income may be reduced or irregular. An emergency fund helps seniors navigate periods of lower income without resorting to high-interest debt or disrupting their long-term financial plans. Financial planners should guide clients in establishing and maintaining an emergency fund that is appropriately sized for their specific income variability, ensuring they have a safety net to support their financial needs when income is less predictable.

In addition, planning for variable income requires a proactive approach to cash flow management and expense control. Seniors should regularly review their financial situation and adjust their spending as needed to align with changes in income. This might involve prioritizing essential expenses, reducing discretionary spending, or finding additional sources of income during periods of financial shortfall. Financial planners can assist clients in developing strategies to balance their budget, manage cash flow effectively, and make informed decisions that support their financial stability despite income fluctuations. By incorporating these practices into their financial planning, seniors can better handle income variability and maintain a secure and stable financial future.

These tools and techniques are crucial for effectively managing the income and cash flow of elderly clients, ensuring they can comfortably meet their financial needs throughout retirement.

TABLE 15.1 Income and Cash Flow Management for the Elderly

TOPIC	DESCRIPTION	KEY CONSIDERATIONS
Strategic budgeting	How elderly individuals can adjust their budgets to accommodate both fixed and variable expenses while maintaining financial stability.	- Balancing necessities and discretionary spending. - Adjusting to changes in health and mobility.
Managing income streams	The importance of balancing multiple income streams such as Social Security, pensions, and part-time work in managing overall cash flow for retirees.	- Synchronizing different income sources for steady cash flow. - Planning withdrawals to minimize tax impact.
Emergency fund utilization	Why an emergency fund is critical for the elderly and how it should be sized and managed.	- Sizing the fund to cover 3–6 months of expenses. - Quick accessibility and liquidity
Impact of variable income	Challenges and strategies associated with managing variable income sources like dividends or rental income in retirement.	- Estimating variable income conservatively. - Creating buffers to manage income fluctuation.
Cash flow timing techniques	Benefits and challenges of aligning income receipts with expense payments to prevent financial shortfalls.	- Timing income to cover periodic and lump sum expenses. - Using automated payments to manage timing issues.
Role of financial technology	How financial technology tools can aid elderly individuals in managing their income and cash flow.	- Benefits: Simplified tracking, automated budgeting. - Drawbacks: Requires technological proficiency, potential security risks.

DISCUSSION QUESTIONS

1. How can elderly individuals strategically adjust their budgets to accommodate both fixed and variable expenses while maintaining financial stability?
2. Discuss the importance of balancing multiple income streams, such as Social Security, pensions, and part-time work, in managing overall cash flow for retirees. What strategies can be employed to stabilize income effectively?
3. Why is an emergency fund particularly critical for the elderly, and how should it be sized and managed to ensure it covers unexpected expenses without compromising long-term financial stability?
4. What are the challenges and strategies associated with managing variable income sources, such as dividends or rental income, in retirement?
5. Explore the benefits and challenges of aligning income receipts with expense payments. How can this practice help prevent financial shortfalls for the elderly?
6. How can financial technology tools aid elderly individuals in managing their income and cash flow more effectively? Discuss the benefits and potential drawbacks of using tech-based financial tools in retirement planning.

CONTINUING CASE—THE HARMONS—HOUSING MORTGAGE AFFORDABILITY/ANALYSIS

Chapter 15 Case Assignment 15.1

Objective:

The purpose of this exercise is to determine how much Darin and Lisa can afford to spend on a home by comparing traditional financial guidelines with the affordability criteria used by lending institutions. This analysis will help them understand the difference between general affordability rules and the more detailed calculations used by lenders.

Instructions:

1. Calculate the Maximum Home Purchase Price Using the Traditional Financial Guideline:

- **Traditional Financial Guideline Calculation:**
  - Darin and Lisa have estimated that they can use $40,000 from their savings as a down payment for their home purchase.
  - According to the traditional financial guidelines, a person can afford to purchase a home that costs "two and a half times their annual salary plus their down payment."
  - Calculate the maximum home purchase price that Darin and Lisa can afford using this guideline.
  - **Formula:** Maximum Home Price = (2.5 × Combined Annual Salary) + Down Payment
  - Clearly show all steps in your calculation and provide the final amount that Darin and Lisa can spend on a home according to this guideline.

2. Calculate the Affordable Mortgage Amount Using Lending Institution Guidelines:

Mortgage Affordability Calculation:

- Use the following data to calculate the affordable mortgage amount for Darin and Lisa:
  - **Down Payment:** 10% of the home purchase price.

  - **Principal, Interest, Taxes, and Insurance (PITI):** 28% of their gross monthly income.
  - **Property Taxes and Insurance:** Estimated at $500.00 per month combined.
  - **Interest Rate:** 5% interest rate for a 30-year mortgage term.

- **Step 1:** Determine the maximum monthly payment that Darin and Lisa can afford based on 28% of their gross monthly income.
- **Step 2:** Subtract the estimated property taxes and insurance ($500.00 per month) from the maximum monthly payment to find the amount available for principal and interest.
- **Step 3:** Using the remaining amount for principal and interest, calculate the total affordable mortgage amount over a 30-year period at a 5% interest rate.
- Clearly show all steps in your calculation and provide the final affordable mortgage amount.

3. Compare the Affordable Mortgage Amount with the Traditional Financial Guideline:

- **Comparison Analysis:**
  - Compare the maximum home purchase price calculated using the traditional financial guideline (from Question 1) with the affordable mortgage amount calculated using the lending institution's guidelines (from Question 2).
  - Discuss the differences between these two amounts.
  - Consider whether the amount suggested by the traditional guideline or the lending institution is more conservative or more realistic for Darin and Lisa's financial situation.
  - Provide recommendations for Darin and Lisa based on the findings of your comparison.

16

Special Considerations for Blended Families and Multiple Generations

Special considerations for blended families and multiple generations are crucial in family financial planning, as these dynamics introduce unique challenges and opportunities that require thoughtful strategies. Blended families, where individuals with children from previous relationships come together, must navigate complexities such as inheritance planning, asset distribution, and financial responsibilities toward both biological and stepchildren. Addressing these considerations early on can help mitigate potential conflicts and ensure equitable treatment of all family members.

Moreover, multiple generations living under one roof or sharing financial resources present additional planning considerations. This may include supporting elderly parents' healthcare needs, funding college education for grandchildren, or balancing financial support across various stages of life. Each generation may have distinct financial goals and priorities, requiring a customized approach to wealth management and estate planning that considers the needs and aspirations of each family member while promoting unity and financial harmony.

Effective financial planning for blended families and multiple generations often involves open communication, transparency, and collaboration among family members and trusted advisors. Discussions should encompass shared values, goals, and concerns related to wealth transfer, retirement planning, and long-term care. By addressing special considerations proactively and integrating them into a comprehensive financial plan, families can navigate complex family dynamics with confidence, promote financial well-being across generations, and foster a legacy of unity and support (Van Cleve & Klontz, 2022).

FINANCIAL CHALLENGES AND DYNAMICS OF BLENDED FAMILIES

Blended families bring unique financial challenges and dynamics that necessitate careful consideration and planning in family monetary management. One of the primary challenges involves navigating inheritance and estate planning to ensure fair and equitable distribution of assets among biological and stepchildren. Differences in familial relationships and legal obligations may influence decisions on beneficiary designations, wills, and trusts. Addressing these complexities requires open communication among family members and consultation with legal and financial professionals to develop strategies that respect each family member's wishes while minimizing potential conflicts.

Financial responsibilities within blended families can also be complex, particularly when balancing support for biological children from previous relationships and shared financial obligations with new spouses or stepchildren. Managing budgets, expenses, and saving priorities may require negotiation and compromise to align financial goals across different household dynamics. Clear agreements on financial responsibilities, such as contributions to household expenses, educational costs, and healthcare needs, can help foster transparency and cooperation among family members.

Moreover, blended families may face emotional and psychological factors that impact financial decision-making. Building trust and fostering positive relationships among all family members is essential for successful financial planning. This may involve addressing concerns about financial security, inheritance expectations, and children's educational and future needs. Establishing mutual respect and understanding can help create a supportive environment where financial challenges are navigated collaboratively, enhancing the overall well-being and stability of the blended family unit. By addressing these financial challenges proactively and fostering open communication, blended families can develop effective strategies that promote financial harmony and long-term success.

STRATEGIES FOR MANAGING FINANCIAL RESOURCES ACROSS GENERATIONS

Strategically managing financial resources across generations is essential in family financial planning to ensure each family member's needs are met while fostering long-term financial stability and harmony. One effective strategy is to establish clear financial goals and priorities through open dialogue among family members of different generations. This includes discussing short-term needs such as education expenses for younger generations, retirement planning for middle-aged adults, and healthcare and long-term care considerations for elderly parents or grandparents. By understanding each generation's financial aspirations and responsibilities, families can develop a comprehensive plan that allocates resources efficiently and equitably.

Another critical aspect of managing financial resources across generations is to promote financial education and literacy. Educating younger family members about budgeting, saving, and investing empowers them to make informed financial decisions and prepares them for future responsibilities. Likewise, providing financial guidance to older generations on retirement income strategies, health-care planning, and estate planning ensures that resources are managed effectively to support their needs throughout retirement and beyond. By fostering a culture of financial education within the family, each generation can build upon the financial knowledge and practices established by their predecessors, promoting financial resilience and continuity across generations.

Furthermore, integrating technology and financial tools can streamline monetary management across generations. Utilizing digital platforms for budgeting, investment tracking, and estate planning can facilitate collaboration and transparency among family members spread across various locations. These tools enable real-time access to financial information and allow families to coordinate financial decisions and monitor progress toward shared goals effectively. By leveraging technology alongside personalized financial advice from professionals, families can optimize their financial resources and navigate life's milestones with confidence, ensuring a secure and prosperous future for all generations involved.

INHERITANCE PLANNING AND ASSET DISTRIBUTION IN BLENDED FAMILY SITUATIONS

Inheritance planning and asset distribution in blended family situations require careful consideration and initiative-taking strategies to navigate complex familial dynamics and ensure fair treatment of all beneficiaries. One of the primary challenges involves addressing potential conflicts between biological children, stepchildren, and spouses from previous marriages. Clear communication and transparency are essential to establish mutual understanding and respect among all family members regarding inheritance intentions and the distribution of assets.

A crucial step in inheritance planning for blended families is to update legal documents such as wills, trusts, and beneficiary designations to reflect current relationships and intentions accurately. This includes specifying how assets should be divided among biological children, stepchildren, and any new children born into the blended family. Consulting with estate planning attorneys who specialize in blended family dynamics can provide valuable insights and strategies for structuring these documents in ways that minimize disputes and ensure that each beneficiary's interests are protected.

Moreover, considering the use of trusts can offer additional benefits in managing asset distribution in blended families. Trusts can provide flexibility in specifying how and when assets are distributed to beneficiaries, ensuring that financial support is provided according to individual needs and circumstances. For example, discretionary trusts can be used to allocate funds for educational expenses or healthcare needs of younger beneficiaries while protecting assets from potential creditors or divorce settlements. By tailoring trust structures to address specific family dynamics and financial goals, blended families can enhance financial security, promote harmony among beneficiaries, and preserve their legacy across generations effectively (Farmer, 2023).

COMMUNICATION AND ADDRESSING FINANCIAL CONCERNS

Effective communication is crucial in family financial planning to address financial concerns, align goals, and foster transparency among family members. Open dialogue enables families to discuss financial priorities, responsibilities, and challenges openly, promoting a shared understanding of each member's financial situation and aspirations. Regular family meetings dedicated to financial planning provide opportunities to review budgets, savings goals, investment strategies, and estate planning considerations. These discussions empower family members to voice their concerns, ask questions, and collaborate on decisions that impact their collective financial future.

Addressing financial concerns involves initiative-taking, planning, and contingency strategies to mitigate risks and uncertainties. Families should identify potential financial challenges, such as unexpected expenses, job loss, or changes in economic conditions, and develop strategies to manage these situations effectively. Establishing emergency funds and insurance coverage, such as health insurance and life insurance policies, can provide financial security and peace of mind during unexpected life events. By addressing potential risks and implementing precautionary measures, families can minimize financial stress and maintain stability in their long-term financial planning.

Furthermore, seeking professional guidance from financial advisors or planners can provide expertise and objective insights to navigate complex financial decisions and challenges. Advisors can offer personalized recommendations tailored to the family's unique circumstances, helping to optimize investment strategies, tax planning, and retirement savings goals. They can also facilitate discussions on sensitive topics such as inheritance planning and wealth transfer, ensuring that decisions are made thoughtfully and in accordance with legal and ethical considerations. By leveraging professional expertise and fostering open communication, families can strengthen their financial resilience, achieve their financial goals, and build a solid foundation for future generations (Van Cleve & Klontz, 2022).

DISCUSSION QUESTIONS

1. How can blended families navigate the complexities of inheritance planning and asset distribution to ensure equitable treatment among biological children and stepchildren while maintaining family harmony?
2. What strategies can families with multiple generations under one roof implement to balance financial support between the needs of elderly parents and the aspirations of younger generations, such as education and home ownership?
3. What are the effective communication techniques that blended families can use to address sensitive financial topics, such as estate planning and living arrangements, to ensure clarity and prevent conflicts?
4. How should blended families approach legal and financial planning differently compared to traditional families to protect the interests of all family members, especially when dealing with wills, trusts, and legal guardianship?
5. In blended families with multiple generations, what unique challenges arise in retirement planning, and how can these be addressed to ensure sufficient resources and quality of life for the elderly family members?
6. How can blended and multigenerational families utilize financial technology tools to improve budgeting, investment decisions, and overall financial management across different age groups and financial literacy levels?

CONTINUING CASE—THE HARMONS—PLANNING FOR BLENDED FAMILIES AND MULTIPLE GENERATIONS

Chapter 16 Case Assignment 16.1

Objective:

The purpose of this exercise is to evaluate and address the unique financial challenges and dynamics that arise in planning for retirement in blended families and multigenerational households. This will involve developing strategies for managing financial resources across generations, inheritance planning and asset distribution in blended family situations, and ensuring open communication to address financial concerns.

Instructions:

1. Understanding the Financial Challenges and Dynamics of Blended Families:

- **Blended Family Dynamics:**
  - Begin by analyzing the dynamics of blended families, particularly how they might apply to Darin and Lisa's situation. Consider aspects such as multiple marriages, stepchildren, and different financial obligations across the family.
  - Identify potential financial challenges that blended families face, such as differing expectations for financial support, complexities in asset distribution, and conflicts over inheritance.
- **Multigenerational Considerations:**
  - Consider the impact of multigenerational living arrangements, such as providing support to aging parents, helping adult children, or caring for grandchildren.
  - Discuss how these dynamics might affect Darin and Lisa's financial planning, including the potential strain on retirement resources and the need for long-term care planning.

2. Strategies for Managing Financial Resources Across Generations:

- **Financial Resource Management:**
  - Develop strategies for managing financial resources across different generations within the family. Consider how to balance the financial needs of parents, children, and grandchildren while ensuring that Darin and Lisa's retirement goals are met.

  - Provide recommendations on how to prioritize financial support, whether it be through direct financial assistance, helping with education costs, or providing care.

- **Balancing Obligations:**
  - Explore ways to balance the financial obligations between current retirement needs and future family support. Consider creating a budget or financial plan that allocates resources to various family members while maintaining financial security for Darin and Lisa.
  - Discuss the potential use of financial tools such as trusts, savings plans, or insurance products to manage these obligations.

3. Inheritance Planning and Asset Distribution in Blended Family Situations:

- **Inheritance Planning:**
  - Analyze the complexities of inheritance planning in blended families, particularly how to ensure fair and equitable distribution of assets among biological children, stepchildren, and other family members.
  - Consider the potential for disputes and conflicts over inheritance and discuss strategies to prevent or mitigate these issues.

- **Use of Trusts and Wills:**
  - Provide recommendations on the use of wills and trusts to manage inheritance and asset distribution effectively. Discuss the benefits of using a living trust, a testamentary trust, or other estate planning tools to protect the interests of all family members.
  - Explore the option of creating specific bequests for different family members, ensuring that the wishes of Darin and Lisa are clearly documented and legally binding.

- **Equal versus Equitable Distribution:**
  - Discuss the difference between equal and equitable distribution of assets in a blended family context. Provide strategies for deciding how to distribute assets in a way that feels fair to all parties, considering the unique dynamics of the family.

4. Communication and Addressing Financial Concerns:

- **Open Communication:**
  - Emphasize the importance of open communication in addressing financial concerns within a blended family. Discuss how Darin and Lisa can facilitate conversations about financial planning, inheritance, and support with all relevant family members.

- Provide recommendations for family meetings, financial planning sessions, or involving a neutral third party, such as a financial planner or mediator, to help manage these discussions.

- **Addressing Conflicts:**
  - Explore strategies for addressing and resolving conflicts that may arise from financial decisions, such as differing expectations or misunderstandings about asset distribution.
  - Discuss the importance of transparency in financial planning and how to document decisions to avoid disputes.
- **Long-Term Planning:**
  - Encourage Darin and Lisa to consider long-term planning for potential changes in family dynamics, such as remarriages, divorces, or the birth of new grandchildren.
  - Discuss how to keep their financial plan flexible to accommodate changes in the family structure over time.

5. Write a Comprehensive Blended Family Retirement Planning Report:

- **Report Content:**
  - Prepare a comprehensive report (five to seven pages) that includes:
    - An analysis of the financial challenges and dynamics specific to blended families and multigenerational households.
    - Strategies for managing financial resources across generations while protecting Darin and Lisa's retirement goals.
    - Recommendations for inheritance planning and asset distribution that consider the complexities of a blended family.
    - Communication strategies to ensure that financial concerns are addressed openly and effectively.
    - A long-term plan to accommodate future changes in the family structure.
- **Action Plan:**
  - Include a timeline for implementing the recommended strategies, prioritizing steps that should be taken immediately versus those that can be addressed over time.
  - Suggest regular reviews of their financial plan to adjust for changes in family circumstances, financial goals, or personal preferences.

17

Planning for Disability and Incapacity

Planning for disability and incapacity is a critical aspect of family financial planning, ensuring that individuals and their loved ones are prepared for unforeseen circumstances that may impact their ability to manage financial affairs. Disability can arise from accidents, illnesses, or cognitive decline, making it essential to establish initiative-taking measures to protect assets and ensure ongoing financial stability. Effective planning involves creating legal documents such as powers of attorney, advance directives, and healthcare proxies that designate trusted individuals to make financial and medical decisions on behalf of incapacitated family members.

Moreover, planning for disability includes assessing insurance coverage options to mitigate financial risks associated with loss of income or increased medical expenses. Disability insurance provides income replacement if an individual becomes unable to work due to disability, offering financial support to cover living expenses and maintain quality of life. Long-term care insurance is also important, covering costs associated with nursing home care, assisted living facilities, or home healthcare services in case of prolonged disability or chronic illness. Evaluating insurance policies and ensuring adequate coverage can safeguard against potential financial hardships resulting from disability.

In addition, addressing estate planning considerations is essential in planning for disability and incapacity. Establishing wills, trusts, and beneficiary designations ensures that assets are managed and distributed according to individual wishes in the event of incapacity or death. Trusts can provide structured management of assets for beneficiaries with special needs or those unable to manage finances independently due to disability. Consulting with estate planning attorneys and financial advisors can provide valuable guidance in developing comprehensive plans that protect assets, preserve wealth, and support family members during times of incapacity. By proactively addressing these aspects of financial planning, families can enhance their preparedness for disability-related challenges and ensure continuity of monetary management and support for loved ones.

PLANNING FOR DISABILITY AND INCAPACITY IN FINANCIAL PLANNING

Planning for disability and incapacity is a crucial component of comprehensive family financial planning, ensuring that individuals are prepared for unforeseen circumstances that could affect their ability to manage finances and make decisions. Disability can arise suddenly from accidents or illnesses, or gradually due to aging or cognitive decline, highlighting the need for initiative-taking measures to protect monetary interests and ensure ongoing financial stability. Effective planning involves creating legal documents such as powers of attorney, advance directives, and healthcare proxies that designate trusted individuals to make financial and healthcare decisions on behalf of incapacitated family members.

In financial planning, addressing disability and incapacity also entails evaluating insurance options to mitigate potential financial risks. Disability insurance provides income replacement if an individual becomes unable to work due to a disability, helping to cover daily expenses and maintain financial independence. Long-term care insurance is essential for covering costs associated with extended medical care needs, such as nursing home care or in-home assistance, ensuring that financial resources are protected from being depleted by healthcare expenses during periods of incapacity.

Furthermore, estate planning considerations are integral to planning for disability within financial planning frameworks. Establishing wills, trusts, and beneficiary designations ensures that assets are managed and distributed according to specific wishes, even in the event of incapacity or death. Trusts can be particularly valuable for individuals with disabilities or special needs, providing structured management of assets and financial support over the long term. Consulting with legal and financial professionals can provide guidance in developing comprehensive plans that protect assets, minimize tax implications, and ensure continuity of monetary management in the face of disability or incapacity. By integrating these strategies into family financial planning, individuals can enhance their preparedness and resilience against the financial impacts of disability, promoting peace of mind for themselves and their loved ones (Bebel, 2023).

DURABLE POWERS OF ATTORNEY, HEALTHCARE PROXIES, AND LIVING WILLS

Durable powers of attorney (DPOA), healthcare proxies, and living wills are essential legal instruments in family financial planning, providing critical guidance and decision-making authority in the event of incapacity or inability to manage affairs due to illness or injury. A DPOA designates an individual (known as an attorney-in-fact or agent) to make financial decisions and manage assets on behalf of the incapacitated person. This legal document remains effective even if the person granting the power becomes mentally incompetent, ensuring continuity in monetary management and protection of assets. It is crucial to choose a trustworthy agent who understands the individual's wishes and can act in their best interests.

Similarly, a healthcare proxy, also known as a healthcare power of attorney, designates an agent to make medical decisions on behalf of an incapacitated person when they are unable to communicate their wishes. This document ensures that healthcare decisions align with the individual's preferences for medical treatment, end-of-life care, and other healthcare interventions. Selecting a healthcare proxy involves thoughtful consideration of the individual's values, beliefs, and treatment preferences, ensuring that the designated agent can advocate effectively for their medical care.

In addition to powers of attorney and healthcare proxies, a living will (or advance directive) complements these documents by providing specific instructions about medical treatment preferences and end-of-life decisions. A living will outlines preferences regarding life-sustaining treatments, resuscitation efforts, and organ donation, offering guidance to healthcare providers and family members during critical medical situations. This document helps ensure that the individual's wishes regarding medical care are respected and followed, reducing uncertainty and potential conflicts among family members during stressful times. Together, DPOAs, healthcare proxies, and living wills form a comprehensive framework for managing financial and medical decisions, providing peace of mind, and ensuring that individuals' preferences are honored in times of incapacity or medical crisis. Integrating these legal tools into family financial planning promotes preparedness and continuity of care, safeguarding both monetary interests and personal well-being across generations.

GUARDIANSHIP AND CONSERVATORSHIP CONSIDERATIONS

Guardianship and conservatorship considerations are significant in family financial planning, particularly when addressing the care and management of assets for individuals who are unable to make decisions independently due to incapacity or disability. Guardianship refers to the legal authority granted by a court to a guardian to make personal and medical decisions on behalf of an incapacitated person, known as a ward. This includes decisions related to healthcare, living arrangements, and other personal matters. Guardians are typically appointed when individuals lack the mental capacity to make informed decisions and do not have valid powers of attorney or healthcare proxies in place.

Conversely, conservatorship pertains to the legal authority granted to a conservator to manage the financial affairs and assets of an incapacitated person. A conservator is responsible for handling financial transactions, paying bills, managing investments, and ensuring that the individual's monetary interests are protected and preserved. Like guardianship, conservatorship is established through court proceedings and is intended to safeguard the financial well-being of individuals who are unable to manage their own finances due to incapacity or disability.

Navigating guardianship and conservatorship considerations in family financial planning requires careful assessment of individual needs, legal requirements, and potential alternatives. It is essential for families to proactively plan for these scenarios by establishing DPOAs, healthcare proxies, and living wills to designate trusted individuals to make decisions on their behalf in the event of incapacity. Consulting with legal professionals specializing in elder law or estate planning can provide guidance on the appropriate steps to take and help families navigate the complexities of guardianship and conservatorship proceedings effectively. By addressing these considerations early and developing comprehensive plans, families can ensure that their loved ones' personal and monetary interests are protected and managed in accordance with their wishes during periods of incapacity or disability (Klebnikov, 2023).

DISCUSSION QUESTIONS

1. How should an individual decide between setting up a DPOA, a healthcare proxy, or both? What are the key considerations that should guide these decisions?
2. What types of insurance policies are most crucial for protecting against the financial impacts of disability and incapacity, and how should individuals evaluate their coverage options?
3. How can legal documents such as advance directives or living wills be used effectively in planning for medical decisions during periods of incapacity? What specific medical decisions should be addressed in these documents?
4. What approaches can families take to ensure effective communication about plans and wishes for disability and incapacity among family members?
5. How can families prepare for the potential financial impact of a member's long-term disability or incapacity? What financial planning steps are most critical?
6. Under what circumstances might seeking guardianship or conservatorship become necessary, and what are the processes and challenges associated with these legal structures?

CONTINUING CASE—THE HARMONS—EVALUATING PLANNING FOR DISABILITY AND INCAPACITY

Chapter 17 Case Assignment 17.1

Objective:

The goal of this exercise is to evaluate and develop a comprehensive plan for managing the financial and healthcare needs of Darin and Lisa Harmon in the event of disability or incapacity. This plan will involve the use of DPOAs, healthcare proxies, living wills, and considerations for guardianship and conservatorship. By completing this exercise, Darin and Lisa will ensure that their wishes are respected, and their financial and personal affairs are managed according to their preferences if they become unable to make decisions for themselves.

Instructions:

1. Understanding Durable Powers of Attorney:

- **Definition and Purpose:**
  - Begin by researching the purpose and function of a DPOA. Explain how a DPOA allows someone to act on Darin and Lisa's behalf for financial and legal matters if they become incapacitated.
- **Key Considerations:**
  - Discuss the key considerations when choosing an agent (the person who will hold the DPOA) for both Darin and Lisa. Consider factors such as trustworthiness, financial acumen, and the ability to make decisions in line with their wishes.
  - Explore the types of powers that can be granted under a DPOA, including broad versus limited authority. Explain the implications of granting extensive powers to an agent.
- **Implementation:**
  - Provide recommendations for setting up a DPOA, including the legal steps required to ensure it is valid and enforceable.
  - Discuss the importance of updating the DPOA as life circumstances change, such as if the chosen agent is no longer able or willing to serve.

2. Healthcare Proxies and Living Wills:

- **Healthcare Proxy:**
  - Define what a healthcare proxy is and how it differs from a DPOA. Explain how a healthcare proxy allows someone to make medical decisions on behalf of Darin and Lisa if they are unable to do so.
  - Discuss the importance of selecting a healthcare agent who understands Darin and Lisa's values, beliefs, and preferences regarding medical treatment.
- **Living Will:**
  - Define a living will and its role in outlining Darin and Lisa's wishes regarding end-of-life care and medical treatments they do or do not want to receive.
  - Explain how a living will works in conjunction with a healthcare proxy to ensure that medical decisions are made in accordance with their wishes.
- **Implementation:**
  - Provide recommendations for drafting and legally executing a healthcare proxy and living will. Ensure these documents clearly articulate Darin and Lisa's medical preferences.
  - Discuss the importance of discussing these documents with family members and the selected healthcare agent to avoid misunderstandings or conflicts.

3. Guardianship and Conservatorship Considerations:

- **Definition and Differences:**
  - Explain the concepts of guardianship and conservatorship, focusing on how these legal arrangements provide for the management of personal and financial affairs when an individual is no longer capable of doing so.
  - Discuss the differences between guardianship (related to personal and healthcare decisions) and conservatorship (related to financial and property management).
- **Planning for Guardianship and Conservatorship:**
  - Explore the circumstances under which Darin and Lisa might need a guardian or conservator. Discuss how these arrangements can be avoided or minimized through proactive planning, such as setting up a DPOA and healthcare proxy.

  - Provide recommendations on how to choose a guardian or conservator, if necessary, and the legal process involved in appointing one.

- **Impact on Family Dynamics:**
  - Discuss the potential impact of guardianship and conservatorship on family dynamics. Consider how to prevent conflicts or disputes among family members by clearly outlining their wishes and involving all relevant parties in the planning process.

4. Write a Comprehensive Disability and Incapacity Planning Report:

- **Report Content:**
  - Prepare a comprehensive report (five to seven pages) that includes:
    - An explanation of the role and importance of DPOAs, healthcare proxies, and living wills in the Harmons' financial and medical planning.
    - Recommendations for implementing these documents, including selecting agents and ensuring their legal validity.
    - An analysis of the considerations for guardianship and conservatorship, including the steps to take if these arrangements become necessary.
    - A discussion of the impact of these planning tools on family dynamics and how to communicate plans effectively with family members.

- **Action Plan:**
  - Include a timeline for implementing the recommended planning strategies, prioritizing steps that should be taken immediately versus those that can be addressed over time.
  - Suggest regular reviews of these documents to ensure they remain current and reflective of Darin and Lisa's wishes.

18

Philanthropic Giving and Charitable Planning

Philanthropic giving and charitable planning play integral roles in family financial planning, allowing individuals and families to make a meaningful impact on causes they care about while optimizing their financial strategies. Philanthropy involves donating time, resources, or expertise to charitable organizations or initiatives that aim to improve communities and address societal challenges. For many families, philanthropic giving is a way not only to give back but also to instill values of generosity and social responsibility across generations. Effective charitable planning integrates philanthropic goals with broader financial planning objectives, ensuring that donations are made in a strategic and tax-efficient manner.

One key aspect of charitable planning is identifying charitable goals and determining the most effective ways to support them. This includes researching and selecting charitable organizations or causes aligned with the family's values and interests. Whether supporting education, healthcare, environmental conservation, or other charitable missions, families can establish an unobstructed vision for their philanthropic endeavors and prioritize initiatives that resonate with their collective values.

Moreover, charitable planning involves exploring different giving vehicles and strategies to maximize the impact of donations while optimizing tax benefits. Strategies may include establishing donor-advised funds (DAFs), charitable remainder trusts, or private foundations, each offering unique advantages in terms of flexibility, control over charitable distributions, and potential tax deductions. By collaborating with financial advisors and philanthropic experts, families can tailor charitable planning strategies to align with their financial goals, minimize tax liabilities, and create lasting legacies that reflect their commitment to making a positive difference in the world. Integrating philanthropic giving into family financial planning not only enhances financial stewardship but also strengthens familial bonds through shared values and a shared sense of purpose in contributing to the greater good.

ROLE OF PHILANTHROPIC GIVING IN FINANCIAL PLANNING

Philanthropic giving plays a significant role in family financial planning by providing avenues to align personal values with financial goals while creating a positive impact on society. For families, incorporating philanthropy into financial planning goes beyond mere charitable donations—it serves as a vehicle for expressing shared values, instilling a sense of social responsibility in future generations, and leaving a legacy. By identifying causes and organizations that resonate with their values, families can foster a deeper connection to their communities and contribute meaningfully to causes that matter most to them.

Strategically integrating philanthropic giving into financial planning also offers tax advantages and potential financial benefits. Charitable contributions can provide deductions that reduce taxable income, especially when coordinated with other financial strategies such as estate planning or retirement planning. For example, establishing a DAF allows families to make contributions to the fund and receive an immediate tax deduction, while retaining the flexibility to distribute charitable donations over time to support various charitable initiatives. Such strategies not only maximize the impact of charitable giving but also optimize financial outcomes for the family.

Furthermore, philanthropic giving can serve as a unifying force within families, promoting open communication, collaboration, and shared decision-making. Engaging family members in discussions about philanthropy encourages reflection on values, priorities, and the impact they wish to achieve collectively. By involving younger generations in philanthropic activities and decision-making processes, families can pass down important values of empathy, generosity, and community engagement. This collaborative approach not only strengthens familial bonds but also empowers future generations to become thoughtful stewards of family wealth and philanthropic legacies. Thus, integrating philanthropic giving into financial planning enriches both the family's financial strategy and their collective sense of purpose in making a meaningful difference in the world.

CHARITABLE PLANNING STRATEGIES AND TAX IMPLICATIONS

Charitable planning strategies encompass a range of methods designed to maximize the impact of donations while optimizing tax benefits for families engaged in philanthropy. One effective strategy is the use of DAFs, which allow donors to make contributions to a fund managed by a sponsoring organization, such as a community foundation or financial institution. By donating assets, such as cash, stocks, or real estate, to a DAF, families receive an immediate tax deduction in the year of the contribution. They can then recommend grants from the fund to qualified charitable organizations over time, providing flexibility in timing charitable gifts while potentially reducing tax liabilities.

Another charitable planning strategy involves the establishment of charitable remainder trusts (CRTs) or charitable lead trusts (CLTs), which offer unique benefits in terms of income tax and estate tax planning. A CRT allows donors to transfer assets into a trust that pays income to beneficiaries (typically the donor or their designated beneficiaries) for a specified period. At the end of the trust term, the remaining assets are distributed to designated charitable organizations. This strategy can provide immediate tax benefits through a charitable deduction and potentially reduce estate taxes upon transfer of assets to the trust. Conversely, a CLT pays income to charitable organizations for a specified period, after which the remaining assets pass to noncharitable beneficiaries, such as family members. This strategy can effectively reduce gift and estate taxes while supporting charitable causes.

Moreover, understanding the tax implications of charitable giving is crucial in charitable planning. Charitable contributions to qualified organizations can be deducted from taxable income, subject to certain limitations based on income levels and the type of charitable organization. By coordinating charitable donations with other tax planning strategies, such as maximizing deductions through bundling contributions in high-income years or donating appreciated assets to avoid capital gains taxes, families can optimize tax savings while supporting charitable missions they care about. Consulting with financial advisors or tax professionals specializing in charitable planning can provide insights into effective strategies tailored to individual financial goals and philanthropic objectives, ensuring that charitable giving is integrated seamlessly into overall family financial planning and contributes to both financial and societal impact.

FAMILY PHILANTHROPY AND THE IMPACT OF CHARITABLE GIVING

Family philanthropy holds significant potential to foster unity, purpose, and a legacy within the context of family financial planning. Beyond financial benefits, charitable giving can profoundly impact family dynamics by strengthening bonds across generations and reinforcing shared values. Engaging in philanthropic activities allows families to collectively support causes they are enthusiastic about, whether it is promoting education, healthcare, environmental conservation, or social justice initiatives. By involving family members in the decision-making process and encouraging active participation in philanthropic endeavors, families can cultivate a sense of empowerment and solidarity, fostering a deeper connection to their community and the world at large.

Moreover, family philanthropy serves as a platform for teaching valuable lessons in stewardship, empathy, and responsible wealth management to younger generations. By involving children and grandchildren in discussions about philanthropy and exposing them to charitable activities from an early age, families can instill a sense of social responsibility and inspire future leaders committed to making a positive impact on society. This educational aspect of philanthropy not only prepares younger generations to oversee wealth responsibly but also nurtures their understanding of the importance of giving back to causes that align with their values and beliefs.

Furthermore, the impact of family philanthropy extends beyond financial contributions, influencing societal change and leaving a legacy that reflects the family's values and ideals. By strategically aligning charitable giving with long-term goals and priorities, families can amplify their impact on issues they care deeply about, driving meaningful progress and effecting positive change in communities. Whether through direct donations, volunteerism, or advocacy efforts, family philanthropy embodies a commitment to leaving a meaningful mark on the world while ensuring that future generations continue to uphold the family's philanthropic traditions and values. By integrating family philanthropy into financial planning, families can create a legacy of generosity, compassion, and purpose that extends far beyond their own lifetimes.

DISCUSSION QUESTIONS

1. How can families identify and articulate their philanthropic goals to ensure alignment with their values and interests? What processes or discussions are most effective in establishing these goals?

2. What are the key strategies families can use to maximize both the impact of their charitable contributions and the associated tax benefits? How do different charitable vehicles like DAFs and CRTs fit into these strategies?

3. How can philanthropic activities be used to strengthen familial bonds and instill values of generosity and social responsibility in younger generations?

4. What criteria should families consider when selecting charitable organizations to support? How can they effectively assess the impact and governance of these organizations?

5. How can charitable planning be integrated into broader estate planning to create a legacy that reflects the family's philanthropic vision?

6. What are some common challenges families face in their philanthropic endeavors, and what strategies can be employed to overcome these obstacles?

CONTINUING CASE—THE HARMONS—PHILANTHROPIC GIVING AND CHARITABLE PLANNING FOR THE HARMONS IN FINANCIAL PLANNING ANALYSIS

Chapter 18 Case Assignment 18.1

Objective:

This exercise aims to analyze and develop a comprehensive financial planning strategy for Darin and Lisa Harmon, focusing on integrating philanthropic giving and charitable planning into their financial goals. The exercise will require a deep understanding of the Harmon family's financial background, goals, and values, with a particular emphasis on how they can achieve their philanthropic objectives while securing their financial future.

Background:

Darin (55) and Lisa Harmon (53) have three adult children and have established a stable financial foundation through Darin's academic career as a tenured professor and Lisa's daycare business. They have various financial goals, including saving for retirement, paying off their home, funding their daughter Maranda's education, purchasing a vacation home, and expanding Lisa's business. The Harmons are also interested in ensuring their charitable intentions are incorporated into their financial and estate planning.

Exercise Tasks:

1. Client Profile Analysis:

- Create a detailed profile of Darin and Lisa Harmon, including their current financial situation, assets, liabilities, and financial goals.
- Analyze the potential impact of their financial decisions on their retirement plans, including the funding of Maranda's education and the purchase of a vacation home.

2. Philanthropic Goals:

- Discuss the philanthropic intentions of the Harmons, including any specific causes they wish to support.

- Consider how their values and goals can be reflected in their philanthropic efforts, both during their lifetime and through their estate.

3. Charitable Planning Strategies:

- Research and propose at least three charitable planning strategies that could be appropriate for the Harmons. These may include:
  - DAFs
  - CRTs
  - CLTs
  - Private foundations
  - Direct gifts of appreciated assets
- Evaluate the benefits and drawbacks of each strategy, particularly in terms of tax implications, flexibility, and alignment with the Harmons' financial and personal goals.

4. Integration with Financial Planning:

- Develop a comprehensive financial plan for the Harmons that incorporates their philanthropic goals alongside their other financial objectives.
- Include a cash flow analysis, considering their income, expenses, and anticipated financial needs, including retirement savings, education funding, and the potential purchase of a vacation home.
- Analyze the impact of their charitable contributions on their tax situation and overall financial plan.

5. Estate Planning Considerations:

- Address how the Harmons can incorporate their philanthropic goals into their estate planning, including the designation of beneficiaries and the creation of trusts.
- Consider the implications of leaving a charitable legacy and how it aligns with their desire to provide for their children and grandchildren.

6. Legal and Ethical Considerations:

- Discuss any legal considerations related to charitable giving and estate planning, including compliance with tax laws and the creation of legally binding documents.
- Consider the ethical responsibilities involved in advising clients on large charitable gifts, particularly in ensuring that their financial security is not compromised.

7. Recommendations and Conclusion:

- Provide a set of recommendations for the Harmons, summarizing how they can achieve their philanthropic goals while also meeting their retirement, education funding, and other financial objectives.
- Conclude with a reflection on the importance of integrating charitable planning into a comprehensive financial plan, particularly for clients like the Harmons who have multiple financial goals and obligations.

19

Monitoring and Adjusting the Financial Plan

Monitoring and adjusting the financial plan are essential practices in resource management planning for the elderly, as they ensure that a retirement strategy remains effective and responsive to changing circumstances. As individuals age, their financial situation, health status, and lifestyle needs can evolve, making it crucial to regularly review and update their financial plans. Continuous monitoring allows retirees to track their income and expenses, evaluate the performance of investments, and assess whether their current financial strategy aligns with their goals and needs. By maintaining an up-to-date financial plan, seniors can make informed decisions and adapt to changes proactively, ensuring ongoing financial stability and peace of mind.

Adjusting the financial plan involves making necessary modifications based on the insights gained from monitoring activities. This might include reallocating investments to better match risk tolerance and financial goals, adjusting budgets to accommodate changes in income or expenses, or revising retirement withdrawals to address shifting financial needs. Financial planners play a key role in guiding clients through these adjustments, helping them navigate life changes such as unexpected medical expenses, fluctuations in income, or shifts in housing needs. By regularly revisiting and refining their financial plan, seniors can better manage their resources and maintain financial security throughout retirement (CFP Board, 2019b).

REGULAR REVIEWS OF FINANCIAL GOALS

Regular reviews of financial goals are a fundamental aspect of resource management planning for the elderly, ensuring that retirement strategies remain aligned with evolving personal and financial circumstances. As individuals age, their financial needs, health conditions, and lifestyle preferences can change, making it essential to periodically reassess and update their financial goals. These reviews help retirees evaluate whether their current financial strategies are effectively supporting their objectives, such as maintaining their desired standard of living, covering healthcare costs, or leaving a legacy for their family. By regularly reviewing their goals, seniors can identify any discrepancies between their expectations and their actual financial situation, allowing them to make timely adjustments to their plans.

During these reviews, financial planners should assist clients in assessing various aspects of their financial situation, including income sources, investment performance, and expense patterns. This process involves analyzing current financial data, comparing it to previously set goals, and determining whether adjustments are necessary to stay on track. For example, if unexpected medical expenses arise or there is a significant change in income, seniors may need to revise their savings strategies, adjust their budget, or reallocate their investments. Regular reviews provide an opportunity to make these adjustments and ensure that financial plans continue to support the client's evolving needs and priorities.

Furthermore, regular goal reviews help retirees anticipate and prepare for future financial challenges. As they approach different stages of retirement, such as transitioning from active income to relying solely on savings, their financial priorities and risks may shift. By proactively reviewing and adjusting their financial goals, seniors can better prepare for potential changes in their circumstances, such as increased healthcare needs or adjustments in living arrangements. Financial planners play a crucial role in guiding clients through these reviews, helping them stay adaptable and responsive to their changing needs. This ongoing evaluation process is essential for maintaining financial stability and achieving long-term retirement objectives (CFP Board, 2019b).

ADAPTING TO LIFE CHANGES

Adapting to life changes is a vital component of resource management planning for the elderly, as these changes can significantly impact financial stability and overall well-being. As seniors age, they may face various life transitions such as health issues, changes in living arrangements, or shifts in family dynamics. Each of these transitions can affect their financial situation and require adjustments to their resource management strategies. For instance, a sudden health issue may lead to increased medical expenses, whereas moving to an assisted living facility might alter monthly living costs. By proactively planning for these potential changes, retirees can ensure that their financial strategies remain effective and responsive to their evolving needs.

Financial planners play a crucial role in helping seniors adapt to life changes by providing guidance on how to adjust their financial plans accordingly. This includes revising budgets to accommodate new expenses, such as additional healthcare costs or changes in housing, and updating investment strategies to align with altered risk tolerances or income requirements. For example, if a senior experiences a decline in health, their financial plan might need to incorporate long-term care insurance or adjustments to retirement account withdrawals. Regularly reviewing and adjusting the financial plan allows seniors to manage these transitions smoothly and maintain financial stability despite unforeseen circumstances.

Moreover, adapting to life changes involves not only financial adjustments but also emotional and practical support. Seniors may need assistance in navigating new care options, understanding changes in benefits, or managing the emotional impact of significant life transitions. Financial planners should collaborate closely with clients to provide comprehensive support, including connecting them with resources such as support groups, legal advisors, or healthcare professionals. By addressing both financial and nonfinancial aspects of life changes, retirees can better cope with transitions and ensure that their resource management plan supports their overall quality of life (CFP Board, 2019b).

REBALANCING INVESTMENT PORTFOLIOS

Rebalancing investment portfolios is a crucial aspect of resource management planning for the elderly, ensuring that investment strategies remain aligned with changing financial needs and risk tolerances. As individuals age, their investment objectives typically shift from growth to preservation of capital and income generation. This shift necessitates a reevaluation of the asset allocation within their portfolio to balance risk and return appropriately. Rebalancing involves adjusting the portfolio to maintain the desired allocation between various asset classes, such as stocks, bonds, and cash, in response to changes in market conditions or personal financial circumstances. By periodically rebalancing, seniors can mitigate risk and ensure that their investments continue to support their retirement goals effectively.

One primary reason for rebalancing is to address the changes in risk tolerance that often occur with aging. As seniors approach or enter retirement, their ability to withstand market volatility decreases, making it important to reduce exposure to high-risk assets and increase holdings in more stable, income-producing investments. For instance, shifting from a higher proportion of equities to bonds or fixed-income securities can help preserve capital while still generating necessary income. Financial planners should assist clients in evaluating their current asset allocation and making necessary adjustments to reflect their reduced risk tolerance, ensuring that their portfolio aligns with their evolving financial needs and retirement objectives.

In addition, rebalancing investment portfolios can help take advantage of market opportunities and avoid potential losses. Over time, certain investments may perform better than others, leading to an imbalance in the portfolio that could either expose the individual to higher risk or miss potential returns. By regularly reviewing and rebalancing their investments, seniors can capture gains from outperforming assets and reinvest them into underperforming or less volatile options, thus maintaining a well-diversified and risk-adjusted portfolio. Financial planners play a key role in this process by providing ongoing market analysis, recommending appropriate adjustments, and ensuring that the portfolio remains aligned with the client's long-term financial strategy and goals (CFP Board, 2019b).

TABLE 19.1 Evaluation Criteria for Monitoring and Adjusting Financial Plans

EVALUATION ITEM	DESCRIPTION	IMPORTANCE
Income sources and stability	Reviewing the stability and sufficiency of income sources such as Social Security, pensions, and annuities.	Ensures ongoing income meets living expenses and adjusts for changes such as cost-of-living increases or inflation.
Healthcare needs and costs	Regular assessment of healthcare expenses, insurance coverage, and eligibility for benefits like Medicare.	Addresses rising healthcare costs and changes in health status, ensuring adequate coverage and financial planning.
Investment performance	Analyzing investment portfolio performance against benchmarks and retirement goals.	Adjusts investments to align with risk tolerance, market conditions, and changing financial goals.
Tax implications	Evaluating the tax impact of withdrawals, investments, and income sources.	Optimizes tax efficiency to maximize net income and preserve wealth.
Living arrangements	Assessing the suitability of current living arrangements and potential need for modifications or relocation.	Ensures the living environment is appropriate for the client's health and mobility needs.
Legal and estate planning	Reviewing wills, trusts, powers of attorney, and beneficiary designations for currency and relevance.	Ensures legal documents are up-to-date and reflect current wishes, protecting assets and legacy.
Long-term care planning	Evaluating the need for long-term care insurance or savings to cover potential future care costs.	Prepares financially for the possibility of needing long-term or specialized care.
Budget adjustments	Regular review of the client's budget to adjust for changes in expenses and income.	Keeps spending in line with income changes and financial priorities, preventing financial strain.
Emergency fund adequacy	Checking the sufficiency of emergency funds to manage unexpected expenses.	Provides a safety net for unforeseen costs, reducing the need to liquidate investments under duress.
Family and dependent support	Considering the financial support provided to dependents or changes in family dynamics.	Adjusts financial assistance to family members based on need and the client's financial capacity.
Risk management and insurance review	Evaluating insurance coverage (health, life, long-term care) to ensure it meets current needs.	Protects against emerging risks and financial vulnerabilities as the client ages.

DISCUSSION QUESTIONS

1. What are the key indicators that suggest a financial plan needs adjustment, and what are the most effective strategies for making these adjustments as a retiree's needs and market conditions change?
2. How do financial advisors facilitate the process of monitoring and adjusting a financial plan for the elderly, and what tools or resources do they commonly use to ensure the plan remains aligned with the client's evolving needs?
3. How should changes in a retiree's health status influence the adjustments made to their financial plan, particularly in terms of healthcare costs and long-term care planning?
4. Why is rebalancing an investment portfolio crucial as individuals age, and what factors should guide the rebalancing process to ensure it aligns with a retiree's changing risk tolerance and financial goals?
5. How often should a financial plan be reviewed and potentially adjusted as one ages, and what events or changes in circumstances typically trigger these reviews?
6. How should new financial products or changes in tax laws influence the adjustments made to an elderly person's financial plan, and what role do these products play in enhancing financial security?

20

Ethical and Legal Considerations

Ethical and legal considerations are fundamental aspects of resource management planning for the elderly, ensuring that financial decisions are made with integrity and in compliance with relevant regulations. As individuals age, they often face complex financial situations that require careful handling to protect their interests and uphold their rights. Ethical considerations involve respecting the autonomy and preferences of elderly clients while providing transparent and unbiased financial advice. This includes ensuring that financial plans are developed with the client's best interests in mind, avoiding conflicts of interest and maintaining confidentiality. Addressing these ethical concerns is crucial for building trust and ensuring that the financial planning process is both respectful and equitable.

Legal considerations also play a significant role in resource management planning for the elderly, encompassing adherence to laws and regulations that affect financial planning and elder care. This includes understanding and implementing legal documents such as wills, powers of attorney, and healthcare directives, which are essential for managing an elderly individual's affairs and making decisions on their behalf when necessary. Financial planners must be well-versed in relevant laws, including those related to tax regulations, estate planning, and elder abuse prevention, to provide accurate and compliant advice. By addressing both ethical and legal aspects, planners can ensure that their clients' financial plans are not only effective but also aligned with legal requirements and ethical standards, supporting the well-being and protection of elderly individuals (CFP Board, 2019a).

ETHICAL RESPONSIBILITIES OF FINANCIAL PLANNERS

Ethical responsibilities of financial planners are paramount in resource management planning for the elderly, as they guide the provision of advice and the management of clients' assets with integrity and respect. One fundamental responsibility is to act in the best interest of the client, ensuring that all recommendations and decisions prioritize the elderly individual's needs and goals over any personal gain or external pressures. This involves providing transparent and unbiased advice, clearly disclosing any potential conflicts of interest, and avoiding actions that could exploit or disadvantage clients. Upholding these ethical standards is essential for maintaining trust and ensuring that the financial planning process is conducted with honesty and fairness.

Another critical ethical responsibility is to ensure that all financial strategies and recommendations are appropriate for the client's specific circumstances and risk tolerance. Financial planners must be diligent in understanding the unique needs, preferences, and financial situations of elderly clients, which may include dealing with limited income, health-related expenses, or changing family dynamics. By tailoring their advice to each client's individual situation, planners can help ensure that financial plans are both realistic and effective, while also safeguarding the client's financial well-being. This personalized approach reflects a commitment to ethical practice and client-centered care.

Moreover, financial planners have an ethical duty to protect the privacy and confidentiality of their elderly clients. This responsibility entails handling sensitive financial information with the utmost care and ensuring that client data is secure from unauthorized access or misuse. In addition, planners should educate their clients about the importance of safeguarding personal information and make informed decisions regarding data sharing and storage. By adhering to these ethical principles, financial planners not only comply with legal requirements but also foster a supportive and trustworthy relationship with their clients, contributing to a more secure and respectful financial planning process (CFP Board, 2019a).

These ethical and legal considerations are crucial for CFPs to navigate effectively to maintain professionalism, comply with regulations, and provide the highest level of service and protection to elderly clients.

TABLE 20.1 Key Considerations in Financial Planning

CONSIDERATION	DESCRIPTION	IMPACT ON FINANCIAL PLANNING
Capacity and competence	Assessing the client's ability to understand the financial decisions and implications of those decisions.	Ensures that financial decisions are made by clients who are competent to do so, avoiding legal disputes.
Financial abuse prevention	Implementing safeguards to protect clients from financial abuse, including scams and exploitation.	Protects the client's assets and ensures financial decisions are in their best interest.
Informed consent	Ensuring the client fully understands and agrees to all aspects of the financial planning process.	Legally and ethically necessary to ensure that all actions are transparent and agreed upon by the client.
Confidentiality	Maintaining the privacy of client information and only sharing with consent or when legally required.	Builds trust and adheres to legal standards concerning data protection and privacy laws.
Conflict of interest	Identifying and disclosing any potential conflicts of interest that might impact the advisor's recommendations.	Promotes transparency and trust by ensuring the planner acts in the client's best interest, not their own.
Durable power of attorney	Establishing a legal document that grants a trusted individual the authority to make decisions if the client is unable to do so.	Provides continuity in financial management during periods of incapacity.
Regular legal document review	Periodic review of wills, trusts, healthcare directives, and power of attorney to ensure they are current.	Keeps legal documents up to date with the client's wishes and current laws, avoiding legal issues in the future.
Fair treatment	Ensuring that all clients are treated fairly and equitably, regardless of age, health, or financial status.	Maintains ethical standards and compliance with antidiscrimination laws.
End-of-life planning	Discussing and planning for issues such as estate distribution, healthcare directives, and funeral arrangements.	Helps ensure that end-of-life wishes are respected and legally documented, providing peace of mind for the client and their family.
Elder law consultation	Involving legal professionals specializing in elder law to address specific concerns like Medicaid planning or guardianship.	Ensures that financial planning aligns with current laws and best practices in elder care and estate planning.

LEGAL ISSUES IN ELDER FINANCIAL PLANNING

Legal issues in elder financial planning are crucial considerations that ensure the effective management of resources while adhering to relevant laws and regulations. One primary concern is the creation and maintenance of essential legal documents, such as wills, trusts, and powers of attorney. These documents are vital for outlining how a person's assets should be managed and distributed upon their death, as well as for designating individuals who can make financial and healthcare decisions on their behalf if they become incapacitated. Financial planners must ensure that these documents are properly drafted, legally valid, and regularly updated to reflect any changes in the client's wishes or circumstances, thereby preventing potential disputes and ensuring that the client's intentions are honored.

Another significant legal issue involves understanding and complying with the complex regulations surrounding tax implications and estate planning. Effective estate planning requires knowledge of federal and state tax laws, including potential estate taxes, inheritance taxes, and gift taxes, which can impact the transfer of assets and overall financial strategy. Financial planners should guide clients in structuring their estates in a tax-efficient manner, utilizing strategies such as tax exemptions and deductions to minimize the tax burden on heirs. Staying informed about changes in tax legislation and ensuring compliance with current laws are essential for optimizing the financial outcomes of the estate planning process.

In addition, elder financial planning must address legal protections against elder abuse and financial exploitation. Seniors are particularly vulnerable to scams and fraudulent schemes, making it imperative for financial planners to be vigilant and implement safeguards to protect their clients. This includes monitoring for signs of financial abuse, such as unauthorized transactions or changes in account activity, and educating clients about potential risks and protective measures. Planners should also be aware of legal frameworks designed to protect seniors, such as reporting requirements for suspected abuse and collaborating with legal professionals to address any issues that arise. By addressing these legal concerns, financial planners help ensure the security and integrity of their clients' financial plans while safeguarding their well-being.

Addressing these legal issues is crucial in developing a comprehensive and effective financial plan for elderly clients, ensuring their finances are secure and their wishes respected as they age.

TABLE 20.2 Legal Issues and Their Impact on Financial Planning

LEGAL ISSUE	DESCRIPTION	IMPACT ON FINANCIAL PLANNING
Capacity and competence evaluations	Determining the client's ability to make informed financial decisions due to potential cognitive decline.	Ensures financial decisions are valid and protect the client from making legally questionable choices.
Estate planning and wills	Creating or updating wills to reflect current wishes for asset distribution.	Prevents legal disputes among beneficiaries and ensures assets are distributed according to the client's wishes.
Powers of attorney	Establishing legal authority for a trusted person to act on behalf of the client in financial and health matters.	Provides for continuity of financial management and personal care decisions in case of incapacity.
Guardianship/conservatorship	Legal processes to appoint someone to manage financial and personal affairs if the client is deemed incompetent.	Protects clients who can no longer manage their own affairs, though it can limit personal autonomy.
Healthcare directives	Documents that specify decisions about healthcare interventions and end-of-life care preferences.	Ensures that healthcare wishes are respected and legally upheld, especially when clients cannot make decisions themselves.
Beneficiary designations	Ensuring that all accounts with beneficiary designations (like IRAs, 401(k)s, life insurance) are up to date.	Avoids outdated designations that can lead to unintended disbursements of assets.
Medicaid planning	Structuring assets and income to qualify for Medicaid, which often involves spending down or creating trusts.	Helps cover long-term care costs without depleting all the client's assets, while adhering to legal standards.
Tax implications	Addressing the tax consequences of distributions from retirement accounts and gifts.	Optimizes tax efficiency for retirement withdrawals and estate transfers.
Scam and fraud protection	Establishing safeguards to protect against scams and financial abuse, which the elderly are particularly vulnerable to.	Protects assets and reduces the risk of financial exploitation by third parties.
Long-term care insurance policies	Reviewing and advising on long-term care insurance options, considering the client's health and financial situation.	Provides financial support for long-term care needs, avoiding significant out-of-pocket expenses.

ENSURING COMPLIANCE WITH FINANCIAL REGULATIONS

Ensuring compliance with financial regulations is a critical aspect of resource management planning for the elderly, as it helps protect both the integrity of the financial plan and the well-being of the client. Financial planners must be well-versed in various regulations that govern retirement accounts, investments, and estate planning to provide accurate and lawful advice. This includes adhering to rules set forth by regulatory bodies such as the Securities and Exchange Commission (SEC), the Financial Industry Regulatory Authority (FINRA), and the Internal Revenue Service (IRS). Compliance with these regulations ensures that financial strategies are not only effective but also legally sound, reducing the risk of penalties and legal issues for both the planner and the client.

In addition to federal regulations, financial planners must also be knowledgeable about state-specific laws that can affect elder financial planning. These may include regulations related to state income taxes, Medicaid eligibility, and estate laws. Each state may have its own rules governing asset protection, inheritance rights, and long-term care planning, which can impact how a financial plan is structured. By staying informed about state regulations and integrating them into the planning process, financial planners can help ensure that their clients' plans comply with all relevant legal requirements, thereby avoiding complications and ensuring smooth execution of the financial strategy.

Moreover, ensuring compliance with financial regulations involves regular updates and ongoing education. Financial regulations are subject to frequent changes, and staying current with new laws and amendments is essential for maintaining compliance. Financial planners should participate in continuing education programs, attend industry seminars, and review updates from regulatory agencies to keep their knowledge current. In addition, regular audits and reviews of clients' financial plans can help identify and address any compliance issues before they become problematic. By proactively managing compliance, financial planners safeguard their clients' financial well-being and enhance the credibility and effectiveness of their advisory services.

In conclusion, resource management planning for the elderly is a multifaceted discipline that requires a careful balance of financial acumen, ethical considerations, and legal compliance. As we have explored throughout this textbook, effective resource management involves not only understanding and managing financial assets but also adapting to the evolving needs and circumstances of elderly clients. By employing comprehensive planning strategies—from budgeting and investment management to estate planning and healthcare considerations—financial planners can help seniors achieve financial stability, maintain their quality of life, and navigate the complexities of retirement with confidence and security.

The goal of resource management for the elderly is to provide a holistic approach that addresses both the financial and emotional well-being of clients. As financial professionals, it is imperative to stay informed about current regulations, continuously reassess financial plans, and approach each client with empathy and respect. By integrating these principles into practice, planners can offer invaluable support to elderly individuals, ensuring that their resources are managed effectively and their retirement years are lived with dignity and peace of mind. The principles and strategies outlined in this textbook are designed to equip financial planners with the tools and knowledge necessary to make a meaningful difference in the lives of their clients (CFP Board, 2019a).

CONTINUING CASE—THE HARMONS—ETHICAL AND LEGAL CONSIDERATIONS FOR THE ELDERLY AND THE IMPORTANCE OF MONITORING AND ADJUSTING THE FINANCIAL PLAN PRE- AND POST-RETIREMENT

Chapter 20 Case Assignment 20.1

Objective:

The purpose of this exercise is to evaluate the ethical and legal considerations that Darin and Lisa Harmon must consider as they approach and enter retirement. In addition, the exercise will emphasize the importance of ongoing monitoring and adjustments to their financial plan both before and after retirement to ensure it remains aligned with their evolving needs and circumstances.

Instructions:

1. Understanding Ethical and Legal Considerations for the Elderly:

- **Ethical Considerations:**
  - Discuss the ethical responsibilities involved in financial planning for the elderly, including ensuring that Darin and Lisa's autonomy, dignity, and wishes are respected.
  - Explore the potential ethical challenges they might face, such as protecting against financial exploitation, addressing cognitive decline, and ensuring that financial decisions reflect their best interests.

    - Consider the ethical implications of involving family members in financial decision-making, balancing the need for support with the Harmons' right to privacy and independence.

- **Legal Considerations:**
    - Outline the key legal considerations that Darin and Lisa must address as they approach retirement, including updating wills, establishing powers of attorney, and ensuring that estate plans are in place and legally binding.
    - Discuss the importance of complying with relevant laws and regulations related to retirement accounts, taxes, healthcare decisions, and inheritance.
    - Highlight the potential legal risks they might encounter, such as challenges to their estate plan, disputes over guardianship or conservatorship, and the need for legal representation in complex financial matters.

2. Protecting Against Financial Exploitation and Abuse:

- **Identifying Risks:**
    - Identify the common risks of financial exploitation and abuse that the elderly may face, including scams, fraud, and undue influence from others.
    - Discuss how Darin and Lisa can recognize the signs of financial abuse and take proactive steps to protect themselves.
- **Preventative Measures:**
    - Recommend strategies for safeguarding their financial assets, such as setting up alerts on financial accounts, regularly reviewing bank statements, and limiting access to sensitive financial information.
    - Discuss the role of legal documents, such as a durable power of attorney, in protecting against financial exploitation, and ensure that the agent chosen for this role is trustworthy and aligned with their best interests.

3. The Importance of Monitoring and Adjusting the Financial Plan Pre-Retirement:

- **Pre-Retirement Planning:**
    - Emphasize the importance of regularly monitoring Darin and Lisa's financial plan as they approach retirement. Discuss how market changes, health developments, or shifts in personal goals may necessitate adjustments to their plan.

- Provide recommendations for key areas to monitor, such as investment performance, retirement account contributions, and tax planning strategies.
- Suggest tools and techniques for staying informed about their financial situation, including working with a financial advisor, using financial planning software, and setting up regular check-ins to review their plan.

- **Adjustments Before Retirement:**
  - Identify potential adjustments that might be necessary before they retire, such as reallocating investments to reduce risk, increasing savings to meet retirement goals, or updating their estate plan to reflect current wishes.
  - Discuss the importance of planning for healthcare costs, including long-term care, and ensuring that they have adequate insurance coverage as they transition into retirement.

4. The Importance of Monitoring and Adjusting the Financial Plan Post-Retirement:

- **Post-Retirement Monitoring:**
  - Discuss the need for ongoing monitoring of their financial plan after retirement to ensure it continues to meet their needs as circumstances change.
  - Highlight key areas to focus on post-retirement, such as managing retirement income, monitoring expenses, and adjusting withdrawal strategies to preserve their savings.
- **Adjustments After Retirement:**
  - Provide recommendations for adjustments that may be necessary after retirement, such as revising their budget, updating their will and beneficiary designations, and reassessing their insurance needs.
  - Consider how changes in health, family dynamics, or economic conditions might impact their financial plan and the importance of remaining flexible in their approach.
- **Communication and Transparency:**
  - Emphasize the importance of maintaining open communication with family members and financial advisors to ensure that their financial plan remains transparent and aligned with their long-term goals.
  - Discuss the benefits of documenting their financial decisions and sharing relevant information with trusted individuals to avoid misunderstandings or conflicts in the future.

5. Draft a Comprehensive Report on Ethical and Legal Considerations and the Importance of Monitoring and Adjusting the Financial Plan:

- **Report Content:**
  - Prepare a comprehensive report (five to seven pages) that includes:
    - An analysis of the ethical and legal considerations specific to Darin and Lisa as they approach and enter retirement.
    - Recommendations for protecting against financial exploitation and abuse, including preventative measures and the use of legal tools.
    - A discussion of the importance of monitoring and adjusting their financial plan both pre- and post-retirement, including specific areas to focus on and potential adjustments to consider.
    - Strategies for maintaining open communication and transparency in financial planning, especially as their circumstances evolve.
- **Action Plan:**
  - Include a timeline for implementing the recommended strategies, prioritizing steps that should be taken immediately versus those that can be addressed over time.
  - Suggest regular reviews of their financial plan to adjust for changes in personal circumstances, financial goals, or legal considerations.

21

Resource Management for the Elderly Cases

CASE 1: THE RETIRED TEACHER

Background:

Margaret, a 68-year-old retired schoolteacher, is living a comfortable but modest lifestyle. After dedicating more than 35 years to education, she now enjoys her retirement with the security of a modest pension and Social Security benefits. Margaret owns her home outright, which gives her a strong foundation of financial stability. She also has a substantial amount saved in her 401(k) account. Margaret's primary concern is ensuring that her savings last throughout her retirement years, allowing her to maintain her current lifestyle and effectively manage any healthcare costs that may arise.

Planning Process:

1. **Establishing Goals:** Margaret wants to continue traveling and engage in community activities but is worried about unexpected healthcare costs.
2. **Gathering Data:** Review her income sources, expenses, and current investments.
3. **Developing the Plan:** Create a budget that includes a plan for healthcare expenses and establish an emergency fund.
4. **Implementation:** Set up a systematic withdrawal plan from her 401(k) and adjust her asset allocation to a more conservative mix to preserve capital.
5. **Monitoring and Adjusting:** Review her financial situation annually and adjust the withdrawal strategy based on changes in expenses or investment performance.

Financial Information:

- **Income Sources:**
    - o **Pension:** $1,800 per month
    - o **Social Security:** $1,600 per month
    - o **Total Monthly Income:** $3,400
- **Assets:**
    - o **Home:** Valued at $350,000 (fully paid off)
    - o **401(k) Account:** $450,000
    - o **Emergency Savings:** $25,000 in a high-yield savings account
- **Liabilities:**
    - o **None:** Margaret has no outstanding debts or mortgages.
- **Monthly Expenses:**
    - o **Living Expenses (including utilities, groceries, transportation, etc.):** $2,500
    - o **Healthcare Costs (Medicare premiums, supplemental insurance, out-of-pocket costs):** $400
    - o **Discretionary Spending (entertainment, hobbies, travel):** $500
    - o **Total Monthly Expenses:** $3,400
- **Net Worth:**
    - o **Total Assets:** $825,000
    - o **Total Liabilities:** $0
    - o **Net Worth:** $825,000

Financial Goals:

1. **Longevity of Savings:** Margaret's primary goal is to ensure that her 401(k) savings last throughout her retirement years, providing her with financial security and peace of mind.

2. **Maintain Lifestyle:** She wants to maintain her current lifestyle, including occasional travel, hobbies, and social activities, without the fear of outliving her resources.
3. **Healthcare Management:** Margaret is concerned about potential healthcare costs as she ages. She wants to make sure she has sufficient coverage to manage both routine medical expenses and any unforeseen health issues.
4. **Estate Planning:** Margaret wishes to leave a financial legacy for her two adult children, ensuring that her estate is distributed according to her wishes.

Investment and Retirement Information:

- **401(k) Account Allocation:**
  - **Stocks:** 50%
  - **Bonds:** 40%
  - **Cash/Cash Equivalents:** 10%
- **Withdrawal Strategy:**
  - Margaret is currently withdrawing 4% annually from her 401(k) account, which amounts to $18,000 per year. This withdrawal supplements her pension and Social Security income.
  - She plans to review her withdrawal strategy annually to ensure it aligns with her retirement needs and market conditions.
- **Risk Tolerance:**
  - Moderate: Margaret is comfortable with some market volatility but wants to avoid taking excessive risks that could jeopardize her savings.

Medical and Long-Term Care Insurance Information:

- **Medicare:**
  - Margaret is enrolled in Medicare Part A (hospital insurance) and Part B (medical insurance).
- **Medicare Supplement Insurance (Medigap):**
  - She has a Medigap policy that covers additional costs not covered by Medicare, such as copayments, coinsurance, and deductibles.

- **Long-Term Care Insurance:**
    - Margaret does not currently have long-term care insurance but is considering whether it would be a wise investment to protect against the potential costs of long-term care services, such as in-home care or a nursing home.
- **Healthcare Concerns:**
    - Margaret is concerned about rising healthcare costs, particularly as she ages, and wants to ensure her insurance coverage is sufficient to manage these expenses.

Estate Information:

- **Will:**
    - Margaret has a current will in place that outlines the distribution of her assets to her two adult children equally. She also named her eldest child as the executor of her estate.
- **Power of Attorney:**
    - Margaret has established a durable power of attorney, giving her eldest child the authority to make financial decisions on her behalf if she becomes incapacitated.
- **Healthcare Proxy:**
    - She has also designated a healthcare proxy to ensure her medical wishes are followed if she is unable to make decisions for herself.
- **Beneficiary Designations:**
    - Margaret's 401(k) account and life insurance policy have her children listed as equal beneficiaries.
- **Trust Consideration:**
    - Margaret is considering setting up a revocable living trust to avoid probate and ensure a smooth transfer of her assets to her children.

CASE 2: THE WIDOW WITH A COMPLEX ESTATE

BACKGROUND:

John, a 72-year-old widower, is facing the complexities of estate planning following the death of his wife. John has three stepchildren from his late wife's previous marriage, whom he considers his own. He has accumulated significant wealth over his lifetime, including a large family home, various investments, and a substantial life insurance policy. John's primary concern is to ensure that his assets are distributed according to his wishes while minimizing estate taxes and avoiding potential conflicts among his heirs.

PLANNING PROCESS:

1. **Establishing Goals:** Ensure the estate is divided fairly among his children and minimize estate taxes.
2. **Gathering Data:** Review existing wills, trusts, and insurance policies.
3. **Developing the Plan:** Update the will and create a trust to manage the distribution of assets. Explore tax-saving strategies, such as gifting and charitable donations.
4. **Implementation:** Work with an estate attorney to finalize the trust and update beneficiary designations.
5. **Monitoring and Adjusting:** Review the estate plan regularly to ensure it aligns with current laws and family dynamics.

FINANCIAL INFORMATION:

- **Income Sources:**
    - **Pension:** $4,000 per month
    - **Social Security:** $2,500 per month
    - **Investment Income:** $50,000 annually from dividends and interest
    - **Total Monthly Income:** $8,167

- **Assets:**
  - **Family Home:** Valued at $1,200,000 (fully paid off)
  - **Investment Portfolio:** $3,000,000 (diversified across stocks, bonds, and mutual funds)
  - **Life Insurance:** $1,000,000 policy with stepchildren as beneficiaries
  - **Cash and Savings:** $200,000 in various savings accounts and CDs.
- **Liabilities:**
  - **None:** John has no outstanding debts or mortgages.
- **Monthly Expenses:**
  - **Living Expenses (including utilities, groceries, transportation, etc.):** $4,000
  - **Healthcare Costs (Medicare premiums, supplemental insurance, out-of-pocket costs):** $800
  - **Discretionary Spending (travel, hobbies, gifts to family):** $1,000
  - **Total Monthly Expenses:** $5,800
- **Net Worth:**
  - **Total Assets:** $5,400,000
  - **Total Liabilities:** $0
  - **Net Worth:** $5,400,000

Financial Goals:

1. **Asset Distribution:** John wants to ensure that his estate is distributed fairly among his three stepchildren according to his wishes, with specific bequests and allocations clearly defined.
2. **Minimizing Estate Taxes:** John is concerned about the potential impact of estate taxes on his heirs and wants to minimize this burden through effective estate planning strategies.
3. **Preserving Wealth:** He aims to preserve as much of his wealth as possible for his heirs while maintaining sufficient resources to cover his own needs during retirement.
4. **Legacy Planning:** John is interested in leaving a charitable legacy, through donations to causes important to him and his late wife.

Investment and Retirement Information:

- **Investment Portfolio Allocation:**
    - **Stocks:** 60% ($1,800,000)
    - **Bonds:** 30% ($900,000)
    - **Cash/Cash Equivalents:** 10% ($300,000)
- **Investment Strategy:**
    - John has adopted a growth-oriented investment strategy, with a significant portion of his portfolio in equities to provide long-term growth. He balances this with bonds and cash to reduce risk and provide income.
- **Retirement Income Strategy:**
    - John's retirement income is primarily derived from his pension, Social Security, and investment income. He is withdrawing approximately 2% annually from his investment portfolio to supplement his other income sources.
- **Risk Tolerance:**
    - Moderate: Although John is willing to take on some risk to achieve growth, he is also concerned about preserving his capital, particularly as he ages.

Medical and Long-Term Care Insurance Information:

- **Medicare:**
    - John is enrolled in Medicare Part A and Part B, covering hospital and medical expenses.
- **Medicare Supplement Insurance (Medigap):**
    - He has a Medigap policy that helps cover additional costs not covered by Medicare, such as copayments and deductibles.
- **Long-Term Care Insurance:**
    - John holds a long-term care insurance policy that covers up to $200 per day for nursing home care, in-home care, and assisted living facilities. This policy provides peace of mind should he require extended care in the future.

- **Healthcare Concerns:**
    - John's main healthcare concern is ensuring that he can afford quality long-term care without depleting his estate, thereby protecting the inheritance of his stepchildren.

Estate Information:

- **Will:**
    - John has a will in place that outlines his wishes for the distribution of his assets, including specific bequests to each of his stepchildren and a charitable donation to a local hospital.
- **Trusts:**
    - **Revocable Living Trust:** John has established a revocable living trust that holds his primary residence and a portion of his investment portfolio. This trust is designed to avoid probate and allow for easier management of his assets if he becomes incapacitated.
    - **Irrevocable Life Insurance Trust (ILIT):** His life insurance policy is held within an irrevocable life insurance trust, ensuring that the $1,000,000 death benefit will pass to his stepchildren free of estate taxes.
- **Power of Attorney:**
    - John has designated his eldest stepchild as the durable power of attorney for financial matters, granting them authority to manage his financial affairs if he becomes incapacitated.
- **Healthcare Proxy:**
    - He has also established a healthcare proxy, assigning his second stepchild to make medical decisions on his behalf if he is unable to do so.
- **Charitable Giving:**
    - John plans to leave a portion of his estate to charity, including a $200,000 bequest to a hospital that provided care for his late wife. He is considering setting up a charitable remainder trust (CRT) to provide income to his heirs with the remainder going to charity.

- **Tax Planning:**
    - John is working with an estate planning attorney to minimize estate taxes. He is considering additional strategies, such as gifting assets to his stepchildren during his lifetime, setting up a family limited partnership (FLP), or making charitable contributions to reduce the size of his taxable estate.

CASE 3: THE AGING COUPLE WITH LONG-TERM CARE NEEDS

BACKGROUND:

Helen and George are both 75 years old and have started to consider the possibility that one or both may require long-term care in the future. Although they have a solid foundation of savings and investments, they are concerned about how potential nursing home or in-home care costs could impact their financial stability and their ability to leave an inheritance for their children. They are unsure how to plan effectively for these potential costs while also maintaining their current lifestyle.

PLANNING PROCESS:

1. **Establishing Goals:** Secure a plan for long-term care that does not deplete their savings.
2. **Gathering Data:** Assess their current financial situation, including savings, investments, and insurance coverage.
3. **Developing the Plan:** Explore long-term care insurance options and evaluate state Medicaid programs for potential coverage.
4. **Implementation:** Purchase a long-term care insurance policy and set up a budget to allocate funds for potential care needs.
5. **Monitoring and Adjusting:** Review the insurance policy and financial plan annually, especially as health conditions or costs change.

FINANCIAL INFORMATION:

- **Income Sources:**
    - **Pension (George):** $3,200 per month

  - **Social Security (Helen):** $1,800 per month
  - **Social Security (George):** $2,200 per month
  - **Total Monthly Income:** $7,200
- **Assets:**
  - **Primary Residence:** Valued at $400,000 (fully paid off)
  - **Investment Portfolio:** $1,200,000 (includes stocks, bonds, and mutual funds)
  - **IRA (George):** $350,000
  - **IRA (Helen):** $250,000
  - **Cash and Savings:** $150,000 in a savings account
  - **Total Assets:** $2,350,000
- **Liabilities:**
  - **None:** Helen and George have no outstanding debts or mortgages.
- **Monthly Expenses:**
  - **Living Expenses (including utilities, groceries, transportation, etc.):** $3,500
  - **Healthcare Costs (Medicare premiums, supplemental insurance, out-of-pocket costs):** $800
  - **Discretionary Spending (travel, hobbies, gifts to family):** $1,200
  - **Total Monthly Expenses:** $5,500
- **Net Worth:**
  - **Total Assets:** $2,350,000
  - **Total Liabilities:** $0
  - **Net Worth:** $2,350,000

Financial Goals:

1. **Long-Term Care Planning:** Helen and George want to ensure they have a plan in place to cover potential long-term care costs, whether it be nursing home care or in-home care, without depleting their savings.

2. **Preserving Wealth:** They wish to preserve as much of their wealth as possible to leave an inheritance for their two adult children.
3. **Maintaining Lifestyle:** Helen and George want to continue enjoying their current lifestyle, including travel and hobbies, while also being financially prepared for future healthcare needs.
4. **Minimizing Financial Risk:** They are concerned about the potential financial risk that long-term care costs could pose to their retirement savings and want to explore options to mitigate this risk.

Investment and Retirement Information:

- **Investment Portfolio Allocation:**
  - **Stocks:** 50% ($600,000)
  - **Bonds:** 40% ($480,000)
  - **Cash/Cash Equivalents:** 10% ($120,000)
- **IRA Allocations:**
  - **George's IRA:**
    - Stocks: 60% ($210,000)
    - Bonds: 40% ($140,000)
  - **Helen's IRA:**
    - Stocks: 50% ($125,000)
    - Bonds: 50% ($125,000)
- **Withdrawal Strategy:**
  - Helen and George are withdrawing 3% annually from their investment portfolio and IRAs to supplement their pension and Social Security income. This amounts to approximately $45,000 per year.
- **Risk Tolerance:**
  - Conservative to Moderate: They are focused on preserving their capital and generating steady income, with some growth potential to keep pace with inflation.

Medical and Long-Term Care Insurance Information:

- **Medicare:**
  - o Helen and George are both enrolled in Medicare Part A and Part B.
- **Medicare Supplement Insurance (Medigap):**
  - o They each have a Medigap policy to cover additional healthcare costs not included in Medicare, such as copayments and deductibles.
- **Long-Term Care Insurance:**
  - o They have not yet purchased long-term care insurance but are considering whether it would be beneficial to cover potential future costs for nursing home care, assisted living, or in-home care.
- **Healthcare Concerns:**
  - o Helen and George are particularly concerned about the rising costs of long-term care and how it could impact their financial situation if one or both require extended care.

Estate Information:

- **Wills:**
  - o Helen and George both have wills that specify the distribution of their assets to their two children. They have named each other as the primary beneficiaries and executors, with their children as secondary beneficiaries.
- **Trusts:**
  - o **Revocable Living Trust:** They have established a revocable living trust that includes their primary residence and a portion of their investment portfolio. The trust is designed to avoid probate and simplify asset management if they become incapacitated.
- **Power of Attorney:**
  - o Each has designated the other as their durable power of attorney for financial and legal matters, with their eldest child named as a secondary agent.

- **Healthcare Proxy:**
  - They have healthcare proxies in place, giving each other the authority to make medical decisions if one becomes incapacitated. Their youngest child is named as the secondary proxy.
- **Beneficiary Designations:**
  - Their IRAs and life insurance policies list their children as equal beneficiaries.
- **Charitable Giving:**
  - Helen and George are interested in leaving a portion of their estate to charity, specifically to a local environmental organization they have supported for many years.
- **Estate Tax Planning:**
  - They are working with an estate planning attorney to minimize estate taxes and ensure their assets are distributed according to their wishes. They are considering additional strategies, such as gifting assets to their children during their lifetime or setting up a charitable remainder trust (CRT).

CASE 4: THE SELF-EMPLOYED RETIREE

Background:

Tom, a 70-year-old recently retired self-employed consultant, spent most of his career running a successful consulting business. Over the years, he has accumulated significant assets in both taxable investment accounts and retirement accounts. However, as he transitions into retirement, Tom is uncertain about how to effectively manage and withdraw from these accounts to support his lifestyle while optimizing tax efficiency and preserving his wealth for future generations.

Planning Process:

1. **Establishing Goals:** Maximize tax efficiency while ensuring a steady income stream during retirement.
2. **Gathering Data:** Review all financial accounts, including tax implications of withdrawals.

3. **Developing the Plan:** Develop a tax-efficient withdrawal strategy, considering both taxable and retirement accounts.
4. **Implementation:** Implement a strategy to withdraw from taxable accounts first, and then from retirement accounts, to minimize tax impact.
5. **Monitoring and Adjusting:** Review tax implications and portfolio performance annually to adjust the withdrawal strategy as needed.

FINANCIAL INFORMATION:

- **Income Sources:**
    - o **Social Security:** $2,800 per month
    - o **Business Sale Proceeds:** $300,000 (received upon selling his consulting business)
    - o **Rental Income:** $1,500 per month from a commercial property he owns
    - o **Total Monthly Income:** $4,300 (excluding withdrawals from investment accounts)
- **Assets:**
    - o **Primary Residence:** Valued at $600,000 (fully paid off)
    - o **Commercial Property:** Valued at $400,000 (generating $1,500/month in rental income)
    - o **Taxable Investment Accounts:** $1,200,000 (stocks, bonds, and mutual funds)
    - o **IRA Accounts:** $800,000 (Traditional IRA: $600,000, Roth IRA: $200,000)
    - o **Emergency Fund:** $100,000 in a high-yield savings account
    - o **Total Assets:** $3,100,000
- **Liabilities:**
    - o **None:** Tom has no outstanding debts or mortgages.
- **Monthly Expenses:**
    - o **Living Expenses (including utilities, groceries, transportation, etc.):** $3,000

  - **Healthcare Costs (Medicare premiums, supplemental insurance, out-of-pocket costs):** $600
  - **Discretionary Spending (travel, hobbies, dining out):** $1,000.
  - **Total Monthly Expenses:** $4,600
- **Net Worth:**
  - **Total Assets:** $3,100,000
  - **Total Liabilities:** $0
  - **Net Worth:** $3,100,000

Financial Goals:

1. **Efficient Withdrawal Strategy:** Tom's primary goal is to develop an effective withdrawal strategy that balances withdrawals from taxable and tax-advantaged accounts to minimize taxes and ensure that his savings last throughout his retirement.
2. **Tax Efficiency:** He wants to optimize tax efficiency by managing how and when he withdraws from his various accounts, taking advantage of favorable tax treatments and minimizing unnecessary tax liabilities.
3. **Preserving Wealth:** Tom aims to preserve as much of his wealth as possible to leave an inheritance for his children and grandchildren.
4. **Maintaining Lifestyle:** He wants to maintain his current lifestyle, including travel, hobbies, and social activities, while ensuring that his financial resources can support him through his retirement years.

Investment and Retirement Information:

- **Investment Portfolio Allocation:**
  - **Taxable Investment Accounts:**
    - Stocks: 60% ($720,000)
    - Bonds: 30% ($360,000)
    - Cash/Cash Equivalents: 10% ($120,000)

- **Traditional IRA:**
  - Stocks: 50% ($300,000)
  - Bonds: 50% ($300,000)
- **Roth IRA:**
  - Stocks: 70% ($140,000)
  - Bonds: 30% ($60,000)

- **Withdrawal Strategy:**
  - Tom has not yet established a systematic withdrawal strategy. He is considering the best approach to drawing down from his taxable accounts, traditional IRA, and Roth IRA in a tax-efficient manner.
- **Required Minimum Distributions (RMDs):**
  - Tom is aware that he must begin taking RMDs from his traditional IRA but is unsure how to incorporate these withdrawals into his overall financial plan.
- **Risk Tolerance:**
  - Moderate: Tom is comfortable with some market risk to achieve growth but wants to ensure that his portfolio remains balanced to protect his principal.

Medical and Long-Term Care Insurance Information:

- **Medicare:**
  - Tom is enrolled in Medicare Part A and Part B, covering hospital and medical expenses.
- **Medicare Supplement Insurance (Medigap):**
  - He has a Medigap policy that covers additional healthcare costs not included in Medicare, such as copayments, coinsurance, and deductibles.
- **Long-Term Care Insurance:**
  - Tom has a long-term care insurance policy that covers up to $250 per day for nursing home care, assisted living, and in-home care. This policy provides him with peace of mind regarding potential future healthcare costs.

- **Healthcare Concerns:**
    - o Tom's main concern is ensuring that his healthcare and long-term care needs are fully covered without depleting his assets. He is particularly focused on balancing the costs of care with the need to preserve his estate.

ESTATE INFORMATION:

- **Wills:**
    - o Tom has an updated will that outlines the distribution of his assets to his two children and four grandchildren. He has named his eldest child as the executor of his estate.
- **Trusts:**
    - o **Revocable Living Trust:** Tom has established a revocable living trust that holds his primary residence and a portion of his taxable investment accounts. This trust is intended to avoid probate and simplify asset management in case of incapacity.
    - o **Charitable Remainder Trust (CRT):** Tom is considering establishing a CRT to provide income during his lifetime, with the remainder going to a charity of his choice after his death.
- **Power of Attorney:**
    - o Tom has designated his eldest child as the durable power of attorney for financial matters, granting them the authority to manage his financial affairs if he becomes incapacitated.
- **Healthcare Proxy:**
    - o He has appointed his youngest child as his healthcare proxy to make medical decisions on his behalf if he is unable to do so.
- **Beneficiary Designations:**
    - o His IRAs and life insurance policies have his children listed as equal beneficiaries.
- **Estate Tax Planning:**
    - o Tom is working with an estate planning attorney to minimize estate taxes. He is considering additional strategies, such as lifetime gifting to his children and grandchildren and leveraging charitable donations to reduce the size of his taxable estate.

CASE 5: THE DIVORCED SENIOR WITH ADULT CHILDREN

Background:

Linda, a 66-year-old divorced senior, is navigating her retirement years with a strong focus on two primary concerns: ensuring her financial security and well-being while also making sure her two adult children receive her assets in the future. Linda's priorities include covering her living expenses, managing her healthcare needs, and establishing an effective estate plan that reflects her wishes. She is particularly concerned about balancing her desire to leave a legacy for her children with the need to maintain her financial independence.

Planning Process:

1. **Establishing Goals:** Provide financial support for her children and ensure she has sufficient funds for her own needs.
2. **Gathering Data:** Review her current assets, income sources, and existing estate planning documents.
3. **Developing the Plan:** Update her will and set up a trust to manage and distribute her assets to her children. Create a budget that accounts for her expenses and potential healthcare costs.
4. **Implementation:** Work with an estate planning attorney to finalize the trust and update beneficiary designations.
5. **Monitoring and Adjusting:** Regularly review and adjust her financial plan and estate documents to reflect changes in her situation or family dynamics.

Financial Information:

- **Income Sources:**
  - **Social Security:** $2,200 per month
  - **Alimony:** $1,500 per month (set to continue until she turns 70)
  - **Part-Time Work:** $1,000 per month (Linda works part-time as a consultant)
  - **Total Monthly Income:** $4,700

- **Assets:**
  - **Primary Residence:** Valued at $450,000 (mortgage balance: $50,000)
  - **Retirement Accounts (IRA and 401(k)):** $550,000
  - **Taxable Investment Accounts:** $200,000 (stocks, bonds, and mutual funds)
  - **Emergency Fund:** $50,000 in a high-yield savings account
  - **Cash Savings:** $25,000 in a checking account
  - **Total Assets:** $1,275,000
- **Liabilities:**
  - **Mortgage:** $50,000 (monthly payment: $600)
  - **Credit Card Debt:** $5,000 (interest rate: 18%)
  - **Total Liabilities:** $55,000
- **Monthly Expenses:**
  - **Mortgage Payment:** $600
  - **Living Expenses (including utilities, groceries, transportation, etc.):** $2,500
  - **Healthcare Costs (Medicare premiums, supplemental insurance, out-of-pocket costs):** $700
  - **Discretionary Spending (entertainment, dining out, travel):** $1,000.
  - **Debt Payments (credit card):** $200
  - **Total Monthly Expenses:** $5,000
- **Net Worth:**
  - **Total Assets:** $1,275,000
  - **Total Liabilities:** $55,000
  - **Net Worth:** $1,220,000

Financial Goals:

1. **Financial Security:** Linda's primary goal is to ensure she has enough income and savings to cover her living expenses and medical needs throughout her retirement.
2. **Debt Reduction:** She wants to eliminate her remaining mortgage and credit card debt as soon as possible to reduce financial stress and free up more income for savings and discretionary spending.
3. **Legacy Planning:** Linda aims to leave a meaningful inheritance for her two adult children, ensuring that her assets are passed on according to her wishes.
4. **Healthcare and Long-Term Care Planning:** She is concerned about potential healthcare costs and wants to make sure she is adequately covered, including the possibility of long-term care needs.

Investment and Retirement Information:

- **Investment Portfolio Allocation:**
    - **Taxable Investment Accounts:**
        - Stocks: 50% ($100,000)
        - Bonds: 40% ($80,000)
        - Cash/Cash Equivalents: 10% ($20,000)
    - **Retirement Accounts (IRA and 401(k)):**
        - Stocks: 60% ($330,000)
        - Bonds: 35% ($192,500)
        - Cash/Cash Equivalents: 5% ($27,500)
- **Withdrawal Strategy:**
    - Linda is not currently withdrawing from her retirement accounts, as she is relying on Social Security, alimony, and part-time work for her income. She plans to start withdrawing from her retirement accounts at age 70, or sooner, if necessary, to supplement her income.

- **Debt Repayment Strategy:**
    - Linda is considering using a portion of her savings or investment income to pay off her mortgage and credit card debt more quickly, reducing her monthly expenses.
- **Risk Tolerance:**
    - Moderate: Linda is willing to take on some market risk to achieve growth, but she prioritizes preserving her capital, especially given her age and the need to ensure her savings last through retirement.

Medical and Long-Term Care Insurance Information:

- **Medicare:**
    - Linda is enrolled in Medicare Part A and Part B, covering hospital and medical expenses.
- **Medicare Supplement Insurance (Medigap):**
    - She has a Medigap policy that covers additional healthcare costs not included in Medicare, such as copayments, coinsurance, and deductibles.
- **Long-Term Care Insurance:**
    - Linda does not currently have long-term care insurance but is exploring whether it would be a wise investment to protect her savings and provide for potential future care needs.
- **Healthcare Concerns:**
    - Linda is concerned about the rising costs of healthcare as she ages and wants to ensure she is adequately covered, particularly if she needs long-term care. She is exploring her options for either purchasing long-term care insurance or creating a financial plan that accounts for these potential costs.

Estate Information:

- **Will:**
    - Linda has a will in place that outlines her wishes for the distribution of her assets to her two children. She has named her eldest child as the executor of her estate.

- **Trusts:**
    - o **Revocable Living Trust:** Linda is considering establishing a revocable living trust to avoid probate and simplify the transfer of her assets to her children. She is also thinking about setting up a trust to protect her assets from potential creditors and to ensure her children receive their inheritance as she intends.
- **Power of Attorney:**
    - o Linda has designated her youngest child as her durable power of attorney for financial matters, granting them the authority to manage her financial affairs if she becomes incapacitated.
- **Healthcare Proxy:**
    - o She has also established a healthcare proxy, assigning her eldest child to make medical decisions on her behalf if she is unable to do so.
- **Beneficiary Designations:**
    - o Her retirement accounts and life insurance policies have her children listed as equal beneficiaries.
- **Estate Tax Planning:**
    - o Although Linda's estate is not large enough to be subject to federal estate taxes, she is still working with an estate planning attorney to ensure her assets are distributed according to her wishes and to minimize any potential state taxes or probate fees.

CASE 6: THE RETIRED VETERAN WITH SPECIAL BENEFITS

Background:

Richard, a 74-year-old retired military veteran, served in the military for more than 25 years and is now enjoying his retirement. He receives a military pension and has access to various veterans' benefits, including healthcare coverage through the VA. Richard is focused on maximizing the benefits available to him and ensuring that his financial resources are managed effectively to cover his living expenses, healthcare needs, and estate planning goals. Richard is particularly interested in understanding how to best utilize his veterans' benefits in conjunction with his other assets to secure his financial future.

Planning Process:

1. **Establishing Goals:** Ensure full utilization of veterans' benefits and plan for any additional financial needs.
2. **Gathering Data:** Review all veterans' benefits, including pension, healthcare, and any additional support programs.
3. **Developing the Plan:** Develop a plan to maximize the use of benefits and explore additional financial strategies to complement them.
4. **Implementation:** Utilize benefits effectively and adjust the financial plan to include additional savings or investments.
5. **Monitoring and Adjusting:** Regularly review benefits and financial plans to adapt to any changes in available benefits or personal needs.

Financial Information:

- **Income Sources:**
  - **Military Pension:** $3,500 per month
  - **Social Security:** $2,200 per month
  - **Total Monthly Income:** $5,700
- **Assets:**
  - **Primary Residence:** Valued at $350,000 (fully paid off)
  - **Taxable Investment Accounts:** $250,000 (stocks, bonds, and mutual funds)
  - **Retirement Accounts (IRA and 401(k)):** $400,000
  - **Savings Account:** $50,000
  - **Life Insurance Cash Value:** $30,000 (whole life insurance policy)
  - **Total Assets:** $1,080,000
- **Liabilities:**
  - **None:** Richard has no outstanding debts or mortgages.

- **Monthly Expenses:**
    - **Living Expenses (including utilities, groceries, transportation, etc.):** $3,000
    - **Healthcare Costs (including premiums, out-of-pocket costs, etc.):** $300 (for services not covered by VA)
    - **Discretionary Spending (travel, hobbies, dining out):** $1,000.
    - **Total Monthly Expenses:** $4,300
- **Net Worth:**
    - **Total Assets:** $1,080,000
    - **Total Liabilities:** $0
    - **Net Worth:** $1,080,000

Financial Goals:

1. **Maximizing Veterans' Benefits:** Richard's primary goal is to maximize the use of his veterans' benefits, including healthcare and pension benefits, to reduce out-of-pocket expenses and ensure his financial security.
2. **Wealth Preservation:** He aims to preserve his wealth to ensure he can maintain his lifestyle throughout retirement and leave a legacy for his children.
3. **Healthcare Planning:** Richard wants to ensure that his healthcare needs are fully covered, especially as he ages and his healthcare requirements increase.
4. **Estate Planning:** He is concerned about ensuring his estate is in order, including setting up an effective plan for the distribution of his assets to his children and minimizing any potential estate taxes.

Investment and Retirement Information:

- **Investment Portfolio Allocation:**
    - **Taxable Investment Accounts:**
        - Stocks: 60% ($150,000)
        - Bonds: 30% ($75,000)
        - Cash/Cash Equivalents: 10% ($25,000)

  - **Retirement Accounts (IRA and 401(k)):**
    - Stocks: 50% ($200,000)
    - Bonds: 40% ($160,000)
    - Cash/Cash Equivalents: 10% ($40,000)
- **Withdrawal Strategy:**
  - Richard is not currently withdrawing from his retirement accounts, as his military pension and Social Security cover his living expenses. He is considering how to structure withdrawals to minimize taxes and ensure his savings last throughout his retirement.
- **Risk Tolerance:**
  - Moderate: Richard is comfortable with some market risk to achieve growth, but he also prioritizes protecting his capital to ensure his long-term financial security.

Medical and Long-Term Care Insurance Information:

- **VA Healthcare Benefits:**
  - Richard is eligible for comprehensive healthcare through the VA, which covers most of his medical needs, including hospital care, medical services, and prescription drugs.
- **Medicare:**
  - Richard is also enrolled in Medicare Part A and Part B, which provides additional coverage for hospital and medical expenses not covered by the VA.
- **Medicare Supplement Insurance (Medigap):**
  - He has a Medigap policy that helps cover additional healthcare costs not included in Medicare, such as copayments, coinsurance, and deductibles.
- **Long-Term Care Insurance:**
  - Richard does not currently have long-term care insurance but is exploring whether he should purchase a policy to cover potential future costs, such as nursing home care or in-home assistance.

- **Healthcare Concerns:**
    - Richard is concerned about potential gaps in coverage, particularly for long-term care, and wants to ensure he is fully protected without depleting his assets.

ESTATE INFORMATION:

- **Will:**
    - Richard has a will that specifies the distribution of his assets to his two children. He has named his eldest child as the executor of his estate.
- **Trusts:**
    - **Revocable Living Trust:** Richard is considering establishing a revocable living trust to avoid probate and ensure that his estate is managed according to his wishes. This trust will also help streamline the process if he becomes incapacitated.
- **Power of Attorney:**
    - Richard has designated his eldest child as his durable power of attorney for financial matters, giving them the authority to manage his financial affairs if he becomes incapacitated.
- **Healthcare Proxy:**
    - He has established a healthcare proxy, assigning his youngest child to make medical decisions on his behalf if he is unable to do so.
- **Beneficiary Designations:**
    - His retirement accounts and life insurance policies list his children as equal beneficiaries.
- **Estate Tax Planning:**
    - Richard is working with an estate planning attorney to minimize estate taxes. He is considering gifting assets to his children during his lifetime and setting up a charitable remainder trust (CRT) to reduce the size of his taxable estate while benefiting a charity he supports.

CASE 7: THE EARLY RETIREE WITH INVESTMENT INCOME

Background:

Nancy, a 62-year-old early retiree, has been able to retire comfortably thanks to substantial investment income generated from her portfolio of rental properties and dividend-yielding investments. Although she enjoys the freedom of early retirement, Nancy is mindful of the need to effectively manage her income, prepare for future healthcare costs, and plan for potential changes in her income streams as she ages. Her goals include maintaining her current lifestyle, ensuring her healthcare needs are met, and preserving her wealth for her heirs.

Planning Process:

1. **Establishing Goals:** Sustain her lifestyle with investment income and prepare for future healthcare costs.
2. **Gathering Data:** Analyze income sources, investment performance, and projected healthcare costs.
3. **Developing the Plan:** Create a diversified investment strategy and budget that accounts for potential healthcare expenses.
4. **Implementation:** Implement the investment strategy and allocate funds for healthcare and other future needs.
5. **Monitoring and Adjusting:** Regularly review investment performance and healthcare cost projections to adjust the financial plan as needed.

Financial Information:

- **Income Sources:**
    - **Rental Income:** $6,000 per month (from three rental properties)
    - **Dividend Income:** $3,000 per month
    - **Total Monthly Income:** $9,000
- **Assets:**
    - **Primary Residence:** Valued at $500,000 (fully paid off)

- **Rental Properties:**
  - Property 1: Valued at $300,000 (net rental income: $2,000/month)
  - Property 2: Valued at $250,000 (net rental income: $2,000/month)
  - Property 3: Valued at $250,000 (net rental income: $2,000/month)
- **Investment Portfolio (stocks, bonds, mutual funds):** $1,200,000
- **Cash Savings:** $100,000 in a high-yield savings account
- **Total Assets:** $2,600,000

- **Liabilities:**
  - **None:** Nancy has no outstanding debts or mortgages.
- **Monthly Expenses:**
  - **Living Expenses (including utilities, groceries, transportation, etc.):** $4,500
  - **Property Management and Maintenance Costs:** $1,500
  - **Healthcare Costs (including premiums and out-of-pocket costs):** $800.
  - **Discretionary Spending (travel, hobbies, dining out):** $1,500.
  - **Total Monthly Expenses:** $8,300
- **Net Worth:**
  - **Total Assets:** $2,600,000
  - **Total Liabilities:** $0
  - **Net Worth:** $2,600,000

Financial Goals:

1. **Income Management:** Nancy's primary goal is to effectively manage her rental and investment income to ensure it continues to support her lifestyle throughout retirement. She wants to prepare for potential changes in income, such as fluctuations in rental income or market downturns.
2. **Healthcare Planning:** Nancy is concerned about future healthcare costs, particularly as she ages and may require more comprehensive care. She wants to ensure she has adequate coverage and savings to manage these costs.

3. **Wealth Preservation:** She aims to preserve her wealth to maintain her lifestyle and leave a financial legacy for her children and grandchildren.

4. **Tax Efficiency:** Nancy is focused on minimizing her tax liability by optimizing her income streams and taking advantage of tax-efficient strategies for her rental and investment income.

Investment and Retirement Information:

- **Investment Portfolio Allocation:**
    - **Stocks:** 60% ($720,000)
    - **Bonds:** 30% ($360,000)
    - **Cash/Cash Equivalents:** 10% ($120,000)
- **Income from Investments:**
    - **Dividend Yield:** 3% on stocks, generating $21,600 annually ($1,800/month)
    - **Bond Interest:** 4% on bonds, generating $14,400 annually ($1,200/month)
- **Risk Tolerance:**
    - Moderate: Nancy is comfortable with a balanced portfolio that provides growth while also preserving capital. She is cautious about taking on too much risk given her reliance on investment income for her retirement.
- **Property Management:**
    - Nancy manages her rental properties with the help of a property management company, which manages day-to-day operations, tenant relations, and maintenance. She budgets for periodic repairs and potential vacancies.

Medical and Long-Term Care Insurance Information:

- **Health Insurance:**
    - Nancy is currently on a private health insurance plan, as she is not yet eligible for Medicare. She pays premiums of $600 per month with additional out-of-pocket costs for medical care.

- **Long-Term Care Insurance:**
    - o Nancy has not yet purchased long-term care insurance but is considering it as part of her strategy to cover potential future healthcare costs, such as nursing home care or in-home assistance.
- **Healthcare Concerns:**
    - o Nancy is particularly concerned about the potential for rising healthcare costs as she ages and the possibility of requiring long-term care. She wants to explore options for managing these costs without depleting her savings.

Estate Information:

- **Will:**
    - o Nancy has an updated will that specifies the distribution of her assets to her two children and two grandchildren. She has named her eldest child as the executor of her estate.
- **Trusts:**
    - o **Revocable Living Trust:** Nancy has established a revocable living trust that holds her primary residence and a portion of her investment portfolio. This trust is designed to avoid probate and simplify the transfer of assets to her heirs.
- **Power of Attorney:**
    - o Nancy has designated her eldest child as her durable power of attorney for financial matters, allowing them to manage her financial affairs if she becomes incapacitated.
- **Healthcare Proxy:**
    - o She has also established a healthcare proxy, assigning her youngest child to make medical decisions on her behalf if she is unable to do so.
- **Beneficiary Designations:**
    - o Her retirement accounts and life insurance policies list her children as equal beneficiaries.
- **Estate Tax Planning:**
    - o Although Nancy's estate is not large enough to be subject to federal estate taxes, she is working with an estate planning attorney to ensure her assets are distributed according to her wishes and to minimize any potential state taxes or probate.

CASE 8: THE COUPLE PLANNING FOR A LEGACY

BACKGROUND:

Ella and Robert, both 78 years old, are focused on leaving a meaningful financial legacy for their grandchildren while ensuring they have sufficient resources to cover their current living expenses and healthcare needs. They have carefully managed their finances throughout their lives and are now at a stage where they want to make sure their wealth benefits future generations without compromising their own financial security.

PLANNING PROCESS:

1. **Establishing Goals:** Ensure a meaningful legacy for their grandchildren and maintain their current standard of living.
2. **Gathering Data:** Review assets, income sources, and current estate planning documents.
3. **Developing the Plan:** Create a strategy to distribute assets to their grandchildren through trusts or other mechanisms, while also setting up a sustainable budget for their own expenses.
4. **Implementation:** Work with estate planning professionals to finalize trusts or other legacy plans and adjust their investment strategy to support their goals.
5. **Monitoring and Adjusting:** Regularly review the legacy plan and financial situation to adjust based on changes in financial needs or market conditions.

FINANCIAL INFORMATION:

- **Income Sources:**
    - **Rental Income:** $6,000 per month (from three rental properties)
    - **Dividend Income:** $3,000 per month
    - **Total Monthly Income:** $9,000
- **Assets:**
    - **Primary Residence:** Valued at $500,000 (fully paid off)

  - **Rental Properties:**
    - Property 1: Valued at $300,000 (net rental income: $2,000/month)
    - Property 2: Valued at $250,000 (net rental income: $2,000/month)
    - Property 3: Valued at $250,000 (net rental income: $2,000/month)
  - **Investment Portfolio (stocks, bonds, mutual funds):** $1,200,000
  - **Cash Savings:** $100,000 in a high-yield savings account.
  - **Total Assets:** $2,600,000
- **Liabilities:**
  - **None:** Nancy has no outstanding debts or mortgages.
- **Monthly Expenses:**
  - **Living Expenses (including utilities, groceries, transportation, etc.):** $4,500
  - **Property Management and Maintenance Costs:** $1,500
  - **Healthcare Costs (including premiums and out-of-pocket costs):** $800.
  - **Discretionary Spending (travel, hobbies, dining out):** $1,500
  - **Total Monthly Expenses:** $8,300
- **Net Worth:**
  - **Total Assets:** $2,600,000
  - **Total Liabilities:** $0
  - **Net Worth:** $2,600,000

Financial Goals:

1. **Income Management:** Nancy's primary goal is to effectively manage her rental and investment income to ensure it continues to support her lifestyle throughout retirement. She wants to prepare for potential changes in income, such as fluctuations in rental income or market downturns.
2. **Healthcare Planning:** Nancy is concerned about future healthcare costs, particularly as she ages and may require more comprehensive care. She wants to ensure she has adequate coverage and savings to manage these costs.

3. **Wealth Preservation:** She aims to preserve her wealth to maintain her lifestyle and leave a financial legacy for her children and grandchildren.

4. **Tax Efficiency:** Nancy is focused on minimizing her tax liability by optimizing her income streams and taking advantage of tax-efficient strategies for her rental and investment income.

Investment and Retirement Information:

- **Investment Portfolio Allocation:**
  - **Stocks:** 60% ($720,000)
  - **Bonds:** 30% ($360,000)
  - **Cash/Cash Equivalents:** 10% ($120,000)
- **Income from Investments:**
  - **Dividend Yield:** 3% on stocks, generating $21,600 annually ($1,800/month)
  - **Bond Interest:** 4% on bonds, generating $14,400 annually ($1,200/month)
- **Risk Tolerance:**
  - Moderate: Nancy is comfortable with a balanced portfolio that provides growth while also preserving capital. She is cautious about taking on too much risk given her reliance on investment income for her retirement.
- **Property Management:**
  - Nancy manages her rental properties with the help of a property management company, which manages day-to-day operations, tenant relations, and maintenance. She budgets for periodic repairs and potential vacancies.

Medical and Long-Term Care Insurance Information:

- **Health Insurance:**
  - Nancy is currently on a private health insurance plan, as she is not yet eligible for Medicare. She pays premiums of $600 per month with additional out-of-pocket costs for medical care.

- **Long-Term Care Insurance:**
    - o Nancy has not yet purchased long-term care insurance but is considering it as part of her strategy to cover potential future healthcare costs, such as nursing home care or in-home assistance.
- **Healthcare Concerns:**
    - o Nancy is particularly concerned about the potential for rising healthcare costs as she ages and the possibility of requiring long-term care. She wants to explore options for managing these costs without depleting her savings.

Estate Information:

- **Will:**
    - o Nancy has an updated will that specifies the distribution of her assets to her two children and two grandchildren. She has named her eldest child as the executor of her estate.
- **Trusts:**
    - o **Revocable Living Trust:** Nancy has established a revocable living trust that holds her primary residence and a portion of her investment portfolio. This trust is designed to avoid probate and simplify the transfer of assets to her heirs.
- **Power of Attorney:**
    - o Nancy has designated her eldest child as her durable power of attorney for financial matters, allowing them to manage her financial affairs if she becomes incapacitated.
- **Healthcare Proxy:**
    - o She has also established a healthcare proxy, assigning her youngest child to make medical decisions on her behalf if she is unable to do so.
- **Beneficiary Designations:**
    - o Her retirement accounts and life insurance policies list her children as equal beneficiaries.
- **Estate Tax Planning:**
    - o Although Nancy's estate is not large enough to be subject to federal estate taxes, she is working with an estate planning attorney to ensure her assets are distributed according to her wishes and to minimize any potential state taxes or probate fees.

Appendix

CFP Board Practice Standards for the Financial Planning Process

1. Understanding the Client's Personal and Financial Circumstances
    - Gather quantitative information (e.g., assets, liabilities, cash flow).
    - Collect qualitative information (e.g., goals, priorities, values).
2. Identifying and Selecting Goals
    - Determine the client's short-term and long-term financial goals.
    - Prioritize goals based on the client's circumstances and values.
3. Analyzing the Client's Current Course of Action and Potential Alternatives
    - Evaluate the client's current financial situation.
    - Identify potential financial strategies and alternatives.
4. Developing the Financial Planning Recommendations
    - Formulate recommendations based on the analysis.
    - Ensure recommendations align with client goals and circumstances.
5. Presenting the Financial Planning Recommendations
    - Communicate the recommendations to the client.
    - Explain the rationale behind each recommendation.
6. Implementing the Financial Planning Recommendations
    - Put the agreed-upon recommendations into action.
    - Coordinate with other professionals as needed.
7. Monitoring Progress and Updating
    - Regularly review the client's situation.
    - Adjust the plan as necessary to ensure it stays aligned with the client's goals.

Certified Family Life Educator (CFLE)

The Certified Family Life Educator (CFLE) designation is awarded by the National Council on Family Relations (NCFR) to professionals who demonstrate expertise in the field of family life education. This certification ensures that individuals are well-equipped to support and educate families across a range of issues. The CFLE designation is built upon ten core competencies, which encompass the essential knowledge and skills required to effectively educate and assist families. Below is a summary of these core competencies:

Families and Individuals in Societal Contexts: This competency involves understanding the diversity and dynamics of families in relation to societal influences, such as culture, community, and social institutions. Professionals must be able to recognize how these factors shape family structures, roles, and relationships, and apply this knowledge to support and strengthen families.

Internal Dynamics of Families: Focused on the internal processes and relationships within families, this competency includes understanding communication patterns, conflict resolution, decision-making, and the impact of stress on family functioning. Professionals are trained to help families navigate these dynamics to promote healthy relationships and functioning.

Human Growth and Development Across the Lifespan: This area covers the stages of human development from birth through old age, emphasizing the physical, emotional, cognitive, and social changes that individuals experience. CFLEs apply this knowledge to support family members at different life stages and to address age-specific challenges.

Human Sexuality: This competency involves understanding human sexuality and sexual development across the lifespan, including the biological, psychological, and social aspects. CFLEs are equipped to educate individuals and families on sexual health, relationships, and the impact of sexuality on family dynamics.

Interpersonal Relationships: This area focuses on the development and maintenance of healthy interpersonal relationships, including communication skills, empathy, and conflict resolution. Professionals work to enhance individuals' relationship skills, contributing to stronger family bonds and improved social interactions.

Family Resource Management: This competency involves understanding the management of family resources, including time, money, and energy. CFLEs are trained to help families set goals, budget, make financial decisions, and utilize resources effectively to meet their needs and achieve long-term stability.

Parenting Education and Guidance: This area focuses on parenting practices and child-rearing strategies that promote healthy child development and family well-being. CFLEs provide education and support to parents, helping them to navigate the challenges of raising children and to foster positive parent–child relationships.

Family Law and Public Policy: This competency encompasses knowledge of family-related laws, policies, and ethical considerations. CFLEs understand the legal rights and responsibilities of family members and the impact of public policy on family life. They are trained to advocate for families and to navigate the legal and policy frameworks that affect them.

Professional Ethics and Practice: This area emphasizes the ethical standards and professional practices that guide family life educators. CFLEs are committed to maintaining confidentiality, respecting cultural diversity, and adhering to ethical guidelines in their work with families.

Family Life Education Methodology: This competency involves the design, implementation, and evaluation of educational programs that address family life issues. CFLEs are skilled in creating and delivering educational materials and programs that are responsive to the needs of families, utilizing evidence-based practices to achieve desired outcomes.

These core competencies collectively ensure that CFLE are well-prepared to support and educate families in a holistic and professional manner, promoting healthy family functioning and contributing to the well-being of individuals and communities (CFLE Credential | National Council on Family Relations, n.d.).

Monthly Budget Example

CATEGORY	MONTHLY BUDGET
Income	
Pension	$1,800
Social Security	$1,600
Investment income	$500
Total monthly income	$3,900
Expenses	
Housing (utilities, maintenance)	$800
Groceries	$400
Transportation (gas, insurance)	$200
Healthcare (Medicare, Medigap)	$400
Entertainment and recreation	$200
Insurance (home, auto, etc.)	$150
Discretionary spending	$300
Savings	$350
Total monthly expenses	$2,800
Net surplus	$1,100

Monthly Budget Worksheet

CATEGORY	PLANNED AMOUNT	ACTUAL AMOUNT	DIFFERENCE
Income			
Pension	$	$	$
Social Security	$	$	$
Investment income	$	$	$
Total monthly income	$	$	$
Expenses			
Housing (rent/mortgage, utilities, maintenance)	$	$	$
Groceries	$	$	$
Transportation (gas, insurance)	$	$	$
Healthcare (Medicare, Medigap, out-of-pocket)	$	$	$
Insurance (home, auto, etc.)	$	$	$
Entertainment and recreation	$	$	$
Discretionary spending (dining out, hobbies)	$	$	$
Savings	$	$	$
Total monthly expenses	$	$	$
Net surplus/deficit	$	$	$

Instructions:

Fill in the "Planned Amount" column with your expected income and expenses.

Track your "Actual Amount" spent in each category throughout the month.

Calculate the "Difference" to see if you are staying within your budget.

Use the "Net surplus/deficit" to determine if you need to adjust your spending or savings.

Net Worth Statement Example

NET WORTH STATEMENT

As of [Date]

Assets	Amount
Cash and cash equivalents	
Checking account	$5,000
Savings account	$25,000
Investments	
401(k) account	$450,000
IRA account	$200,000
Brokerage account	$100,000
Real estate	
Primary residence	$350,000
Personal property	
Automobile	$15,000
Personal belongings (furniture, jewelry, etc.)	$10,000
Total assets	$1,155,000
Liabilities	Amount
Current liabilities	
Credit card debt	$2,000
Long-term liabilities	
Mortgage (none, house paid off)	$0
Total liabilities	$2,000
Net worth	$1,153,000

Net Worth Statement Worksheet

NET WORTH STATEMENT WORKSHEET		
As of [Date]		
Assets		
Category	**Description**	**Value**
Cash and cash equivalents	Checking account	$
	Savings account	$
	Money market accounts	$
Investments	401(k) account	$
	IRA account	$
	Brokerage account	$
Real estate	Primary residence	$
	Rental property	$
Personal property	Automobile	$
	Furniture, jewelry, etc.	$
Other assets	Annuities	$
	Life insurance (cash value)	$
Total assets		**$**
Liabilities		
Category	**Description**	**Value**
Current liabilities	Credit card debt	$
	Medical bills	$
Long-term liabilities	Mortgage	$
	Home equity loan	$
	Other loans	$
Total liabilities		**$**

Net worth calculation		
Description	**Value**	
Total assets	$	
Total liabilities	$	
Net worth	$	

Instructions:

1. Fill in the value of each asset and liability.
2. Calculate the total assets and liabilities.
3. Subtract total liabilities from total assets to determine the net worth.
4. Review and update the worksheet periodically to reflect any changes in assets or liabilities.

Personal Statement of Cash Flows Example

PERSONAL STATEMENT OF CASH FLOWS

For the Month Ending [Date]

Cash Inflows

Source	Amount
Pension	$1,800
Social Security	$1,600
Investment income (dividends, interest)	$500
Rental income	$0
Other income (annuities, part-time work)	$0
Cash Outflows	
Category	**Amount**
Housing (utilities, maintenance)	$800
Groceries	$400
Transportation (gas, insurance)	$200
Healthcare (Medicare, Medigap, out-of-pocket)	$400
Insurance (home, auto, etc.)	$150
Entertainment and recreation	$200
Discretionary spending (dining out, hobbies)	$300
Savings contributions	$350
Total cash outflows	$2,800
Net cash flow	
Description	**Amount**
Total cash inflows	$3,900
Total cash outflows	$2,800
Net cash flow	$1,100

Personal Statement of Cash Flows Worksheet

PERSONAL STATEMENT OF CASH FLOWS WORKSHEET

For the Month Ending [Date]

Cash Inflows

Source	Planned Amount	Actual Amount	Difference
Pension	$	$	$
Social Security	$	$	$
Investment income (dividends, interest)	$	$	$
Rental income	$	$	$
Other income (annuities, part-time work)	$	$	$
Total cash inflows	**$**	**$**	**$**
Cash outflows			
Category	**Planned Amount**	**Actual Amount**	**Difference**
Housing (rent/mortgage, utilities, maintenance)	$	$	$
Groceries	$	$	$
Transportation (gas, insurance)	$	$	$
Healthcare (Medicare, Medigap, out-of-pocket)	$	$	$
Insurance (home, auto, etc.)	$	$	$
Entertainment and recreation	$	$	$
Discretionary spending (dining out, hobbies)	$	$	$
Savings contributions	$	$	$
Total cash outflows	**$**	**$**	**$**
Net cash flow calculation			
Description	**Amount**		
Total cash inflows	$		
Total cash outflows	$		
Net cash flow	$		

Instructions:

1. Fill in the "Planned Amount" for each source of income and expense category at the start of the month.
2. Track the "Actual Amount" throughout the month.
3. Calculate the "Difference" to see if you are staying within your budget.
4. Use the "Net cash flow" to assess whether your income covers your expenses or if adjustments are needed.

Estimate Your Annual Cost of Living Worksheet

Complete the first column with your current spending. Then calculate the Inflation Factor based on the steps listed above the Inflation Factor Table on page 3. Place the inflation factor in the second column either for the total or for each category of costs.) Multiply column 1 by column 2 to compute the income you wil lneed during your first year of retirement.

	Current Spending	**Inflation Factor**	**Future Budget at Retirement in_____ years**
Housing			
Household Maintenance			
Automobile/Transportation			
Food			
Clothing			
Personal			
Medical/Health			
Recreation/Education			
Contributions			
Taxes/Insurance			
Savings, investments			
Variable Essential Expenses (ex. gifts, license plates, holiday spending, etc.)			
ANNUAL TOTAL			

Inflation Factor Table

(1) Choose the number of years until your retirement starts from the "Years to Retirement" column on the left of Table 1.
(2) Then select an estimated annual inflation rate from the row across the top. Inflation cannot be predicted from year to year. In 1980, it was 12.4%. In 2001, it was 1.6%. In 2007, it was 4.1%. You must make an educated guess.
(3) Read across and down to find the appropriate inflation factor corresponding to your predicted rate of inflation. For example, 10 years at 6% inflation gives a factor of 1.79.
(4) Multiply your estimated annual cost of living expenses from the first column of Worksheet 2 by the inflation factor to get an idea of the amount of income you will need for your first year of retirement if you want to maintain your current lifestyle. (Example: $14,000 × 1.79 = $25,060.)

	ANNUAL INFLATION RATE									
YEARS TO RETIREMENT	2%	3%	4%	5%	6%	7%	8%	9%	10%	11%
1	1.02	1.03	1.04	1.05	1.06	1.07	1.08	1.09	1.10	1.11
2	1.04	1.06	1.08	1.10	1.12	1.15	1.17	1.19	1.21	1.23
3	1.06	1.09	1.13	1.16	1.19	1.23	1.60	1.30	1.33	1.37
4	1.08	1.13	1.17	1.22	1.26	1.31	1.36	1.41	1.46	1.52
5	1.10	1.16	1.22	1.28	1.34	1.40	1.47	1.54	1.61	1.69
6	1.13	1.19	1.27	1.34	1.42	1.50	1.59	1.68	1.77	1.87
7	1.15	1.23	1.32	1.41	1.50	1.59	1.71	1.83	1.95	2.08
8	1.17	1.27	1.37	1.48	1.59	1.71	1.85	1.99	2.14	2.30
9	1.20	1.31	1.42	1.55	1.69	1.85	2.00	2.17	2.36	2.56
10	1.22	1.34	1.48	1.63	1.79	1.97	2.16	2.37	2.59	2.84
11	1.24	1.38	1.54	1.71	1.90	2.11	2.33	2.58	2.85	3.15
12	1.27	1.43	1.60	1.80	2.01	2.25	2.52	2.81	3.14	3.50
13	1.29	1.47	1.67	1.89	2.13	2.41	2.72	3.07	3.45	3.88
14	1.32	1.51	1.73	1.98	2.26	2.58	2.94	3.34	3.80	4.31
15	1.35	1.56	1.80	2.08	2.40	2.76	3.17	0.36	4.18	4.78
16	1.37	1.61	1.87	2.18	2.54	2.95	3.43	3.97	4.60	5.31
17	1.40	1.65	1.95	2.29	2.69	3.16	3.70	4.33	5.05	5.90
18	1.43	170.00	2.03	2.41	2.85	0.38	4.00	4.72	5.56	6.54
19	1.46	1.75	2.11	2.53	3.03	3.62	4.32	5.14	6.12	7.26
20	1.49	1.81	2.19	2.65	3.21	3.87	4.66	5.60	6.73	8.06

Financial Risk Tolerance Worksheet for Elderly Clients

Client Name:	
Date:	
Planner Name:	
Part 1: Client Profile	
1. Age:	
2. Health Status (e.g., Excellent, Good, Fair, Poor):	
3. Expected Retirement Duration (Years in Retirement):	
4. Key Financial Goals (List and prioritize):	
5. Primary Income Sources:	
6. Monthly Income vs. Expenses Overview:	
Part 2: Investment Experience	
1. Describe your previous investment experience (None, Limited, Moderate, Extensive):	
2. Types of investments	
3. Reaction to previous market downturns (Sold, Held, Bought More):	
Part 3: Financial Goals and Priorities	
1. Rank Financial Goals (e.g., Maintaining lifestyle, Healthcare, Legacy):	
2. Investment Time Horizon for Major Goals:	
3. Importance of Liquidity (Ability to quickly convert to	

Part 4: Risk Tolerance Assessment

1. How would you react if your investment balance fell by 10% in one year?

Sell all investments

Sell some

Do nothing

Buy more

2. What return do you expect from your investments? (Low, Moderate, High):

3. Are you willing to accept high volatility for potentially higher returns? (Yes, No, Unsure):

Part 5: Scenario Analysis

1. If your investments did well and grew 20% in one year, what would you do?

Sell all and secure gains

Sell a portion and rebalance

Keep all and do nothing

Invest more

2. If your investments perform poorly for multiple years, would you adjust your lifestyle? (Yes, No, Unsure?):

Part 6: Conclusion and Planning

1. Overall Risk Tolerance Level (Assign based on responses):

Low

Moderate

High

2. Financial Planner's Recommendations (Based on risk tolerance and financial goals):

Instructions for Use:

Preparation: Have clients fill this out before the meeting to allow for preliminary analysis.

Discussion: Use this worksheet as a discussion guide during client meetings to explore responses and clarify financial goals and risk tolerance.

Review: Regularly revisit this worksheet to adjust the financial plan as client situations or market conditions change.

Estimating Changes in Retirement Spending Worksheet

Use this worksheet to calculate possible changes in your expenses. For each expense category, figure the difference between what you are spending now and what you expect to spend after retirement. If the retirement expense will be lower, put the difference in the "less" column; if it will be higher, put the difference in the "more" column. Add the figures in both columns and compare the totals. Which total is larger? What does that suggest about your future spending? Will you need to make some changes in what you expect to spend?

Expense	**Spending How**	**Spending Expected in Retirement**	**Less After Retirement**	**More After Retirement**
Work related:				
Transportation				
Clothing				
Dues				
Meals				
Other				
Social Security Taxes Withheld				
Income Taxes				
Pension Plan Contributions				
Contributions to other Retirement Accounts (IRAs, etc)				
Savings, investments for retirement				
Travel				
Entertainment, leisure activities				
Health insurance				
Other health care costs				
TOTALS				

Adapted from Financial Planning for Retirement, NCR-265, Field and Hathaway, Michigan State University CES.

Estimated Annual Cost of Living ____Years After Retirement

	Current Spending	Inflation Factor	Future Budget at Retirement in_____ years
Housing			
Household Maintenance			
Automobile/Transportation			
Food			
Clothing			
Personal			
Medical/Health			
Recreation/Education			
Contributions			
Taxes/Insurance			
Savings, investments			
Variable Essential Expenses (ex. gifts, license plates, holiday spending, etc.)			
ANNUAL TOTAL			

Expectation of Life by Age and Sex

ALL RACES			
Age	**Total**	**Male**	**Female**
0	77.4	74.7	80.0
1	77.0	74.3	79.5
5	73.1	70.4	75.6
10	68.1	65.5	70.6
15	63.2	60.5	65.7
20	58.4	55.8	60.8
25	53.6	51.2	56.0
30	48.9	46.5	51.1
35	44.1	41.8	46.3
40	39.5	37.2	41.5
45	34.9	32.8	36.9
50	30.5	28.5	32.3
55	26.2	24.3	27.9
60	22.2	20.4	23.7
65	18.4	16.8	19.7
70	14.8	13.4	15.9
75	11.7	10.5	12.5
80	8.9	7.9	9.5
85	6.6	5.9	7.0
90	4.8	4.3	5.0
95	3.5	3.1	3.5
100	2.5	2.2	2.5

Source: National Vital Statistics Report, Vol. 54, No. 14, April 19, 2006, Report revised March 28, 2007. Retrieved August 5, 2009
www.cdc.gov/nchs/data/nvsr/nvsr54/nvsr54_14.pdf

Estimated Annual Cost of Living ____Years After Retirement

	CURRENT SPENDING	INFLATION FACTOR	FUTURE BUDGET AT RETIREMENT IN____ YEARS
Housing			
Household maintenance			
Automobile/transportation			
Food			
Clothing			
Personal			
Medical/health			
Recreation/education			
Contributions			
Taxes/insurance			
Savings, investments			
Variable essential expenses (e.g., gifts, license plates, holiday spending, etc.)			
ANNUAL TOTAL			

Large Future Irregular Expenses Worksheet

	YEAR BOUGHT	AVERAGE EXPECTED YEARS OF LIFE	YEAR TO REPLACE	PRESENT REPLACEMENT PRICE	ESTIMATED PRICE IN REPLACEMENT YEAR*
Vehicles:					
Car		?		–	–
Other vehicles		?			–
Appliances:				–	–
Range		12-13			
Refrigerator		15			
Dishwasher		11			
Washer		11			
Dryer		13–14			
Freezer		20			
Furnace		25–30			
Water heater		12			
Other					
House:					
Roof (varies with type)		15-30			
Fencing		20–30			
Other					
Furnishings:					
Carpet		8-15			
Drapes, window treatments		10			
Flooring, hard surface		15			
Furniture		Will vary			
Other					

* Calculate by counting the number of years until the replacement year. Then, choose an inflation factor from the chart and multiply by the "Present Replacement Price."

Source: Adapted from *Financial Planning for Retirement*, NCR-264, Field and Hathaway, Michigan State University CES, 5/87.

Age to Receive Full Social Security Benefits

YEAR OF BIRTH	FULL RETIREMENT AGE	AGE 62 REDUCTION IN MONTHS	MONTHLY % REDUCTION	TOTAL % REDUCTION
1937 or earlier	65	36	0.555	20
1938	65 and 2 months	38	0.548	20.83
1939	65 and 4 months	40	0.541	21.67
1940	65 and 6 months	42	0.535	22.5
1941	65 and 8 months	44	0.53	23.33
1942	65 and 10 months	46	0.525	24.17
1943-1954	66	48	0.52	25
1955	66 and 2 months	50	0.516	25.84
1956	66 and 4 months	52	0.512	26.66
1957	66 and 6 months	54	0.509	27.5
1958	66 and 8 months	56	0.505	28.33
1959	66 and 10 months	58	0.502	29.17
1960 and later	67	60	0.5	30

Note: This information is also available on the Internet at www.ssa.gov/pubs/#retirement.

Benefit Increases for Delayed Retirement

YEAR OF BIRTH	YEARLY PERCENTAGE INCREASE
1933-1934	5.50%
1935-1936	6.00%
1937-1938	6.50%
1939-1940	7.00%
1941-1942	7.50%
1943 or later	8.00%

Source: U.S. Department of Health and Human Services, Washington, D.C.: Retirement Benefits. Retrieved August 2006 from www.ssa.gov/retire2/delayret.htm

Estimated Annual Income After Retirement Worksheet

Estimated Annual Income After Retirement Worksheet			
Look 10 years into retirement and see how your estimated income will keep up with inflation. In the first column, copy your figures from "Estimated Annual Income After Retirement." Then, for each source of income, estimate how it will grow over the next 10 years. Some sources, like a pension or fixed annuity, will not change. For those sources that could change, use the same inflation rate from the table. Compare your estimated income 10 years after retirement with your estimated expenses 10 years after retirement.			
Inflation Rate = ______________ %			
	Yearly Income at Retirement	Inflation Factor	Yearly Income 10 Years After Retirement
1. Social Security:			
Man's age			
Woman's age			
2. Pensions and Employer Benefits:			
Company			
State or federal government Veteran's			
Union or other Profit-sharing Deferred pay Other			
3. Savings and Investments: IRA/Roth IRA			
Keogh or SEP			
Savings account (interest) Money market (interest) Treasury securities (interest)			
Mutual funds (dividends, capital gains) Stocks (dividends)			
Bonds (dividends) Real estate			
Farm/business rent or installment payments home equity conversion			
Annuities Other			
4. Earnings:			
Salary, wages			
Commissions, royalties, fees Partnership income			
5. Income from Assets That Could Be Liquidated Real estate			
Mutual funds Stocks Bonds			
Antiques, collectibles Farm/business			
Anticipated gifts or inheritance			
ESTIMATED TOTAL GROSS INCOME			
6. Possible Deductions from Income			
Federal income tax			
State/county tax			
Social Security tax			
ESTIMATED TOTAL DEDUCTIONS **(Subtract total tax deductions from total gross income to estimate your total net income.)** TOTAL ESTIMATED NET INCOME			
Compare estimated income 10 years after retirement to estimated expenses 10 years after retirement (calculated at inflation rate % with inflation factor of). Will you have a positive balance of $ extra income? OR A negative balance of $ less income than expenses? TOTAL ESTIMATED NET INCOME			

Adapted from *Financial Planning for Retirement*, NCR-264, Field and Hathaway, Michigan State University CES, 5/87.

Monthly Cost of Living Worksheet

Shelter		**Medical and Health**	
Rent or mortgage payments		Medications	
Real estate taxes		Physician, dentist, hospital	
Home insurance		Eyeglasses, hearing aids	
		Health insurance	
Household Operation and		**Recreation, Education, and Other**	
Home repair, yard care		Books, newspapers, magazines	
Water		Club memberships, dues	
Telephone, TV dish/cable		Movies, sports events, concerts	
Waste disposal		Sport and hobby equipment, supplies	
Cleaning and laundry supplies		Vacations, celebrations, weekend trips	
Electric		Adult continuing education	
Gas, fuel oil		Pets: care, food, license	
Furniture, fixtures		Other	
Garden, yard equipment, supplies			
Other			
Food, Beverages		**Contributions**	
Food at home		Church	
Food away from home		Charities	
Entertaining expenses		Gifts	
Automobile and Transportation		**Taxes and Insurance**	
Car payment		U.S. taxes	
Repairs		State taxes	
Gasoline and oil		Local taxes	
License, registration Insurance		Life insurance	
Other transportation		Property insurance (not homeowners)	
Clothing		**Savings, Investments**	
New clothing		Banks, savings and loan, credit union	
Laundry not done at home		Company pension, profit-sharing plan	
Dry cleaning		Stocks, bonds, real estate Retirement: Keogh, IRA	
Shoe repair			
Personal		**Irregular Expenses**	
Cosmetics and toiletries			
Barber and beauty shops			
Smoking supplies, alcohol			
Stationery, postage			
TOTAL MONTHLY EXPENSES			

Adapted from *Ready. Set. Retire: Financial Planning*, PM-1167a. Danes, Dippold, Schuchardt, Iowa State University CES, 11/85 (based on information from the original *Financial Planning for Retirement*, NCR-264 by Anne Field and Irene Hathaway.

Time Value of Money (TVM) Tables

Table 1 - Future value interest factors for single cash flows. Formula: FV = (1 + k)^n

Period (n) / per cent	1%	2%	3%	4%	5%	6%	7%	8%	9%	10%	11%	12%	13%	14%	15%	16%	20%
1	1.0100	1.0200	1.0300	1.0400	1.0500	1.0600	1.0700	1.0800	1.0900	1.1000	1.1100	1.1200	1.1300	1.1400	1.1500	1.1600	1.2000
2	1.0201	1.0404	1.0609	1.0816	1.1025	1.1236	1.1449	1.1664	1.1881	1.2100	1.2321	1.2544	1.2769	1.2996	1.3225	1.3456	1.4400
3	1.0303	1.0612	1.0927	1.1249	1.1576	1.1910	1.2250	1.2597	1.2950	1.3310	1.3676	1.4049	1.4429	1.4815	1.5209	1.5609	1.7280
4	1.0406	1.0824	1.1255	1.1699	1.2155	1.2625	1.3108	1.3605	1.4116	1.4641	1.5181	1.5735	1.6305	1.6890	1.7490	1.8106	2.0736
5	1.0510	1.1041	1.1593	1.2167	1.2763	1.3382	1.4026	1.4693	1.5386	1.6105	1.6851	1.7623	1.8424	1.9254	2.0114	2.1003	2.4883
6	1.0615	1.1262	1.1941	1.2653	1.3401	1.4185	1.5007	1.5869	1.6771	1.7716	1.8704	1.9738	2.0820	2.1950	2.3131	2.4364	2.9860
7	1.0721	1.1487	1.2299	1.3159	1.4071	1.5036	1.6058	1.7138	1.8280	1.9487	2.0762	2.2107	2.3526	2.5023	2.6600	2.8262	3.5832
8	1.0829	1.1717	1.2668	1.3686	1.4775	1.5938	1.7182	1.8509	1.9926	2.1436	2.3045	2.4760	2.6584	2.8526	3.0590	3.2784	4.2998
9	1.0937	1.1951	1.3048	1.4233	1.5513	1.6895	1.8385	1.9990	2.1719	2.3579	2.5580	2.7731	3.0040	3.2519	3.5179	3.8030	5.1598
10	1.1046	1.2190	1.3439	1.4802	1.6289	1.7908	1.9672	2.1589	2.3674	2.5937	2.8394	3.1058	3.3946	3.7072	4.0456	4.4114	6.1917
11	1.1157	1.2434	1.3842	1.5395	1.7103	1.8983	2.1049	2.3316	2.5804	2.8531	3.1518	3.4785	3.8359	4.2262	4.6524	5.1173	7.4301
12	1.1268	1.2682	1.4258	1.6010	1.7959	2.0122	2.2522	2.5182	2.8127	3.1384	3.4985	3.8960	4.3345	4.8179	5.3503	5.9360	8.9161
13	1.1381	1.2936	1.4685	1.6651	1.8856	2.1329	2.4098	2.7196	3.0658	3.4523	3.8833	4.3635	4.8980	5.4924	6.1528	6.8858	10.6993
14	1.1495	1.3195	1.5126	1.7317	1.9799	2.2609	2.5785	2.9372	3.3417	3.7975	4.3104	4.8871	5.5348	6.2613	7.0757	7.9875	12.8392
15	1.1610	1.3459	1.5580	1.8009	2.0789	2.3966	2.7590	3.1722	3.6425	4.1772	4.7846	5.4736	6.2543	7.1379	8.1371	9.2655	15.4070
16	1.1726	1.3728	1.6047	1.8730	2.1829	2.5404	2.9522	3.4259	3.9703	4.5950	5.3109	6.1304	7.0673	8.1372	9.3576	10.7480	18.4884
17	1.1843	1.4002	1.6528	1.9479	2.2920	2.6928	3.1588	3.7000	4.3276	5.0545	5.8951	6.8660	7.9861	9.2765	10.7613	12.4677	22.1861
18	1.1961	1.4282	1.7024	2.0258	2.4066	2.8543	3.3799	3.9960	4.7171	5.5599	6.5436	7.6900	9.0243	10.5752	12.3755	14.4625	26.6233
19	1.2081	1.4568	1.7535	2.1068	2.5270	3.0256	3.6165	4.3157	5.1417	6.1159	7.2633	8.6128	10.1974	12.0557	14.2318	16.7765	31.9480
20	1.2202	1.4859	1.8061	2.1911	2.6533	3.2071	3.8697	4.6610	5.6044	6.7275	8.0623	9.6463	11.5231	13.7435	16.3665	19.4608	38.3376
21	1.2324	1.5157	1.8603	2.2788	2.7860	3.3996	4.1406	5.0338	6.1088	7.4002	8.9492	10.8038	13.0211	15.6676	18.8215	22.5745	46.0051
22	1.2447	1.5460	1.9161	2.3699	2.9253	3.6035	4.4304	5.4365	6.6586	8.1403	9.9336	12.1003	14.7138	17.8610	21.6447	26.1864	55.2061
23	1.2572	1.5769	1.9736	2.4647	3.0715	3.8197	4.7405	5.8715	7.2579	8.9543	11.0263	13.5523	16.6266	20.3616	24.8915	30.3762	66.2474
24	1.2697	1.6084	2.0328	2.5633	3.2251	4.0489	5.0724	6.3412	7.9111	9.8497	12.2392	15.1786	18.7881	23.2122	28.6252	35.2364	79.4968
25	1.2824	1.6406	2.0938	2.6658	3.3864	4.2919	5.4274	6.8485	8.6231	10.8347	13.5855	17.0001	21.2305	26.4619	32.9190	40.8742	95.3962

Table 2 - Future value interest factors for an annuity. Formula: FV = [(1 + k)^n - 1] / k

Period (n) / per	1%	2%	3%	4%	5%	6%	7%	8%	9%	10%	11%	12%	13%	14%	15%	16%	20%
1	1.0000	1.0200	1.0300	1.0400	1.0500	1.0600	1.0700	1.0800	1.0800	1.1000	1.1100	1.1200	1.1300	1.1400	1.1500	1.1600	1.2000
2	2.0100	2.0200	2.0300	2.0400	2.0500	2.0600	2.0700	2.0800	2.0900	2.1000	2.1100	2.1200	2.1300	2.1400	2.1500	2.1600	2.2000
3	3.0301	3.0604	3.0909	3.1216	3.1525	3.1836	3.2149	3.2464	3.2781	3.3100	3.3421	3.3744	3.4069	3.4396	3.4725	3.5056	3.6400
4	4.0604	4.1216	4.1836	4.2465	4.3101	4.3746	4.4399	4.5061	4.5731	4.6410	4.7097	4.7793	4.8498	4.9211	4.9934	5.0665	5.3680
5	5.1010	5.2040	5.3091	5.4163	5.5256	5.6371	5.7507	5.8666	5.9847	6.1051	6.2278	6.3528	6.4803	6.6101	6.7424	6.8771	7.4416
6	6.1520	6.3081	6.4684	6.6330	6.8019	6.9753	7.1533	7.3359	7.5233	7.7156	7.9129	8.1152	8.3227	8.5355	8.7537	8.9775	9.9299
7	7.2135	7.4343	7.6625	7.8983	8.1420	8.3938	8.6540	8.9228	9.2004	9.4872	9.7833	10.0890	10.4047	10.7305	11.0668	11.4139	12.9159
8	8.2857	8.5830	8.8923	9.2142	9.5491	9.8975	10.2598	10.6366	11.0285	11.4359	11.8594	12.2997	12.7573	13.2328	13.7268	14.2401	16.4991
9	9.3685	9.7546	10.1591	10.5828	11.0266	11.4913	11.9780	12.4876	13.0210	13.5795	14.1640	14.7757	15.4157	16.0853	16.7858	17.5185	20.7989
10	10.4622	10.9497	11.4639	12.0061	12.5779	13.1808	13.8164	14.4866	15.1929	15.9374	16.7220	17.5487	18.4197	19.3373	20.3037	21.3215	25.9587
11	11.5668	12.1687	12.8078	13.4864	14.2068	14.9716	15.7836	16.6455	17.5603	18.5312	19.5614	20.6546	21.8143	23.0445	24.3493	25.7329	32.1504
12	12.6825	13.4121	14.1920	15.0258	15.9171	16.8699	17.8885	18.9771	20.1407	21.3843	22.7132	24.1331	25.6502	27.2707	29.0017	30.8502	39.5805
13	13.8093	14.6803	15.6178	16.6268	17.7130	18.8821	20.1406	21.4953	22.9534	24.5227	26.2116	28.0291	29.9847	32.0887	34.3519	36.7862	48.4966
14	14.9474	15.9739	17.0863	18.2919	19.5986	21.0151	22.5505	24.2149	26.0192	27.9750	30.0949	32.3926	34.8827	37.5811	40.5047	43.6720	59.1959
15	16.0969	17.2934	18.5989	20.0236	21.5786	23.2760	25.1290	27.1521	29.3609	31.7725	34.4054	37.2797	40.4175	43.8424	47.5804	51.6595	72.0351
16	17.2579	18.6393	20.1569	21.8245	23.6575	25.6725	27.8881	30.3243	33.0034	35.9497	39.1899	42.7533	46.6717	50.9804	55.7175	60.9250	87.4421
17	18.4304	20.0121	21.7616	23.6975	25.8404	28.2129	30.8402	33.7502	36.9737	40.5447	44.5008	48.8837	53.7391	59.1176	65.0751	71.6730	105.931
18	19.6147	21.4123	23.4144	25.6454	28.1324	30.9057	33.9990	37.4502	41.3013	45.5992	50.3959	55.7497	61.7251	68.3941	75.8364	84.1407	128.117
19	20.8109	22.8406	25.1169	27.6712	30.5390	33.7600	37.3790	41.4463	46.0185	51.1591	56.9395	63.4397	70.7494	78.9692	88.2118	98.6032	154.740
20	22.0190	24.2974	26.8704	29.7781	33.0660	36.7856	40.9955	45.7620	51.1601	57.2750	64.2028	72.0524	80.9468	91.0249	102.444	115.380	186.688
21	23.2392	25.7833	28.6765	31.9692	35.7193	39.9927	44.8652	50.4229	56.7645	64.0025	72.2651	81.6987	92.4699	104.768	118.810	134.841	225.026
22	24.4716	27.2990	30.5368	34.2480	38.5052	43.3923	49.0057	55.4568	62.8733	71.4027	81.2143	92.5026	105.491	120.436	137.632	157.415	271.031
23	25.7163	28.8450	32.4529	36.6179	41.4305	46.9958	53.4361	60.8933	69.5319	79.5430	91.1479	104.603	120.205	138.297	159.276	183.601	326.237
24	26.9735	30.4219	34.4265	39.0826	44.5020	50.8156	58.1767	66.7648	76.7898	88.4973	102.174	118.155	136.831	158.659	184.168	213.978	392.484
25	28.2432	32.0303	36.4593	41.6459	47.7271	54.8645	63.2490	73.1059	84.7009	98.3471	114.413	133.334	155.620	181.871	212.793	249.214	471.981

Table 3 - Present value interest factors for single cash flows, PV = 1/(1 + k)^n)

Period (n) # per	1%	2%	3%	4%	5%	6%	7%	8%	9%	10%	11%	12%	13%	14%	15%	16%	20%
1	0.9901	0.9804	0.9709	0.9615	0.9524	0.9434	0.9346	0.9259	0.9174	0.9091	0.9009	0.8929	0.8850	0.8772	0.8696	0.8621	0.8333
2	0.9803	0.9612	0.9426	0.9246	0.9070	0.8900	0.8734	0.8573	0.8417	0.8264	0.8116	0.7972	0.7831	0.7695	0.7561	0.7432	0.6944
3	0.9706	0.9423	0.9151	0.8890	0.8638	0.8396	0.8163	0.7938	0.7722	0.7513	0.7312	0.7118	0.6931	0.6750	0.6575	0.6407	0.5787
4	0.9610	0.9238	0.8885	0.8548	0.8227	0.7921	0.7629	0.7350	0.7084	0.6830	0.6587	0.6355	0.6133	0.5921	0.5718	0.5523	0.4823
5	0.9515	0.9057	0.8626	0.8219	0.7835	0.7473	0.7130	0.6806	0.6499	0.6209	0.5935	0.5674	0.5428	0.5194	0.4972	0.4761	0.4019
6	0.9420	0.8880	0.8375	0.7903	0.7462	0.7050	0.6663	0.6302	0.5963	0.5645	0.5346	0.5066	0.4803	0.4556	0.4323	0.4104	0.3349
7	0.9327	0.8706	0.8131	0.7599	0.7107	0.6651	0.6227	0.5835	0.5470	0.5132	0.4817	0.4523	0.4251	0.3996	0.3759	0.3538	0.2791
8	0.9235	0.8535	0.7894	0.7307	0.6768	0.6274	0.5820	0.5403	0.5019	0.4665	0.4339	0.4039	0.3762	0.3506	0.3269	0.3050	0.2326
9	0.9143	0.8368	0.7664	0.7026	0.6446	0.5919	0.5439	0.5002	0.4604	0.4241	0.3909	0.3606	0.3329	0.3075	0.2843	0.2630	0.1938
10	0.9053	0.8203	0.7441	0.6756	0.6139	0.5584	0.5083	0.4632	0.4224	0.3855	0.3522	0.3220	0.2946	0.2697	0.2472	0.2267	0.1615
11	0.8963	0.8043	0.7224	0.6496	0.5847	0.5268	0.4751	0.4289	0.3875	0.3505	0.3173	0.2875	0.2607	0.2366	0.2149	0.1954	0.1346
12	0.8874	0.7885	0.7014	0.6246	0.5568	0.4970	0.4440	0.3971	0.3555	0.3186	0.2858	0.2567	0.2307	0.2076	0.1869	0.1685	0.1122
13	0.8787	0.7730	0.6810	0.6006	0.5303	0.4688	0.4150	0.3677	0.3262	0.2897	0.2575	0.2292	0.2042	0.1821	0.1625	0.1452	0.0935
14	0.8700	0.7579	0.6611	0.5775	0.5051	0.4423	0.3878	0.3405	0.2992	0.2633	0.2320	0.2046	0.1807	0.1597	0.1413	0.1252	0.0779
15	0.8613	0.7430	0.6419	0.5553	0.4810	0.4173	0.3624	0.3152	0.2745	0.2394	0.2090	0.1827	0.1599	0.1401	0.1229	0.1079	0.0649
16	0.8528	0.7284	0.6232	0.5339	0.4581	0.3936	0.3387	0.2919	0.2519	0.2176	0.1883	0.1631	0.1415	0.1229	0.1069	0.0930	0.0541
17	0.8444	0.7142	0.6050	0.5134	0.4363	0.3714	0.3166	0.2703	0.2311	0.1978	0.1696	0.1456	0.1252	0.1078	0.0929	0.0802	0.0451
18	0.8360	0.7002	0.5874	0.4936	0.4155	0.3503	0.2959	0.2502	0.2120	0.1799	0.1528	0.1300	0.1108	0.0946	0.0808	0.0691	0.0376
19	0.8277	0.6864	0.5703	0.4746	0.3957	0.3305	0.2765	0.2317	0.1945	0.1635	0.1377	0.1161	0.0981	0.0829	0.0703	0.0596	0.0313
20	0.8195	0.6730	0.5537	0.4564	0.3769	0.3118	0.2584	0.2145	0.1784	0.1486	0.1240	0.1037	0.0868	0.0728	0.0611	0.0514	0.0261
21	0.8114	0.6598	0.5375	0.4388	0.3589	0.2942	0.2415	0.1987	0.1637	0.1351	0.1117	0.0926	0.0768	0.0638	0.0531	0.0443	0.0217
22	0.8034	0.6468	0.5219	0.4220	0.3418	0.2775	0.2257	0.1839	0.1502	0.1228	0.1007	0.0826	0.0680	0.0560	0.0462	0.0382	0.0181
23	0.7954	0.6342	0.5067	0.4057	0.3256	0.2618	0.2109	0.1703	0.1378	0.1117	0.0907	0.0738	0.0601	0.0491	0.0402	0.0329	0.0151
24	0.7876	0.6217	0.4919	0.3901	0.3101	0.2470	0.1971	0.1577	0.1264	0.1015	0.0817	0.0659	0.0532	0.0431	0.0349	0.0284	0.0126
25	0.7798	0.6095	0.4776	0.3751	0.2953	0.2330	0.1842	0.1460	0.1160	0.0923	0.0736	0.0588	0.0471	0.0378	0.0304	0.0245	0.0105

Table 4 - Present value interest factors for an annuity, Formula: PV = [1 - 1/(1 + k)^n] / k

Period (n) # per	1%	2%	3%	4%	5%	6%	7%	8%	9%	10%	11%	12%	13%	14%	15%	16%	20%
1	0.9901	0.9804	0.9709	0.9615	0.9524	0.9434	0.9346	0.9259	0.9174	0.9091	0.9009	0.8929	0.8850	0.8772	0.8696	0.8621	0.8333
2	1.9704	1.9416	1.9135	1.8861	1.8594	1.8334	1.8080	1.7833	1.7591	1.7355	1.7125	1.6901	1.6681	1.6467	1.6257	1.6052	1.5278
3	2.9410	2.8839	2.8286	2.7751	2.7232	2.6730	2.6243	2.5771	2.5313	2.4869	2.4437	2.4018	2.3612	2.3216	2.2832	2.2459	2.1065
4	3.9020	3.8077	3.7171	3.6299	3.5460	3.4651	3.3872	3.3121	3.2397	3.1699	3.1024	3.0373	2.9745	2.9137	2.8550	2.7982	2.5887
5	4.8534	4.7135	4.5797	4.4518	4.3295	4.2124	4.1002	3.9927	3.8897	3.7908	3.6959	3.6048	3.5172	3.4331	3.3522	3.2743	2.9906
6	5.7955	5.6014	5.4172	5.2421	5.0757	4.9173	4.7665	4.6229	4.4859	4.3553	4.2305	4.1114	3.9975	3.8887	3.7845	3.6847	3.3255
7	6.7282	6.4720	6.2303	6.0021	5.7864	5.5824	5.3893	5.2064	5.0330	4.8684	4.7122	4.5638	4.4226	4.2883	4.1604	4.0386	3.6046
8	7.6517	7.3255	7.0197	6.7327	6.4632	6.2098	5.9713	5.7466	5.5348	5.3349	5.1461	4.9676	4.7988	4.6389	4.4873	4.3436	3.8372
9	8.5660	8.1622	7.7861	7.4353	7.1078	6.8017	6.5152	6.2469	5.9952	5.7590	5.5370	5.3282	5.1317	4.9464	4.7716	4.6065	4.0310
10	9.4713	8.9826	8.5302	8.1109	7.7217	7.3601	7.0236	6.7101	6.4177	6.1446	5.8892	5.6502	5.4262	5.2161	5.0188	4.8332	4.1925
11	10.3676	9.7868	9.2526	8.7605	8.3064	7.8869	7.4987	7.1390	6.8052	6.4951	6.2065	5.9377	5.6869	5.4527	5.2337	5.0286	4.3271
12	11.2551	10.5753	9.9540	9.3851	8.8633	8.3838	7.9427	7.5361	7.1607	6.8137	6.4924	6.1944	5.9176	5.6603	5.4206	5.1971	4.4392
13	12.1337	11.3484	10.6350	9.9856	9.3936	8.8527	8.3577	7.9038	7.4869	7.1034	6.7499	6.4235	6.1218	5.8424	5.5831	5.3423	4.5327
14	13.0037	12.1062	11.2961	10.5631	9.8986	9.2950	8.7455	8.2442	7.7862	7.3667	6.9819	6.6282	6.3025	6.0021	5.7245	5.4675	4.6106
15	13.8651	12.8493	11.9379	11.1184	10.3797	9.7122	9.1079	8.5595	8.0607	7.6061	7.1909	6.8109	6.4624	6.1422	5.8474	5.5755	4.6755
16	14.7179	13.5777	12.5611	11.6523	10.8378	10.1059	9.4466	8.8514	8.3126	7.8237	7.3792	6.9740	6.6039	6.2651	5.9542	5.6685	4.7296
17	15.5623	14.2919	13.1661	12.1657	11.2741	10.4773	9.7632	9.1216	8.5436	8.0216	7.5488	7.1196	6.7291	6.3729	6.0472	5.7487	4.7746
18	16.3983	14.9920	13.7535	12.6593	11.6896	10.8276	10.0591	9.3719	8.7556	8.2014	7.7016	7.2497	6.8399	6.4674	6.1280	5.8178	4.8122
19	17.2260	15.6785	14.3238	13.1339	12.0853	11.1581	10.3356	9.6036	8.9501	8.3649	7.8393	7.3658	6.9380	6.5504	6.1982	5.8775	4.8435
20	18.0456	16.3514	14.8775	13.5903	12.4622	11.4699	10.5940	9.8181	9.1285	8.5136	7.9633	7.4694	7.0248	6.6231	6.2593	5.9288	4.8696
21	18.8570	17.0112	15.4150	14.0292	12.8212	11.7641	10.8355	10.0168	9.2922	8.6487	8.0751	7.5620	7.1016	6.6870	6.3125	5.9731	4.8913
22	19.6604	17.6580	15.9369	14.4511	13.1630	12.0416	11.0612	10.2007	9.4424	8.7715	8.1757	7.6446	7.1695	6.7429	6.3587	6.0113	4.9094
23	20.4558	18.2922	16.4436	14.8568	13.4886	12.3034	11.2722	10.3711	9.5802	8.8832	8.2664	7.7184	7.2297	6.7921	6.3988	6.0442	4.9245
24	21.2434	18.9139	16.9355	15.2470	13.7986	12.5504	11.4693	10.5288	9.7066	8.9847	8.3481	7.7843	7.2829	6.8351	6.4338	6.0726	4.9371
25	22.0232	19.5235	17.4131	15.6221	14.0939	12.7834	11.6536	10.6748	9.8226	9.0770	8.4217	7.8431	7.3300	6.8729	6.4641	6.0971	4.9476

Basic Will Example

Last Will and Testament of John Doe

I, **John Doe**, residing at 123 Main Street, Anytown, USA, being of sound mind and body, declare this to be my Last Will and Testament.

1. **Executor**: I appoint my son, **James Doe**, as the Executor of this will. If James is unable or unwilling to serve, I appoint my daughter, **Jane Doe**, as the alternate Executor.
2. **Specific Bequests**:
   - I leave my primary residence located at 123 Main Street, Anytown, USA, to my daughter, **Jane Doe**.
   - I leave my car, a 2018 Toyota Camry, to my son, **James Doe**.
   - I leave the sum of $10,000 to my granddaughter, **Emily Doe**.
3. **Residue of Estate**: I leave the residue of my estate, including all remaining assets not specifically bequeathed, to be divided equally between my two children, **James Doe** and **Jane Doe**.
4. **Guardianship**: If both of my children are minors at the time of my death, I appoint my sister, **Mary Smith**, as the guardian of my children.
5. **Revocation**: I revoke all previous wills and codicils made by me.

In witness whereof, I have signed this Will on this 15th day of August 2024.

John Doe
(Your Signature)

Witness 1:
(Signature)
Name: __________
Address: __________

Witness 2:
(Signature)
Name: __________
Address: __________

Durable Power of Attorney Example

Durable Power of Attorney

Principal:
Name: **John Doe**
Address: 123 Main Street, Anytown, USA

Agent:
Name: **Jane Doe**
Address: 456 Oak Avenue, Anytown, USA

I, **John Doe**, hereby appoint **Jane Doe** as my true and lawful agent to act on my behalf regarding all financial and legal matters. This includes managing bank accounts, real estate transactions, paying bills, and filing taxes. This Power of Attorney shall remain in effect even if I become incapacitated.

Signature of Principal:
(John Doe's Signature)
Date: August 15, 2024

Witness 1:
(Signature)
Name: __________
Address: __________

Witness 2:
(Signature)
Name: __________
Address: __________

Notary Public:
(Signature and Seal)

Revocable Living Trust Example

Revocable Living Trust Agreement

Grantor:
John Doe
123 Main Street, Anytown, USA

Trustee:
John Doe (while living)
Successor Trustee: Jane Doe
456 Oak Avenue, Anytown, USA

Trust Name:
The John Doe Revocable Living Trust dated August 15, 2024.

Article 1: Declaration of Trust
I, John Doe, hereby establish this Revocable Living Trust, transferring all the assets listed in Schedule A (attached) to the Trustee, to be managed according to the terms outlined in this agreement.

Article 2: Revocability
This trust is revocable. As the Grantor, I retain the right to amend, revoke, or terminate this trust in whole or in part at any time during my lifetime.

Article 3: Distribution During Lifetime
If I am capable, I shall serve as the Trustee and manage the trust assets. I may use the trust income and principal for my benefit as needed.

Article 4: Distribution Upon Death
Upon my death, the Successor Trustee, Jane Doe, shall distribute the trust assets as follows:

- To Jane Doe: My primary residence is located at 123 Main Street, Anytown, USA.
- To James Doe: My investment account at ABC Investments.
- To Charity XYZ: $50,000 to be donated.

Any remaining assets shall be distributed equally between Jane Doe and James Doe.

Article 5: Successor Trustee Powers
The Successor Trustee shall have all powers necessary to manage, invest, and distribute the trust assets according to the terms of this trust. This includes the power to sell, lease, or mortgage trust assets.

Article 6: Governing Law
This trust shall be governed by the laws of the state of [State].

Signatures:

John Doe (Grantor/Trustee):
(Signature)
Date: August 15, 2024

Witness 1:
(Signature)
Name: __________
Address: __________

Witness 2:
(Signature)
Name: __________
Address: __________

Healthcare Proxy Example

Healthcare Proxy

Principal:
Name: **John Doe**
Address: 123 Main Street, Anytown, USA

Healthcare Agent:
Name: **Jane Doe**
Address: 456 Oak Avenue, Anytown, USA

Alternate Healthcare Agent:
Name: **James Doe**
Address: 789 Maple Drive, Anytown, USA

I, **John Doe**, hereby appoint **Jane Doe** as my healthcare agent to make medical decisions on my behalf if I am unable to make them myself. If Jane Doe is unable or unwilling to act, I appoint **James Doe** as the alternate agent.

Powers Granted:
My healthcare agent has the authority to make all healthcare decisions for me, including decisions about life-sustaining treatment. This authority includes, but is not limited to, consenting to, or refusing medical treatment, hiring, or firing healthcare providers, and authorizing admission or discharge from any medical facility.

Living Will Directives:
If I am terminally ill or permanently unconscious, I do not wish to be kept alive by artificial means, including mechanical ventilation or artificial nutrition and hydration. I authorize my healthcare agent to ensure that my wishes are followed.

Effective Date and Revocability:
This healthcare proxy becomes effective when I am determined to be incapacitated by my attending physician. I retain the right to revoke or amend this document at any time while I am still competent.

Signature of Principal:
(John Doe's Signature)
Date: August 15, 2024

Witness 1:
(Signature)
Name: __________
Address: __________

Witness 2:
(Signature)
Name: __________
Address: __________

Beneficiary Designation Example

Account Type:
401(k) Retirement Account

Account Holder:
John Doe
Account Number: 123456789

Primary Beneficiary:
Name: **Jane Doe**
Relationship: **Spouse**
Percentage: **100%**
Address: 456 Oak Avenue, Anytown, USA
Social Security Number: --***

Contingent Beneficiary:
Name: **James Doe**
Relationship: **Son**
Percentage: **100% (if the primary beneficiary is deceased)**
Address: 789 Maple Drive, Anytown, USA
Social Security Number: --***

I, **John Doe**, hereby designate the above-named individuals as the beneficiaries of my 401(k)-retirement account. If I am not survived by the primary beneficiary, the contingent beneficiary will receive the account assets.

Signature of Account Holder:
(John Doe's Signature)
Date: August 15, 2024

Witness 1:
(Signature)
Name: __________
Address: __________

Witness 2:
(Signature)
Name: __________
Address: __________

REFERENCES

Bajtelsmit, V. L. (2024). *Personal finance.* https://books.google.com/books/about/Personal_Finance.html?id=SNjzEAAAQBAJ

Bebel, J. (2023, September 7). Financial planning for disabilities and special needs: What to know. *Morningstar.*

CFLE Credential | National Council on Family Relations. (n.d.). https://www.ncfr.org/cfle-certification

CFP Board. (n.d.). CFP Board Practice Standards. https://www.cfp.net/ethics/code-of-ethics-and-standards-of-conduct

CFP Board. (2019a). *Code of ethics and standards of conduct.* Author.

CFP Board. (2019b). *Monitoring and updating progress.* https://www.cfp.net/ethics/compliance-resources/2019/04/focus-on-ethics---monitoring-and-updating-progress

Chambers, B., Walker, R., Feng, J., & Gu, Y. (2021). The silver tsunami: An enquiry into the financial needs, preferences, and behaviors of retirees. *Accounting and Finance, 61*(1), 645–687. https://doi.org/10.1111/ACFI.12589

Farmer, J. (2023, April 19). Considerations for financial and estate planning professionals who work with blended families. *Forbes.*

Flood, F. (2020). Silver tsunami of retirement: Implications for consideration. In *Global encyclopedia of public administration, public policy, and governance* (pp. 1–8). Springer International Publishing. https://doi.org/10.1007/978-3-319-31816-5_3995-1

Kagan, J. (2024). What are social security benefits? Definition, types, and history. *Investopedia.* https://www.investopedia.com/terms/s/social-security-benefits.asp

Klebnikov, S. (2023, April 30). Special needs financial planning: Smart advice for families coping with disabilities. *Forbes.* https://www.forbes.com/sites/sergeiklebnikov/2023/04/30/special-needs-financial-planning-smart-advice-for-families-coping-with-disabilities/

National Council on Aging. (2023). *Addressing the nation's retirement crisis.* https://www.ncoa.org/article/addressing-the-nations-retirement-crisis-the-80-percent-financially-struggling

Social Security Administration. (n.d.-a). *The United States Social Security Administration.* https://www.ssa.gov/

Social Security Administration. (n.d.-b). *What is social security?* Author.

Social Security Administration. (2024). *Medicare.* Author.

Van Cleve, M., & Klontz, B. (2022). The psychology of estate planning with blended families | Financial Planning Association. *Journal of Financial Planning.* https://www.financialplanningassociation.org/learning/publications/journal/AUG22-psychology-estate-planning-blended-families-OPEN

www.ingramcontent.com/pod-product-compliance
Lightning Source LLC
LaVergne TN
LVHW080034210926
848481LV00011B/3185